D0114195

Perspectives on American Furniture

Perspectives on American Furniture

EDITED BY

Gerald W. R. Ward

PUBLISHED FOR
The Henry Francis du Pont Winterthur Museum
WINTERTHUR, DELAWARE

W. W. Norton & Company
NEW YORK   LONDON

First Edition

Production and copy editing by
Patricia R. Lisk, Winterthur Museum.

Library of Congress Cataloging-in-Publication Data

Perspectives on American furniture.

   1. Furniture—United States—History—18th century.
2. Furniture—United States—History—19th century.
3. Furniture—United States—History—20th century.
I. Ward, Gerald W. R.   II. Henry Francis du Pont
Winterthur Museum.
NK2406.P44   1988   749.213   88-12599

ISBN 0-393-02654-X

W. W. Norton & Company, Inc., 500 Fifth Avenue, New York, N. Y. 10110
W. W. Norton & Company Ltd., 37 Great Russell Street, London WC1B 3NU

1 2 3 4 5 6 7 8 9 0

Contents

Perspectives on American Furniture

Introduction

Gerald W. R. Ward

Eleven decades ago Irving Whitall Lyon "began to collect pieces of old furniture in and about Hartford," a genteel pursuit that soon led him to make what he called "a somewhat systematic study" of the objects he and his fellow collectors gathered. To answer his questions, Lyon found it necessary to examine four broad categories of evidence. Foremost in Lyon's mind was the "examination of specimens," or the study of the objects themselves. Next, Lyon found it necessary to gain a familiarity with "what others knew or had written," what today we would call secondary sources. After absorbing this literature, he turned to primary sources, such as inventories, newspapers, account books, and diaries. Last, he found it useful to go abroad and study the seventeenth- and eighteenth-century furniture of England and Holland.[1]

Lyon's logical method remains the standard approach for mainstream furniture historians today. The dozen essays in this volume, an outgrowth of the 1985 Winterthur Conference entitled "Changing Perspectives on American Furniture," demonstrate this point convincingly. Despite the title of the conference, the papers reveal that continuity in furniture scholarship is as strong as change—and perhaps as important.[2]

[1] Irving Whitall Lyon, *The Colonial Furniture of New England: A Study of the Domestic Furniture in Use in the Seventeenth and Eighteenth Centuries* (Boston and New York: Houghton, Mifflin, 1891), pp. iv–v. Bernard D. Cotton emphasized a similar traditional method when laying out the scope of the Regional Furniture Society's new journal devoted to English vernacular furniture. See his introductory essay in *Regional Furniture* 1 (1987): 1–18.

[2] Remarks by the three commentators on the conference sessions—Robert Blair St. George, Kevin M. Sweeney, and Barbara McLean Ward—were helpful in editing the papers in this volume.

1

Nearly all the essays in this book make use of Lyon's four categories of evidence, although each author draws more or less heavily on each type. Several of the papers here, for example, are based primarily on research into objects and bring much new material to light. Others, particularly the surveys of regional studies by Philip D. Zimmerman and of the literature on craftsmen by Edward S. Cooke, Jr., survey secondary sources to identify past trends and suggest future directions for research. Original documents form the core of Nancy Goyne Evans's study of how seating furniture was marketed in the federal period and of William N. Hosley, Jr.'s, monograph on Connecticut joiner Timothy Loomis III. John T. Kirk's essay reflects his long-standing interest in the distinctiveness of American design, an interest grounded in and enriched by his detailed knowledge of contemporaneous English and European furniture. Lyon's trips to England in the 1880s, for example, began a tradition of overseas research resumed by Kirk in the 1960s.

Yet much has changed, of course, and this dynamic quality is also reflected in the papers here. While the means of furniture scholarship have remained constant, the scope and depth of investigation have broadened dramatically. The study of furniture has now widened to include nearly everything from nearly everywhere. While there is still great interest in early American furniture of high aesthetic quality, there is now strong interest in furniture of all periods, from all places, and of all levels of design and craftsmanship. For example, furniture made after 1820 is now examined enthusiastically, as witnessed in this volume by Ellen Marie Snyder's paper on Victorian death furniture, David B. Driscoll's study of patent rockers in the nineteenth century, and Katherine C. Grier's look at Victorian parlors. Furniture of a type previously considered "below the level of historical scrutiny" is now examined seriously, as demonstrated by Edwin A. Churchill and Sheila McDonald's paper on the furniture made and owned in backwoods Maine. Whereas Lyon and other early writers were most interested in the colonial furniture of New England, studies of furniture have expanded to include objects made and used everywhere, as represented by Dean Herrin's work on Appalachian furnishings and Gerald L. Pocius's study of the furniture owned in the Newfoundland outport of Keels. Andrew Passeri's autobiographical essay reflects the current interest in the lives of artisans and labor history.

The biggest change that has come about since Lyon's time lies not in subject matter, however, but in attitudes and goals; not in means, but in ends. Lyon and his colleagues loved old furniture and valued it for itself. They were not given to serious introspection about their motives for collecting and studying such objects. Today furniture scholarship in most quarters has become mannered and self-conscious. The study of furniture *qua* furniture is no longer acceptable to many people interested in furniture in a scholarly way (although it still has great appeal for large and growing numbers of people who collect furniture and who study it avocationally for pleasure). Rather, it is a means toward the goal of a greater understanding of people and how their interaction with furniture reveals fundamental attitudes, beliefs, and patterns of behavior. In imaginative ways, scholars are trying to discover what the manufacture, appearance, and use of furniture can tell us that other sources traditionally used by historians and social scientists cannot.

No one can seriously doubt the importance of asking intelligent questions of the material. Occasionally, however, the emphasis on a search for *meaning* can be carried to an extreme. There can be no escaping Lyon's categories when it comes to developing hypotheses concerning the meaning of objects and the significance of rituals, ceremonies, and customs associated with their use. Such evidence forms the grammar on which theoretical and imaginative studies can be based. Familiarity with American objects of all kinds, with the secondary literature, with primary documents and pictorial sources, and with prototypes and parallels from other cultures are the four cornerstones of a solid foundation on which interpretive constructs, paradigms, and models can be built. Without a knowledge of these four bodies of material, a furniture scholar cannot be said to be culturally literate. Without a grounding in this material, a scholar's work is liable to tell us more about that person's predilections and prejudices than about his or her ostensible subject.

Perhaps the most unusual paper in this book is the sociolinguistic essay by folklorist Gerald Pocius. He draws on the literature of linguistics, folklore, and other disciplines to develop his interpretation of Keels furniture as a type of three-dimensional gossip. On the face of it, one might be tempted to dismiss Pocius's study as a clever bit of academic posturing that has style but no substance. But his work is built on a solid basis of mainstream scholarship, including his familiarity with the objects, with their form, construction, ornament, and finish. Pocius knows the furniture of Keels from firsthand experience: from fieldwork conducted over the course of several years and from maintaining a summer residence there. He has surveyed the secondary literature, particularly the pioneering work of Walter Peddle, and primary sources. He spent a year as a research fellow at Winterthur Museum searching for the factory-made prototypes for local Newfoundland work. This intimacy with Lyon's categories gives Pocius's imaginative and speculative work credibility and represents a blending of the new furniture scholarship with the old. As we go about trying to make Lyon's "somewhat systematic study" into a more systematic one, it would be good to remember that the study of furniture cannot make any *distinctive* contribution to history (or any other discipline) unless we attempt to understand the furniture itself.

The necessity of using furniture as evidence underlines the intellectual importance of museum collections and curators. While all four of Lyon's categories are important, the "examination of specimens" is first among equals.[3] Significant contributions to scholarship are most likely to be made by those most familiar with objects, and curators are in an excellent position to gain such an understanding through long and regular experience with collections. It is ironic that museums rarely provide the necessary time for research to the people in the best situation to make good use of it. Whatever a scholar's institutional affiliation, however, he is most likely to produce innovative and sound work if he holds a strong interest in, and respect for, his subject.

The twelve papers in this volume were prepared by the authors as discrete entities. Although each is designed to stand on its own, they are presented in roughly thematic order.

The first cluster contains four essays primarily concerned with the definition and application of the concept of regionalism, broadly conceived. Philip Zimmerman provides a historiographic overview of the application of regionalism to studies of American furniture, which he

---

[3] The most systematic examination of American furniture yet undertaken is Benjamin A. Hewitt's computer-assisted quantitative study of nearly 400 American federal-period card tables. Hewitt's analysis of some 176 variables of construction and ornament of these tables revealed many insights into shop practices and organization, consumer preferences, economic life, and other issues. His research, however, has generally been overlooked by traditional historians. See Benjamin A. Hewitt, Patricia E. Kane, and Gerald W. R. Ward, *The Work of Many Hands: Card Tables in Federal America, 1790–1820* (New Haven: Yale University Art Gallery, 1982).

traces to the work of William MacPherson Hornor, Clair Franklin Luther, and others writing in the 1930s. He follows changing definitions of the term through the work of Helen Comstock, Charles F. Montgomery, John T. Kirk, and others in the 1960s and 1970s and then examines the usefulness of the concept in current furniture studies. Drawing on related work in other academic disciplines, Zimmerman calls for a more fluid and wide-ranging definition of regionalism, one that is sensitive to changes over time and that embraces issues of geography, social and economic conditions, and broader cultural factors.

While Zimmerman's essay treats regionalism within an American setting, John Kirk's contribution expands the field of inquiry to include the role of American objects within an international context. Returning to themes he has examined in the past, Kirk briefly traces the changing attitudes among scholars toward questions of dependence and independence in American art, noting, "the past ten years have seen the gradual acceptance of the natural dependence of American expressions, cultural and artistic." Acknowledging this dependence, he stresses, in no way diminishes or exalts early American furniture; rather, the placement of American objects in as wide a context as possible enhances our understanding of them. By looking at them as part of a continuum of world-wide production, we can examine questions of patronage, style, quality, and connoisseurship clearly and without prejudice. The design of furniture—furniture as a work of art—is once again used by Kirk as a type of historical evidence as valid as any written record.

Zimmerman's and Kirk's reflective essays are followed by two case studies of furniture produced in specific regions. As part of a research project conducted by Maine State Museum, Edwin Churchill and Sheila McDonald examined the furniture produced in the upper St. John Valley of Maine between about 1820 and 1930. They found a strong tradition of French-inspired joined furniture in this remote, bilingual, and bicultural area. Although much of the furniture was utilitarian, some objects were more style-conscious and carried messages of status and prestige. Other forms were influenced by local demographic conditions; one form popular in the region, the large table, was made in response to the large family size common in the valley. Toward the end of the nineteenth century, this conservative tradition was largely broken by outside influences brought by the lumber industry and the railroads. The old craft died away as the valley people eagerly acquired factory-made furniture marketed through stores and mail-order catalogues. Only one form—the rocker—continued to be made locally in significant numbers, and Churchill and McDonald see the rocker as a key artifactual document in their explanation of the dramatic shifts that occurred in the valley as the twentieth century progressed.

The perhaps equally isolated interiors of Appalachia are the focus of Dean Herrin's paper, which treats the issue of regionalism in a different vein. Herrin is concerned not so much with identifying the products of a region, but with understanding the "outside" world's perception of the Appalachian people. He argues convincingly that the popular press has projected a romantic image of Appalachians as artsy-craftsy, poverty-stricken pioneers. This cultural stereotyping is belied, at least in part, he argues, by a more careful reading of the physical and pictorial documents. Examination of such evidence as photographs of interiors, for example, reveals ways in which misconceptions, both accidental and deliberate, have been perpetuated. These myths have drawn attention away from the true cause of poverty in Appalachia, the "exploitation of natural resources by a capitalist economy."

The second constellation of papers is a group of four essays chiefly concerned with craftsmanship and trade. This group also begins with a broad overview, prepared in this case by Edward Cooke. Cooke summarizes briefly the current state of scholarship concerning craftsmen and argues that we must build on the existing base of documentary material to achieve a "more contextual analysis" of the lives of furniture makers. Noting that scholars should draw on as many different types of evidence as are available, Cooke proposes a sophisticated analytical model that "involves a complex series of interlocking spheres of analysis that focuses on composition, process, and performance." He thus advocates a type of material culture studies in which the *material* (in this case, furniture) is a primary form of evidence. This is a challenging agenda, for it is a time-consuming task to learn how to read three-dimensional evidence, yet it must be followed if material culture studies are to make a unique contribution to scholarship.

Cooke's prescriptive essay is followed by William Hosley's case study of Timothy Loomis III of Windsor, Connecticut. Hosley's rich analysis of this eighteenth-century joiner, based on surviving objects and a rare group of account books and ledgers, approaches the ideal methodology suggested by Cooke. These documents allow him to reconstruct Loomis's world—his training, network of patrons, work rhythms, and daily tasks—within his largely agrarian society.

While Hosley presents an unusually textured look at one artisan, Nancy Evans casts a wider net in her study of how painted seating furniture was marketed from 1750 to 1840. Drawing on an immense familiarity with documents, she presents an overview of the imaginative ways furniture makers sold their chairs. Her analysis of methods of payment, promotion options, advertising, packaging, transportation, and other technical aspects of the domestic, coastal, and overseas trade suggests the existence of a broader and more "modern" furniture industry than we have heretofore suspected at this early date.

The next essay represents a departure in style from the other parts of this book. Unlike the other historical monographs gathered here, this chapter is an engaging autobiography by Andrew Passeri, master upholsterer. Born in Italy in 1909, Passeri came to America and spent nearly fifty years in the upholstery trade in Boston, before embarking on a second career in retirement as a specialist in historic upholstery. His story, transcribed and edited from taped interviews, paints a bleak picture of the context of work within the factory during the mid twentieth century. Low wages, nonexistent benefits, callous employers, and jealous colleagues were only some of the obstacles Passeri encountered in plying his craft. His ability to retain a genuine humanity in the face of deplorable working conditions marks a triumph of the spirit over capitalism. Passeri's narrative provides rich primary material for the type of contextual study advocated by Cooke and brings to a close this group of craftsmen-related papers.

The last group of loosely related essays consists of four monographs on specialized topics that generally concern the interaction of people with furniture in different environments. Three of the essays deal with the nineteenth century, beginning with Katherine Grier's "Imagining the Parlor, 1830–1880." Quasi-public room settings in hotels, photographers' studios, railroad cars, steamboats, and elsewhere, Grier suggests, "served to focus new consumer demand on certain kinds of furnishing practices by allowing people to 'imagine' parlors of their own." These "model interiors" provided an arena where many assumptions, aspirations, and attitudes of Victorian America were brought into play.

The broad relationship between the domestic interior and a public space is also the general theme of Ellen Snyder's study of Victorian death furniture. Snyder examines nineteenth-century ideas about life, death, and the afterlife as revealed in the vocabulary of Victorian cemetery fittings, such as coffins, grave beds, graveside seats, and vacant chairs. Seats for mourners and bedlike tombstones are just two of the objects that reflected Victorian concepts of "true Christian gentility, domesticity, and the role of memory."

David Driscoll's study of nineteenth-century patent rockers also attempts to understand fundamental Victorian beliefs, in this case attitudes toward work, leisure, progress, and technology. In a subtle theoretical analysis, Driscoll examines the documentary record concerning machine rockers (few ever made it past the drawing board) and interprets the patent applications and drawings as a form of nonverbal communication. While recognizing that the material is open to several interpretations, he argues persuasively that the machine rocker is an "optimistic and opportunistic" reflection of Victorian culture. Such rockers emphasized work, not leisure and comfort, and were "extensions of nineteenth-century America's uncritical trust in the virtue of the machine and the promise of abundance."

The final essay in the book is Gerald Pocius's study of the furniture of Keels from 1850 to 1950. Although this paper might well have been included with the first group of essays in this volume, it is an intensely local study that falls outside the usual form of a regional work. Pocius was interested in how the diverse body of furniture found in Keels operated in "socially strategic ways." For purposes of analysis, he compared the uses of furniture to the uses of gossip, especially with regard to "information management and the fostering of self-interest." One of the properties of gossip, for example, is that it contains something new; in Keels, chairs were chosen as a form that introduced new statements. The competitive aspect of gossip is paralleled by the use of decorative elements on furniture, small embellishments that Pocius sees as significant rhetorical devices. Furniture making in Keels was largely a decentralized affair, and each "person making furniture in Keels generally answered to his own personal concerns." Furthermore, furniture, like gossip, was a way of alleviating the crushing boredom of life in a tiny community. Finding a greater degree of richness, diversity, and even cosmopolitanism than one might expect, Pocius suggests that stereotyped ways of looking at isolated folk communities need to be questioned.

The variety of papers here indicates that there is value in an eclectic approach to furniture. If our goal is to learn more about people, then we should expect our studies of furniture to be as varied as our studies of people. These diverse approaches need to be encouraged and tolerated. The different vantage points taken by scholars does not alter the basis of our work, however. As we move forward in the age of analysis and interpretation, there is no escaping the necessity of beginning with Lyon's categories.[4] Whatever our perspective, without a foundation erected upon objects and documents, our shifting paradigms shall be as a house built upon the sand.

[4]Thomas J. Schlereth, comp. and ed., *Material Culture Studies in America* (Nashville, Tenn.: American Association for State and Local History, 1982), pp. 7 ("Age of Analysis") and 32 ("Age of Interpretation").

Regionalism in American Furniture Studies

Philip D. Zimmerman

Dependence on the concept of regionalism to organize our thinking about American furniture has been the rule for decades. A brief outline of the role it has played to date lays the foundations for suggesting its place in the future. The earliest furniture studies were not regional in their approach. Pioneers like Irving Lyon, Esther Singleton, Luke Vincent Lockwood, and Wallace Nutting pursued more elementary concerns, namely, distinguishing forms, establishing chronologies of form and decoration, and suggesting a rudimentary sense of historical context by unearthing period terms, references, and anecdotes.[1] Regional concerns, even those as basic as the country of origin, were secondary. In Lockwood's 1926 edition of *Colonial Furniture in America*, for example, he published the fully inscribed Benjamin Burnham desk of 1769 as an anonymous object even though Lyon had recorded the inscription in his 1891 book.[2] The early scholars saw little need to scrutinize construc-

The author wishes to thank Robert F. Trent, Kevin M. Sweeney, and Louise L. Stevenson for their help in preparing this article and Eugene C. Tate for his photographs.

[1] Irving Whitall Lyon, *The Colonial Furniture of New England: A Study of the Domestic Furniture in Use in the Seventeenth and Eighteenth Centuries* (1891; reprint, New York: E. P. Dutton, 1977); Esther Singleton, *The Furniture of Our Forefathers* (1900 / 1901; reprint, New York: Benjamin Blom, 1970); Luke Vincent Lockwood, *Colonial Furniture in America* (New York: Charles Scribner's Sons, 1901); Wallace Nutting, *Furniture of the Pilgrim Century* (1924; reprint, New York: Dover Publications, 1965).

[2] Luke Vincent Lockwood, *Colonial Furniture in America* (3d ed., 1926; reprint, New York: Castle Books, 1951), pp. 240–42, fig. 264; Lyon, *Colonial Furniture*, p. 121, fig. 50. The desk and inscription are illustrated and discussed in Morrison H. Heckscher,

tion details, secondary woods, and other features as we require today. Consequently, the results of their research contain what appear to our modern ways and purposes to be glaring errors of omission.

William MacPherson Hornor was among the first to recognize the value of studying local and regional craft practices. His *Blue Book: Philadelphia Furniture*, published in 1935, was remarkably advanced and thorough, if somewhat disorganized, in its treatment of the subject. Moreover, Hornor demanded a new standard of accuracy in local history and in identifying the properties of the object. Nothing expresses Hornor's disassociation from earlier work better than a passage from his introduction: "Since the first rediscovered piece of labelled eighteenth century furniture—a William Savery lowboy—was photographed and illustrated in 1918, each new authentic 'find' was accompanied by a doubt, a fear, or an error; with the result that there has been no guide in which a thinking student could have confidence. The Wharton-Lippincott highboy was pictured as the chef-d'oeuvre of Thomas Tufft, whereas it actually bears three labels of William Savery" (figs. 1, 2).[3]

Hornor's introduction identified the basic structure of regional studies. He observed that Philadelphia furniture "developed a distinctive manner" which, "after seeing a few good examples of Provincial Queen Anne or Philadelphia-Chippendale, even an untrained eye [could] distinguish . . . quite readily."[4] Although the statement betrayed Hornor's aesthetic interests, made all the clearer by his intention that his work be "a stepping stone to a higher appreciation" of furniture he considered unparalleled in design and workmanship, he nonetheless postulated the existence of shared characteristics as the primary requirement for regionalizing artifacts. His full discussion of the furniture, makers, owners, local commercial circumstances, and domestic life gives the reader an intimate view of a particular slice of American material culture.

American Furniture in the Metropolitan Museum of Art, vol. 2, *Late Colonial Period: The Queen Anne and Chippendale Styles,* ed. Mary-Alice Rogers (New York: Metropolitan Museum of Art and Random House, 1985), cat. 178 pp. 270–72, 366.

[3] William MacPherson Hornor, *Blue Book: Philadelphia Furniture, William Penn to George Washington* (Philadelphia: Privately printed, 1935), p. ix. The labeled Savery dressing table was published in R. T. H. Halsey, "William Savery, the Colonial Cabinetmaker and His Furniture," *Bulletin of the Metropolitan Museum of Art* 13, no. 12 (December 1918): 254–67. The Wharton-Lippincott high chest, or highboy, was published in Clarence W. Brazer, "Early Pennsylvania Craftsmen: Thomas Tufft 'Joyner,' " *Antiques* 13, no. 3 (March 1928): 202–3 figs. 4–7.

[4] Hornor, *Blue Book,* p. ix.

Hornor was not a lone voice in his selection of a regional approach to furniture. That same year Clair Franklin Luther published his comprehensive study of Hadley chests, a group of furniture first recognized by Lyon and discussed more fully by Lockwood. Both Hornor and Luther built on well-founded interest in regional subjects. Luther himself had written about his Hadley chests in a 1928 *Antiques* article. Other studies in the late 1920s included the compilations by George Francis Dow and Alfred Coxe Prime of craft-related newspaper advertisements drawn from regionalized sources, Henry W. Belknap's study of Essex County craftsmen, and various *Antiques* articles. The Metropolitan Museum of Art recognized the value of a regional subject when it produced a loan exhibition and catalogue of New York State furniture in 1934.[5]

The development of regional interests at this time is not surprising when viewed in a broader context. As far back as the late eighteenth century, books like Jedidiah Morse's *American Geography* (1789 and later editions) divided the United States into discrete sections and ascribed certain characteristics to these areas. Sectional interpretations appeared regularly throughout the nineteenth century in geographies and in the arrangements of many of the United States censuses. By the early twentieth century, scholars began to refine and question existing interpretations based on sectionalism and environmental determinism by studying

[5] Clair F. Luther, *The Hadley Chest* (Hartford, Conn.: Case, Lockwood, and Brainard Co., 1935); Lyon, *Colonial Furniture*, pp. 16–17; Lockwood, *Colonial Furniture*, pp. 26–32; Clair F. Luther, "The Hadley Chest," *Antiques* 14, no. 4 (October 1928): 338–40; George Francis Dow, comp., *The Arts and Crafts in New England, 1704–1775* (1927; reprint, New York: Da Capo Press, 1967); Alfred Coxe Prime, comp., *The Arts and Crafts in Philadelphia, Maryland, and South Carolina, 1721–1785* (1929; reprint, New York: Da Capo Press, 1969); Henry W. Belknap, *Artists and Craftsmen of Essex County, Massachusetts* (Salem, Mass.: Essex Institute, 1927). Representative *Antiques* articles are reprinted in Robert F. Trent, ed., *Pilgrim Century Furniture: An Historical Survey* (New York: Main Street / Universe Books, 1976); and John J. Snyder, Jr., ed., *Philadelphia Furniture and Its Makers* (New York: Main Street / Universe Books, 1975). Joseph Downs and Ruth Ralston, *A Loan Exhibition of New York State Furniture with Contemporary Accessories* (New York: Metropolitan Museum of Art, 1934). Three state tercentenary celebrations followed this exhibition and catalogue format. They were *Three Centuries of Connecticut Furniture, 1635–1935* (Hartford: Tercentenary Commission of the State of Connecticut, 1935); *Harvard Tercentenary Exhibition: Catalogue of Furniture, Silver, Pewter, Glass, Ceramics, Paintings, Prints, Together with Allied Arts and Crafts of the Period 1636–1836* (Cambridge, Mass.: Harvard University Press, 1936); and *Rhode Island Tercentenary Celebration: A Catalogue of an Exhibition of Paintings by Gilbert Stuart, Furniture by the Goddards and Townsends, Silver by Rhode Island Silversmiths* (Providence: Rhode Island School of Design, 1936).

Fig. 1. Dressing table, labeled by Thomas Tufft (ca. 1738–88), Philadelphia, 1773–85. From Samuel W. Woodhouse, Jr., "Thomas Tufft," *Antiques* 12, no. 4 (October 1927): 293. (Winterthur Library.)

Fig. 2. High chest, labeled by William Savery (1722–87), Philadelphia, 1770–85. Mahogany; H. 94″. From William MacPherson Hornor, *Blue Book: Philadelphia Furniture, William Penn to George Washington* (Philadelphia: Privately printed, 1935), frontis. (Winterthur Library.)

the interplay of social, economic, and geographical factors. Their rede-
fined areal divisions emphasized observed natural and human conditions rather than imposed frameworks and ideals and resulted in notably
less precise boundaries. Regionalism, as this refinement of sectionalism
has come to be called, became an issue of great interest to historical
geographers of the 1930s, an academic group whose influence was proportionally greater then than it is today.[6] Their regional studies attempted
to identify the common denominators that bound a settled area together
and, to a lesser extent, to look for movement of ideas across the land.
The related field of linguistic geography also developed in a parallel manner. In an article of 1928, Hans Kurath argued against the prevailing theory that the local dialects of American English represented
substandard modifications of a single form of speech, Southern English
Standard, that developed over 200 years. He suggested instead that
dialectal differences among his twentieth-century American subjects owed
their origin to related differences in England at the time of American
settlement and to the influences of various migratory groups in the
intervening years. In 1939 he published the results of ten years' study
as *The Linguistic Atlas of New England* and its accompanying *Handbook*. The *Atlas* and its satellite publications have provided insight for
furniture scholars since the early 1970s. Finally, it is worth noting that
regionalism was a driving force behind many Works Progress Administration projects and the work of artists such as Grant Wood, John Steuart
Curry, and Thomas Hart Benton.[7]

The early regional studies of furniture established a valuable and
enduring approach to the subject. Regionalism gave structure to schol-

[6] See discussions of Morse's work and the U.S. censuses in Fulmer Mood, "The
Origin, Evolution, and Application of the Sectional Concept, 1750–1900," in *Regionalism in America*, ed. Merrill Jensen (Madison: University of Wisconsin Press, 1951), pp.
38–46, 65–84. Raymond D. Gastil, *Cultural Regions of the United States* (Seattle: University of Washington Press, 1975), p. vii. Concurrent use of regionalism by government
officials is discussed in Robert E. Dickinson, *City and Region: A Geographical Interpretation* (London: Routledge and Kegan Paul, 1964), pp. 508–9.

[7] Hans Kurath, "The Origin of the Dialectal Differences in Spoken American English,"
Modern Philology 25, no. 4 (May 1928): 385–95. Kurath's work shows the conflict between
regionalism and ethnocentrism. Hans Kurath, *The Linguistic Atlas of New England*
(Providence, R.I.: Brown University, 1939); Hans Kurath and B. Bloch, *Handbook of the
Linguistic Geography of New England* (Providence, R.I.: ACLS and Brown University,
1939). Kurath's work is discussed in John T. Kirk, *American Chairs: Queen Anne and
Chippendale* (New York: Alfred A. Knopf, 1972), pp. 195–200. Joshua Taylor, *The Fine
Arts in America* (Chicago: University of Chicago Press, 1979), pp. 192–95.

ars' efforts to identify and interpret similarities in construction, materials, form, and decoration. The results of this approach were sensible and proved to be an effective way to organize the growing corpus of early American furniture in public and private collections and the volume of new information about its makers and owners. Throughout the 1940s and 1950s, articles were published in *Antiques* and elsewhere that identified new furniture schools and traced regional sources. Regional studies assumed new direction and purpose with two 1962 publications. Helen Comstock's *American Furniture* and William R. Johnston's "Anatomy of the Chair" treated the subject comparatively. Each author concentrated on the different ways furniture was constructed or decorated in all the major regions of colonial America. As an interesting aside, each author started with the Queen Anne style as the point in time when regionalism became recognizable.[8] Furniture scholars are still troubled by the nature of regional patterns in William and Mary furniture—a period that links the highly localized patterns of the seventeenth-century production with the broader patterns of the mid eighteenth century. Regardless, the two presentations established a format that is still followed today in which recognition of regional expressions is sharpened through comparison of one region to another.

As comparative regional studies evolved, interregional differences became just as important a subject of inquiry as the similarities within a region. John Kirk brought this concern into sharp focus in his *American Chairs: Queen Anne and Chippendale* published in 1972. In his "regional approach to American furniture," he argued that furniture from his period of study should be evaluated according to the design principles and construction practices common to the region of their origin. "For example," he wrote, "a Connecticut chair should be assessed in relation to its peers and not against the chairs of, say, Philadelphia, for the desires of both makers and buyers in each region were markedly different."[9] Thus, knowing the geographical origin of an object became a critical step in its study and aesthetic appreciation.

Regional studies advanced significantly with Charles F. Montgomery's 1966 catalogue of federal furniture at Winterthur. Like virtually

[8] Helen Comstock, *American Furniture: Seventeenth, Eighteenth, and Nineteenth Century Styles* (1962; reprint, New York: Bonanza Books, n.d.), p. 74; William R. Johnston, "Anatomy of the Chair: American Regional Variations in Eighteenth Century Styles," *Metropolitan Museum of Art Bulletin* 21, no. 3 (November 1962): 118–29.

[9] Kirk, *American Chairs*, p. 3, see also chap. 1.

all such catalogues, it was organized by furniture form, but within each category the objects were arranged by region. Beyond the simple structure of the book, Montgomery presented such depth in his material that time and again he explored the causes and mechanisms of regionalism. He pioneered microanalysis of woods and plotted the presence of certain inlays to determine patterns of use across the land. He also revealed, almost incidentally, why certain patterns existed by citing such evidence as the furniture specialists in Baltimore who supplied the local trade with distinctive inlays. Later, Margaret Burke Clunie provided further documentation of the importance of specialists in her study of the Salem federal furniture trade, especially the career of Joseph True, a turner and carver who supplied table legs and other parts to the major furniture makers of Salem.[10]

Montgomery's search for the causes of regionalism did not end with his book. His essay in the catalogue *American Art: 1750–1800, Towards Independence* of 1976 addressed a series of practical questions about regionalism that asked why these various common denominators existed. He found his answers in craft practices and in changing patterns of taste. Of the two, craft practices are much more fully documented and understood, largely because Montgomery's students and others have unearthed a wealth of references to furniture-making practices as they pursued graduate degrees in the Winterthur Program in Early American Culture at the University of Delaware and other related programs. Recently, Benjamin A. Hewitt of New Haven, spurred by Montgomery's teaching at Yale, quantified and systematically tested regional characteristics of documented federal-period card tables. His computer-assisted study yielded statistically based profiles of regional norms which then served as measures for unidentified card tables.[11] His and others' research pointed again to clearly defined training and employment net-

[10] Charles F. Montgomery, *American Furniture: The Federal Period* (New York: Viking Press, 1966), pp. 27–40. Details about inlay makers in Baltimore appear in John Henry Hill, "The Furniture Craftsmen in Baltimore, 1783–1823" (M.A. thesis, University of Delaware, 1967), pp. 154–55. Hill discovered that Thomas Barrett, who supplied inlays to the trade, called himself "ebonist," thus distinguishing himself from other kinds of craftsmen. Margaret Burke Clunie, "Furniture Craftsmen of Salem, Massachusetts, in the Federal Period," *Essex Institute Historical Collections* 113, no. 3 (July 1977): 91–203; Margaret Burke Clunie, "Joseph True and the Piecework System in Salem," *Antiques* 111, no. 5 (May 1977): 1006–13.

[11] Charles F. Montgomery, "Regional Preferences and Characteristics in American Decorative Arts: 1750–1800," in *American Art: 1750–1800, Towards Independence*, ed. Charles F. Montgomery and Patricia E. Kane (Boston: New York Graphic Society, 1976),

works and specialization within the craft as key sources of regional expressions.

The issue of regional taste (the buyer's side of the marketplace), however, remains less certain. Montgomery's treatment of this issue was essentially descriptive rather than analytical. Ethnicity, he suggested, contributed substantially to regional preferences, but he failed to say how or why.[12] Thus, Pennsylvania Germans, for example, continued to favor certain furniture forms, decorative idioms, and other distinctive features familiar to them from their homelands. In a less identifiable manner, the tastes of various regional style centers reflected their distinct social and ethnic compositions.

In summary, regional studies generally conform to one of three types, each having its own objective. The first kind of regional study, pioneered by Hornor and still very much in evidence today, is an intensive reading of artifacts and written evidence that reconstructs a profile of localized craft practices and patterns of taste. It may or may not compare regions. This kind of study is essentially descriptive, often presenting the first classification of new objects and information. The second kind of study is a comparative examination of regional aesthetics, which is essentially evaluative and which may ultimately become a matter of personal choice.[13] The third, representing Montgomery's concerns and being the latest development, is the most self-consciously regional study in that it seeks answers to why regional traits or practices existed. It is analytical.

This brief survey of past regional studies brings us to the question of the role that regionalism plays in current furniture scholarship. Regionalism, as it applies to nineteenth-century furniture studies, raises a particularly important question, namely, its soundness as an approach to the subject. Many examples of nineteenth-century furniture, like a high-style "rustic" side chair (fig. 3), defy attempts to place them within customary geographical regions. Moreover, when regional origins can be determined, they may not reveal much. Intercity partnerships, large-

pp. 50–65, questions raised pp. 50–51, graduate research credited p. 18 n. 6. Benjamin A. Hewitt, "Regional Characteristics of American Federal-Period Card Tables," in Benjamin A. Hewitt, Patricia E. Kane, and Gerald W. R. Ward, *The Work of Many Hands Card Tables in Federal America, 1790–1820* (New Haven, Conn.: Yale University Ar Gallery, 1982), pp. 55–106.
[12] Montgomery, "Regional Preferences," pp. 56–57.
[13] Kirk, *American Chairs*, p. 3.

Fig. 3. Side chair, probably northeastern United States, 1850–60. Mahogany;
H. 35½″, W. 16½″, D. 20″. (Private
collection: Photo, Eugene C. Tate.)

scale warehousing, inexpensive transportation by railroad, and reduced
postal rates simply broke down the old regional barriers. Mid nineteenth-century furniture made by New Yorker John Henry Belter or his
many competent imitators, for example, was purchased by style-conscious people from all over the eastern half of the United States. In
1872, Montgomery Ward issued its first nationally distributed catalogue
and ensured a further degree of similarity among manufactured goods
and tastes across all regional boundaries.

Fig. 4. Side chair, probably northeastern United States, 1830–50. Mahogany, beech; H. 33″, W. 18½″, D. 20¼″. (Private collection: Photo, Eugene C. Tate).

Regionalism loses its importance during the nineteenth century as a key factor in understanding American furniture. However, the nature and extent of this change remains largely unexplored. Scholars must establish when shifts in manufacturing and marketing practices occurred and how they affect the old patterns of taste and availability. By the 1830s, many style-sensitive furniture forms expressed little, if any, regional character (fig. 4). Indeed, how much empire furniture can be region-alized? And does knowing where something was made at this time in history substantially add to our understanding of the material or of the community in which it was used? If it does enrich our understanding, *how* does it do so? Investigating these new directions and levels of appreciation will also help to clarify the nature of regionalism in earlier periods. A careful look at Hewitt's federal card table results, for instance, suggests that the boundaries of regionalism may have already begun to break down. To achieve the high levels of statistical accuracy needed to establish where undocumented examples were made, he had to expand and generalize his regional groupings of documented tables beyond useful boundaries.[14]

We encounter substantive problems in the eighteenth century as well. Recent research has uncovered instances that contradict or confound conventional interpretations based on regionalism. What distinguishes an example of Maryland Chippendale-style furniture from one made in Pennsylvania (fig. 5)? Many of the distinguishing characteristics cited in years past have since been proved inadequate.[15] Are we gradually discovering that, with the additional factual information that keeps coming to light, regionalism may not be as useful an approach as we thought it to be?

An underlying cause of some of the difficulties encountered in regional studies may stem from limitations in our understanding of the concept of regionalism. Regionalism, as we have seen, has been treated as self-evident.[16] Identification of a body of shared characteristics among

[14] Hewitt, "Regional Characteristics," pp. 58, 103–4, n. 4. Hewitt establishes a region called rural Massachusetts–New Hampshire which includes such locales as Springfield, Mass., in the upper Connecticut River valley; Antrim, in central New Hampshire; and Harvard, in central Massachusetts. A table in this group bears the label of Archelaus Flint of Charlestown, Mass., an area usually associated with, if not undifferentiated from, Boston. Other tables with his label are placed in the Newburyport and Boston area groups. Hewitt relies on Connecticut's political boundaries to define another region. This treatment obscures culturally dissimilar areas within the state, such as the western part, which relates to New York's Hudson River region, and the eastern shore, with its ties to Rhode Island. Some particularly problematic cabinetmaking centers, like Charleston, S. C., Portsmouth, N. H., and New Jersey communities, are omitted from his study. See Hewitt, List of Tables, "Regional Characteristics," pp. 178–83.

[15] This difficulty is acknowledged in Charles F. Hummel, *A Winterthur Guide to American Chippendale Furniture: Middle Atlantic and Southern Colonies* (New York: Rutledge Book/Crown Publishers, 1976), pp. 112, 135. Specific examples involving other regions and periods are common.

[16] Wendy Cooper expressed this idea recently by stating, "Regionalism is inherent and has existed for centuries, not only on this side of the Atlantic, but also all over the world" (Wendy A. Cooper, *In Praise of America* [New York: Alfred A. Knopf, 1980], p. 158).

Fig. 5. Armchair, Maryland or Philadelphia, 1765–80. Mahogany, yellow poplar; H. 41⅜″, W. 28⅞″, D. 23¾″. (Winterthur Museum.)

pieces of furniture not only produces a regional study but also inherently proves the existence of regionalism, or so we are to assume. Implicitly we see regionalism as a single, static fact or idea. It becomes a property of an object to be catalogued or, in unfamiliar examples, to be discovered.

Inquiry into other academic areas, however, reveals complexity in the nature of regionalism. By analyzing this complexity, regionalism can be sorted and tailored to fit historical conditions more exactly, thus becoming a richer tool for understanding early American furniture. Regionalism embodies at least three separate approaches or strategies: regionalism based on geographical characteristics, on social and economic conditions, and on broader cultural factors. These strategies are not mutually exclusive, but each emphasizes a certain set of circumstances. Thus, depending upon historical conditions at a particular time and place, one strategy may have advantages over the other.

Geographical regionalism has roots in historical geography. The relationship between a particular place, identified by physical characteristics of the land, and the people occupying that place is its focus. In the words of Robert E. Dickinson, it "seeks to evaluate the territorial factor in the life and organization of human communities." As adapted to furniture studies, these factors appear as conditions or circumstances that are tied to the land. Isolation or proximity to water routes may affect the movement of ideas or materials, thus influencing craft communities profoundly. Geographical features are evident in our use of secondary woods to indicate regional origin. That technique depends on the distribution of trees and to a lesser extent on commercial movement of wood which itself is influenced by topography. The technique becomes ineffective when some other factor disrupts the pattern, as happened when interregional trade in white pine developed between New England and Charleston and other southern coastal cities. [17]

Another example, also pertaining to the South, is less obvious but no less instructive in showing dependence upon geographical features to establish regional characteristics. Until the work of scholars at the Museum of Early Southern Decorative Arts and at Colonial Williamsburg showed otherwise, the South was thought to have had a poorly developed craft economy and to have exercised a stronger preference for English goods than in the Middle Atlantic or North. In *The Colonial Craftsman* (1950), Carl Bridenbaugh stated, "beyond basic needs almost no crafts developed." His reasoning is pure historical geography, almost

---

[17] Robert E. Dickinson, *Regional Ecology: The Study of Man's Environment* (New York: John Wiley and Sons, 1970), p. 41. See Dorothy Welker, "White Pine—A Northern Immigrant at Home on the Southern Coast," *Journal of Early Southern Decorative Arts* 3, no. 1 (May 1977): 11–26.

bordering on geographical determinism: "Nearly all craftsmen were inexorably drawn into planting or farming, because they could not gain a living from their trades. . . . In fact all the deterrents to the development of crafts have their origins in the topography of the South and its distinctive agricultural economy."[18]

Geographers have sought to explain regions and, in particular, the location and development of centers within those regions. One theory relevant to furniture studies and especially to interest in style centers seeks to explain the development of central places which provide goods and services to an entire region. The center is defined by function (furniture making, for example), rather than by location. The size of the region served by the center depends on transportation costs and other factors based on physical conditions. The theory suggests, for instance, that at a certain distance south of Boston, a buyer will turn to Rhode Island for a stylish chest of drawers. Central-place theory also distinguishes between central functions or professions and those professions that are practiced throughout the region.[19] A parallel in furniture studies exists in the ability of certain communities to support such skills as gilding, ornamental carving, and some kinds of upholstery. Other subtler differences distinguish urban and rural furniture-making practices and products, but precision in this area of study continues to challenge the scholar.

Although central-place theory necessarily involves economic factors, it is essentially a spatial explanation; however, we can also explain regionalism in economic and social terms. Such a framework is most visible in the many discussions of master-apprentice networks and schools.

[18] All kinds of craft activity have appeared regularly in the *Journal of Early Southern Decorative Arts* published by the Museum of Early Southern Decorative Arts. Wallace B. Gusler discussed Virginia cabinetmaking in detail in *Furniture of Williamsburg and Eastern Virginia, 1710–1790* (Richmond: Virginia Museum of Fine Arts, 1979). Carl Bridenbaugh, *The Colonial Craftsman* (4th ed.; Chicago: University of Chicago Press, 1971), pp. 29, 31.

[19] The central-place theory is applied in James T. Lemon, *The Best Poor Man's Country: A Geographical Study of Early Southeastern Pennsylvania* (1972; reprint, New York: W. W. Norton, 1976), pp. 118–19, 184–86, bibliographical references to the theory p. 258, n. 4. A more recent treatment may be found in Bruce C. Daniels, *The Connecticut Town: Growth and Development, 1635–1790* (Middletown, Conn.: Wesleyan University Press, 1979), chap. 6. Walter Christaller, *Central Places in Southern Germany*, trans. Carlisle W. Baskin (Englewood Cliffs, N. J.: Prentice-Hall, 1966), p. 14.

Account-book references document close working relationships among craftsmen and shops. In 1811, New Yorker John Hewitt referred to making Phyfe columns and Lannuier columns. Such terminology suggests that both Duncan Phyfe and Charles-Honoré Lannuier depended to some degree on independent pieceworkers to complete their own shop orders. Cooperation among various craftsmen led to regionalized designs. Similarly, the same carvers might serve many masters. And conversely, a shop owner might employ many carvers to complete an important commission. Supplies of similar parts, whether inlays, turned legs, or other pieces, passed between shops, as did shop tools and patterns, when an owner died or sold his business.[20] All these factors produced the similarities in appearance that we recognize as regional characteristics.

Economic and social factors underlie the well-known example of regional clash and accommodation manifested in the work of Eliphalet Chapin. He carried his Philadelphia training into East Windsor, Connecticut, and built chairs that at first blush look like other New England products but have several Philadelphia characteristics, including "stump" rear legs, through-tenons, and vertical corner blocks (fig. 6). Chapin was not the only tie between the two geographically separated communities. Benjamin Burnham "sarvfed his time in Felledlfey" learning the cabinetmaking trade, if not spelling. Unlike Chapin, however, Burnham did not incorporate Philadelphia design or construction characteristics into the desk he made, the only documented example of his work. Other links between Philadelphia and Connecticut furniture making appear in some Queen Anne–style chairs from New London County, Connecticut, and, especially, from the Wethersfield area. These chairs, which have recently been reassessed by Robert F. Trent, exhibit as many

---

[20] Hewitt quoted in Michael Brown, "Duncan Phyfe" (M.A. thesis, University of Delaware, 1978), pp. 66–67. Clunie, "Furniture Craftsmen," pp. 194–96. One of the best examples of the practice of employing carvers is recorded by a bill from Thomas Affleck to John Cadwalader dated October 13, 1770, and reproduced in Nicholas B. Wainwright, *Colonial Grandeur in Philadelphia: The House and Furniture of General John Cadwalader* (Philadelphia: Historical Society of Pennsylvania, 1964), p. 44. For additional discussion, see Philip D. Zimmerman, "A Methodological Study in the Identification of Some Important Philadelphia Chippendale Furniture," in *American Furniture and Its Makers: Winterthur Portfolio 13*, ed. Ian M. G. Quimby (Chicago: University of Chicago Press, 1979), pp. 200, 206–8. Shop practices of shared supplies are detailed in Philip D. Zimmerman, "Workmanship as Evidence: A Model for Object Study," *Winterthur Portfolio 16*, no. 4 (Winter 1981): 301–5.

Fig. 6. Side chair, attributed to Eliphalet Chapin
(1741–1807), East Windsor, Conn., ca. 1780. Cherry;
H. 38″, W. 22¾″, D. 22″. (Winterthur Museum.)

as three construction features typical of Philadelphia: compass-shape
seat rails laid flat with the front legs secured by round tenons, through-
tenons in the rear legs, and chamfered stump rear legs. Stylistically
earlier than either Chapin's or Burnham's working dates, the chairs

demand another explanation for their structural relationships. Trent and John Kirk have each suggested that craft ties to England may account for the similarities, although confirming evidence has not yet come to light. These common denominators extend into the Chippendale period, too, as shown in a side chair now thought to be from Connecticut with "Pennsylvania"-type tulip-and-vine carving on the rear stiles and across the crest rail (fig. 7).[21]

The last regional strategy uses a broader, anthropological approach based on cultural geography. Here the factors that bind an area together are drawn from a wide range of sources, including religion, language, political, economic, and social structures, and artifacts. Despite the seemingly general or all-inclusive nature of this approach, it functions well in specific ways. It provides the necessary framework for looking at the furniture of Pennsylvania Germans, Shakers, or other culturally detached communities in which economic forces or geographical circumstances simply do not adequately account for unity among a group of people. Benno M. Forman's sensitivity to the cultural foundations of regional characteristics revealed the distinctive qualities of Philadelphia high-style furniture traceable to German influences in a region politically and economically dominated by Englishmen.[22]

[21] For discussion of Chapin's chairs, see Kirk, *American Chairs*, pp. 187–88. Kirk analyzes a high chest attributed to Chapin in *Early American Furniture* (New York: Alfred A. Knopf, 1970), pp. 103–5. Chapin's career is detailed in Ethel Hall Bjerkoe, *The Cabinetmakers of America* (1957; reprint, New York: Bonanza Books, n.d.), pp. 59–62. For biographical information, see Houghton Bulkeley, "Benjamin Burnham of Colchester, Cabinetmaker," in *Contributions to Connecticut Cabinet Making* (Hartford: Connecticut Historical Society, 1967), pp. 28–33, inscription fig. 9. Robert F. Trent, "New London County Joined Chairs," *Connecticut Historical Society Bulletin* 50, no. 4 (Fall 1985): 39–40. Trent's analysis does not associate the chamfered rear legs with Philadelphia work. John T. Kirk, *Connecticut Furniture: Seventeenth and Eighteenth Centuries* (Hartford, Conn.: Wadsworth Atheneum, 1967), p. xiv, cat. 229. The chair, one of a pair, was purchased at a Parke-Bernet auction in 1964 for exhibition in the newly restored General Gates House in York, Pa. All the furnishings were intended to represent the kinds of things a well-to-do Englishman might have owned in a south-central Pennsylvania urban house. The house and furnishings are now owned by the Historical Society of York County.

[22] The standard text on cultural geography is Wilbur Zelinsky, *The Cultural Geography of the United States* (Englewood Cliffs, N.J.: Prentice-Hall, 1973). Related useful ideas may also be found in Henry Glassie, *Pattern in the Material Folk Culture of the Eastern United States* (Philadelphia: University of Pennsylvania Press, 1968), pp. 33ff. Benno M. Forman, "German Influences in Pennsylvania Furniture," in Scott T. Swank et al., *Arts of the Pennsylvania Germans*, ed. Catherine E. Hutchins (New York: W. W. Norton, 1983), pp. 102–70.

Fig. 7. Side chair, Connecticut, 1760–90. Cherry;
H. 39″, W. 20¾″, D. 20½″. (Historical Society of
York County, Pa.: Photo, Eugene C. Tate.)

Awareness of the three regional strategies can be use᠎ to great
advantage both in evaluating regional studies and in pursuing them.
Trent's statement in *New England Begins* that more is known about
English regional sources of seventeenth-century New England joinery
and turning than for any other region or period in American furniture

is true. But he also notes that the scale of life was different from the later periods.[23] In many ways it was smaller, simpler, and more localized. Moreover, its characteristics may defy effective comparison with later periods. Thus his treatment of seventeenth-century objects, which depends heavily on geographical regionalism, may not be appropriate for the study of later objects.

Trent related objects by their structure and decoration, then traced them to a specific locale through family histories, and finally attributed them to the most prominent workman visible in the records.[24] His attributions become compelling upon acceptance of two conditions: that his object analysis and extensive documentary research not only are correct but also accommodate all reasonable possibilities and that seventeenth-century communities were sufficiently isolated that the variables—objects, family histories, and workman—related to one another only. In short, his interpretative method assumes a highly localized regional phenomenon based largely on geographical factors. In other words, distances between settlements or communities impeded interchange of craftsmen or their products. Trent's ability to attribute certain pieces of furniture to individuals is directly related to the numbers of identifiable craftsmen in any one area. His many attributions, which may appear excessive to scholars more familiar with the later periods, may be questioned, but only by the challenging task of discovering new evidence that disproves the geographical regionalism foundation or that introduces reasonable alternatives to one or more of the variables.

If we attempt to use this same method for studying most late eighteenth-century furniture, we will fail. Family histories may still lead the researcher back in time to a locale, but craft practices had changed enough to obscure the individual hand. Ample evidence demonstrates that individual shops were capable of broad ranges in style and technique which overlapped with other shops. Consider the substantial differences in design and technique in two chairs labeled by Benjamin Randolph of Philadelphia (figs. 8, 9). Aside from their differences in proportion, design, and carved decoration, only one (fig. 8) has through-tenons and visible pins securing the seat rails. Conversely, separate shops

---

[23] Robert F. Trent, "New England Joinery and Turning before 1700," in Jonathan L. Fairbanks and Robert F. Trent, *New England Begins: The Seventeenth Century*, vol. 3 (Boston: Museum of Fine Arts, 1982), p. 501.

[24] Trent, "New England Joinery," 3:501.

Fig. 8. Side chair, labeled by Benjamin Randolph (w. 1760–82), Philadelphia, 1760–80. Mahogany; H. 38⅜", W. 23¾", D. 19". (Museum of Fine Arts, Boston, M. and M. Karolik Collection.)

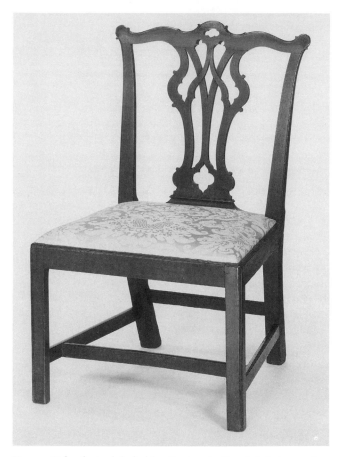

Fig. 9. Side chair, labeled by Benjamin Randolph (w. 1760–82), Philadelphia, 1760–80. Mahogany, Atlantic white cedar; H. 37″, W. 22⅝″, D. 19⁹⁄₁₆″. (Yale University Art Gallery, the Mabel Brady Garvan Collection.)

could produce similar work, like published examples of a labeled Tufft dressing table and a Savery high chest (see figs. 1, 2).

What happened to create this confusion? The geography did not change; it simply was overcome by improved transportation of goods and communication among shops and by increased mobility among workers. Consequently, economic and social factors tend to determine groupings of eighteenth-century furniture. In short, eighteenth-century regionalism is different from that of the seventeenth century. We may discover that assignment of regional origin by the nineteenth century is so difficult in some cases that, in the final analysis, the historical conditions that once supported regionalism must no longer exist. Similarly, objects of a known place of origin, like Belter's New York furniture of the 1860s, may have been so widely distributed throughout America that they lose much of their regional significance.

Acceptance that regionalism is not a constant factor in American furniture history imposes the need to determine the nature and extent of geographical, economic and social, or cultural phenomena before embarking on any study with regional overtones. In each case there are related works in other disciplines that help to sharpen our own methods and interpretations.

Part of our regional interpretation of eighteenth-century Dunlap-style furniture from southern New Hampshire is to call it "country." That label carries more assumed meaning than actual. Does *country* merely identify the dispersed regional services (that is, furniture design) of central-place theory—in essence, a lower grade of cabinetmaking in areas around a style center? Or is there a fundamental difference between a country and a regional style center? Concerning the Dunlaps, we know little about them as individuals, and we may never be able to determine who actually made each object, thereby losing potentially valuable investigative material; however, we can still use different regional approaches to advantage and shed light on our understanding of country furniture.

Distinctive decorative traits characterize Dunlap case furniture. They include the use of multiple shells, pronounced S scrolls along the lower edge of the skirt, and bold "flowered ogee" moldings. A full expression of this group of furniture is a chest-on-chest-on-frame (fig. 10). Its weighty cornice bears an uncanny resemblance (given the differences in time and space) to the crest of a late seventeenth-century armchair made in 1695 by Robert Rhea of Freehold, New Jersey (fig. 11).[25] Parallels between

<hr/>

[25] For thorough discussion of Dunlap furniture, see Charles S. Parsons, *The Dunlaps and Their Furniture* (Manchester, N.H.: Currier Gallery of Art, 1970); for the Rhea armchair, Charles T. Lyle and Philip D. Zimmerman, "Furniture of the Monmouth County Historical Association," *Antiques* 117, no. 1 (January 1980): 187.

Fig. 10. Chest-on-chest-on-frame, attributed to the Dunlap school, Henniker or Salisbury, N.H., 1790–95. Maple, white pine; H. 82½″, W. 41″, D. 18¾″. (Currier Gallery of Art.)

Fig. 11. Armchair, attributed to Robert Rhea (d. 1720), Monmouth County, N.J., 1695. White oak, southern yellow pine; H. 42¾″, W. 25¾″, D. 27¾″. (Monmouth County Historical Association: Photo, Helga Photo Studio.)

the two exist in massing, which strains the limits of pleasing proportion, and in decorative motifs and their placement. The central motif in each is a shell or fan set within a rectangular panel. It is flanked by additional rectangular elements defined by deeply carved striae. Shells or pinwheels terminate each, and scrolls arch over each central shell.

Relationships based solely on visual analysis, especially of such disparate pieces of furniture, must be treated with great skepticism. Nonetheless, they may open fruitful paths of inquiry. Although there is no geographical unity or any economic or social factor tying these two pieces of furniture across such a time span, there is a cultural link. Rhea was a Scot, and he made a Scottish chair, complete with a thistle carved below the initials and date in the back panel. The Dunlaps were born in New Hampshire of a Scotch-Irish father. Whether he or others trained the Dunlaps, it is reasonable to assume that that generation was familiar with late seventeenth-century Scottish furniture similar to the Rhea chair in addition to the newer styles in vogue when they left for America in the 1720s and 1730s. Among the earlier forms is a joined chair with pinwheels and a prominent shell (fig. 12). Dated 1690, it is listed in the 1696 inventory of furnishings in Trinity Hall, Aberdeen.[26] Later furniture, like the early eighteenth-century side chair now in the John Knox House in Edinburgh (fig. 13), suggests additional Dunlap motifs, in this case the counterposed scrolls carved into the crest that may have inspired the bold S scrolls at the base of the chest-on-chest.

The value of this exercise lies in recognizing that traditional decorative schemes inspired the imaginative designs of the Dunlaps. Their work, when considered as a regional school, becomes more comprehensible and informative. It raises the possibility that the Dunlaps and the Scotch-Irish settlers whom they represent retained a significant portion of their cultural identity long after arriving in America. Because they were English-speaking, we may have assumed their assimilation into English ways of life too readily. If, in fact, material culture analysis defines a Scotch-Irish subculture, we not only add to our understanding of this large group of immigrants but also enhance the concept of country. Dunlap furniture designs seem to draw more heavily from traditional Scotch-Irish sources than colonial American style centers. Thus

[26] David Learmont, "The Trinity Hall Chairs, Aberdeen," *Furniture History* 14 (1978): 1–2, 5, pl. 10.

Fig. 12. Armchair, Aberdeen, Scotland, 1690. Oak; H. 50½". In the collection of Trinity Hall, Aberdeen, Scotland. From Margaret Jourdain, *English Decoration and Furniture of the Early Renaissance (1500–1650): An Account of Its Development and Characteristic Forms* (London: B. T. Batsford, 1924), p. 255 fig. 255. (Winterthur Library.)

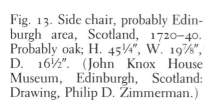

Fig. 13. Side chair, probably Edinburgh area, Scotland, 1720–40. Probably oak; H. 45¼", W. 19⅞", D. 16½". (John Knox House Museum, Edinburgh, Scotland: Drawing, Philip D. Zimmerman.)

they alter the model of provincial craftsmen of uncertain training who reinterpreted regional high-style precedents in their own creative manner.[27]

Regional studies do not always respond directly to the particular questions of the day. But over the long term they have shown their value in organizing our basic understanding of early American furniture and have at times revealed significant insight into early cultural history. Now, more than ever before, we are able to build on past studies and to tighten our interpretations of material evidence while expanding their usefulness to other scholars. The future of regionalism lies in continued pursuit of the historical conditions that led to localized groupings of furniture. Properly applied, regionalism is also a valuable and dynamic tool that can shape our thinking about artifacts and how they inform us of their makers and users.

[27] The concept of country is discussed in Kirk, *Early American Furniture*, pp. 95–98.

American Furniture in an International Context

John T. Kirk

I believe that in most cases American work can be distinguished from European examples, although at times they can be very close in design, materials, and construction. I place American objects in an international context not to diminish their stature, but to increase their aesthetic and cultural significance.

Until twenty years ago few scholars of American objects saw them as so closely allied with European artifacts that they are at times almost interchangeable. Until recently parochialness combined with chauvinism and made it nearly anti-American to think of our culture and its expressions as extensions of European patterns. Many now realize that the view of America as progenitor implied that people got off the boats in the seventeenth and eighteenth centuries, looked around, and said, "Now let's be different." Many of the early settlers did strive for a strict theological stance not shared by most of those they left behind, but they did not seek or quickly achieve a cultural independence. From 1944 until his death in 1949, Waldron Phoenix Belknap, Jr., undertook the first systematic exploration of the link between American and European artistic expressions. In a search for print dependence in American painting, he found that European prints often provided a range of images, from chairs, tables, and urns to entire compositions. For example, major American eighteenth-century portraitist John Singleton Copley freely used printed images, even ones with trees although his own setting was full of them: Copley's *General Joshua Winslow* copies the landscape in a print depicting Sir John Perceval (figs. 1, 2).[1] It has long been accepted that many "American" artists had first, or later, worked on the other side of the Atlantic, but the paintings they made here were held to be more interesting, more important. Copley, who escaped in the other direction, had been deemed great, as an artist and as a person, only to the point of his departure. Belknap's findings pushed European and American work closer together, and this rattled scholars, dealers, and collectors of American art, for it seemed then to deny any American artistic originality. It was nearly heresy when in 1966 Jules Prown, in a two-volume study, treated Copley's English work as seriously as his American oeuvre.[2]

This myopic view of our art gradually broke apart. Thus, in the catalogue for the 1976 bicentennial exhibition at the Yale University Art Gallery and the Victoria and Albert Museum, Prown could show American designs as part of a natural cultural flow from Europe. Still, in that essay Prown leaves the impression that much that is of value in American art began here, particularly an emphasis on line and plainness.[3] This wrongly continued the impression that no other culture has employed surface and line, rather than ornamentation, as a major factor in its creative process. In fact, these design features have been part of many cultures. The serene elegance of early Chinese furniture joined with and quieted European baroque movement in one of the design

---

[1] Belknap's work was published posthumously in a summary in 1955 and his notes in 1959: *The Waldron Phoenix Belknap, Jr., Collection of Portraits and Silver, with a Note on the Discoveries of Waldron Phoenix Belknap, Jr., Concerning the Influence of the English Mezzotint on Colonial Painting*, ed. John Marshall Phillips, Barbara N. Parker, and Kathryn C. Buhler (Cambridge, Mass.: Harvard University Press, 1955), pp. 125–63; Waldron Phoenix Belknap, Jr., *American Colonial Painting: Materials for a History* (Cambridge, Mass.: Harvard University Press, Belknap Press, 1959), pp. 271–330. Trevor J. Fairbrother, "John Singleton Copley's Use of British Mezzotints for His American Portraits: A Reappraisal Prompted by New Discoveries," *Arts* 55, no. 7 (March 1981): 122–30. New discoveries were an occasion to discuss Copley's creative process; a list of all previously published Copley borrowings is included. One of the main contributions of this article is a discussion of the use of prints and old sketches by major London portraitists in helping their clients to establish the kind of portrait they wanted and the use of studio specialists in such details as drapery and clothing. This aligns American artists' use of prints with mainstream London practice.

[2] Today the comparisons are found less shocking, and scholars can concentrate on what is new in the handling of borrowed images. Jules David Prown, *John Singleton Copley*, 2 vols. (Cambridge, Mass.: Harvard University Press, 1966).

[3] Jules David Prown, "Style in American Art: 1750–1800," in *American Art: 1750–1800, Towards Independence*, ed. Charles F. Montgomery and Patricia E. Kane (Boston: New York Graphic Society, 1976), pp. 32–49.

Fig. 1. John Singleton Copley (1738–1815), *General Joshua Winslow*. Boston, dated 1755. Oil on canvas; H. 50″, W. 40″. (Santa Barbara Museum of Art, Preston Morton Collection.)

attitudes of early eighteenth-century Europe and thereby America. Chinese chairs provided crest rails with ears, back posts rounded above the seat, and splats with straight edges from the front and shaped to reverse curves from the side. The base of the chair in figure 3 has a skirt shaped to reverse curves and a raised-edge molding as used on much Queen Anne and early Georgian furniture. The Italian chairs show features associated with China, England, and America, although the form of the parts is just slightly more dramatic (fig. 4). English chairs

Fig. 2. John Smith (1652?–1742), *Sir John Percivale Bart. of Burton in the County of Cork in Ireland*. London, ca. 1708, after a painting by Sir Godfrey Kneller, 1704. Mezzotint; H. 16½", W. 10¼". (Private collection.)

are as unadorned as most American chairs (fig. 5; this chair, one of a set, employs the through-tenon seat construction associated in America with Philadelphia work.[4]) Published furniture designs that stressed line, such as those of George Hepplewhite (1788), for example, inspired related forms in many countries. Upon occasion in the nineteenth century

[4]Colonial Williamsburg's archives record the chairs as being purchased in Bath, England. Dealer David Stockwell reported in a September 1980 conversation that John

Fig. 3. Chair, China, late seventeenth or early eighteenth century. *Hong mu* wood; H. 44⅞", W. 23¼", D. 17¾". (Den Danske Kunstindustri-museum.)

Graham purchased them for Williamsburg in York, England, and that they were considered local chairs. This seat construction appears in about 95 percent of Philadelphia eighteenth-century chairs, a few Connecticut chairs of the same date, a small number of New York Chippendale-style chairs, and some neoclassical Newport chairs. The use of through-tenons in England and on the Continent is discussed in John T. Kirk, *American Furniture and the British Tradition to 1830* (New York: Alfred A. Knopf, 1982), pp. 128–32.

Fig. 4. Set of three chairs, Italy, probably northern, 1720–40. Walnut. (Palazzo Pisani, Stra, near Venice: Photo, John T. Kirk.)

plainness became a feature of European taste, and those styles were reflected in American furniture, as with the "pillar and scroll" designs of the 1830s and 1840s. Other internationally related line-dependent designs emerged about 1900 in the work of Scotland's Charles Rennie Mackintosh, Austria's Josef Hoffmann, and America's Frank Lloyd Wright. In the 1950s Danish designers such as Hans Wegner gave the world a new, lean, wood aesthetic. It is, then, not a plain line or a clean surface that denotes the American design attitude; rather, it is *how* line and surface are used that distinguishes American objects from related European examples.

The past ten years have seen the gradual acceptance of the natural dependence of American expressions, cultural and artistic. American work, English precedents for American pieces, and European pieces used in New England are fully integrated in both text and illustrations in the recent *New England Furniture: The Colonial Era* by Brock Jobe and Myrna Kaye. In 1763 Samuel Walker of London made a set of chairs, and Nathaniel Barrell of York, Maine, brought them to New

Fig. 5. Chair, northern England, 1720–50. Walnut and pine; H. 40¼″, W. 20¼″, D. 16½″. (Courtesy Colonial Williamsburg.)

England where they were copied. In *New England Furniture*, the English and New England versions receive equal attention. But even this excellent study continues the general bias toward American furniture, in part by maintaining some terms that connote separateness. In the text two different versions of corner blocks in chairs are described by form and the direction of their grain, while cross ties are said to be "in an English manner."[5] In fact, all three forms of seat bracing were used in various areas of Europe before becoming standard in these colonies.

With the recent acceptance of the integration of American and European art, there is renewed emphasis on American superiority— aesthetic and cultural. American objects are often described as "more beautiful," "more original," "more significant." Perhaps this bias is an understandable part of a national striving for international artistic and cultural significance. But I do not understand why it is demeaning to America and American art objects to find that at times American expressions are more interesting, at times European work more fascinating, and at other times both are about equal in meriting attention.

The new chauvinism parallels the trend for furniture historians to ask more and more detailed questions. Beginning with European sources, it is logical to move to American regionalism, then contrast the work of two towns and focus on makers and then on shop practices. This process starts with world questions and ends with whether the grain of the drawer bottom runs front to back or side to side. The latter is necessary and important information, but the approach is capable of spiraling to smaller and smaller issues, although it can go in the other direction. A by-product of this approach has been a sometimes unfortunate neo-1920s paper chase to find the name of at least one local person who might have made furniture and link it to the locally made products.[6] In the hands of skillful and careful scholars willing to admit the problems inherent in paper research, this approach has recovered important information. In a few instances the unbridled desire to link maker and

---

[5] Many recent cultural studies have accepted what were previously seen as new American cultural patterns as simply extensions of numerous European practices. Bernard Bailyn establishes the influx into the colonies of individuals and groups as a logical extension of the greater mobility within western Europe than has previously been recognized as people sought "employment, security, and a hopeful future" (*The Peopling of British North America: An Introduction* [New York: Alfred A. Knopf, 1986], p. 20). Brock Jobe and Myrna Kaye, *New England Furniture: The Colonial Era* (Boston: Houghton Mifflin Co., 1984), p. 92.

[6] Two entries in an important exhibition catalogue demonstrate the shortcomings of emphasizing paper evidence over a close look at the object under study: see *The Great River: Art and Society of the Connecticut Valley, 1635–1820* (Hartford: Wadsworth Atheneum, 1985), cats. 78, 99. The first cites numerous documents in an attempt to link the cupboard to the hand of Peter Blin. The exercise in itself is not terribly convincing, while at the same time the entry overlooks one major alteration to the piece which must surely be taken into account before speculating on the possible maker and relating it to other pieces: The top board has the mass and edge shaping associated with seventeenth-

object has allowed distracting leaps of faith and, on occasion, caused the misdating of an object simply to attribute it to a maker who worked before or after the piece's real date. Patricia E. Kane in her judicious study *Furniture of the New Haven Colony* warned us against an over-emphasis on makers' names when she showed how furniture joiners were often listed under less obvious designations and made furniture without being recorded as furniture makers. To understand the history of furniture, the arts in general, and cultural developments, it is more important to have an accurately dated piece than even a secure link between maker and object. In his article "The Origins of the Joined Chest of Drawers," published in Europe in 1981, Benno M. Forman brilliantly integrated documents and objects from the Netherlands, England, and America and broadened our understanding of three mid seventeenth-century cultures. He used the Boston chest of drawers with doors which relates in overall design to a London example, dated 1662 (figs. 6, 7). (The form and the placement of the lower applied turnings suggest that none of the applied turnings on the English chest are orig-inal.) The Boston piece has turnings like those on a London cupboard dated 1654 and initialed I^{W}P and stamped SH (fig. 8). Unfortunately the midcentury dates of the London pieces are now often ignored since a current approach is to identify the Boston example, and an even later related Boston piece without doors, with makers that arrived in Boston in the 1630s.[7]

century chest tops and not contemporary cupboard tops. Physical evidence supports this observation: the right rear edge has a hole with surrounding marks suggesting that it once held a snipe-bill hinge; the right end has holes probably from nails that once held an end cleat when the board was a chest top. Again, for the second entry (a desk and bookcase), stress is placed on histories and inventories in relating it to other pieces. But two features of the piece that relate it to another desk (cat. 107) are overlooked. It is not of cherry (as cited), but is probably of walnut or possibly mahogany, and the raised door panels are cut from solid boards, not constructed of rails and stiles around panels in the normal manner. Thus the door of the desk and bookcase and the deeply shaped lid and front of the desk are similar in construction and aesthetics.

[7]Patricia E. Kane, *Furniture of the New Haven Colony: The Seventeenth-Century Style* (New Haven: New Haven Colony Historical Society, 1973); Benno M. Forman, "The Origins of the Joined Chest of Drawers," *Nederlands Kunst-historisch Jaarboek* 31 (1981): 169–83. After Forman's death, the article was edited and extended: Benno M. Forman, "The Chest of Drawers in America, 1635–1730: The Origins of the Joined Chest of Drawers," *Winterthur Portfolio* 20, no. 1 (Spring 1985): 1–30. It expands For-man's text and number of illustrations and, regrettably, alters Forman's dating scheme and back dates the Boston pieces and some London work to link them with London-trained workers who arrived in Boston at the earlier date.

Fig. 6. Chest of drawers with doors, Boston, Mass., 1650–70. Red oak, white oak, chestnut, walnut, soft maple, eastern white pine, cedar, cedrela *(Cedrela odorata)*, snakewood *(Piratinesa guianensis)*, rosewood *(Dalbergia* spp.), and lignum vitae *(Guaiacum* spp.); H. 48⅞″, 45⅜″, D. 23¾.″ (Courtesy Yale University Art Gallery, the Mabel Brady Garvan Collection.)

The exploitation of countless other informative European documents and objects has hardly begun. For example, the records of the Gillows firm of Lancaster, in the northwest of England, have yet to be

Fig. 7. Chest of drawers with doors, London, dated 1662. Oak, bone, and mother-of-pearl. From Percy Macquoid and Ralph Edwards, *The Dictionary of English Furniture*, vol. 2 (London, New York, 1924), fig. 5. (Winterthur Library.)

mined in any significant manner by American or European scholars. This vast group of papers describes in detail—with accompanying drawings—the making and distribution of thousands of items. They are sources for understanding shop practices, materials, patronage, and the date of introduction and longevity of styles and motifs: one drawing records the

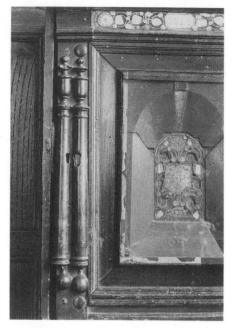

Fig. 8. Detail of small cupboard, London, dated 1654. Oak, other woods, and mother-of-pearl. (Christchurch Mansion, Ipswich, Suffolk: Photo, John T. Kirk.)

use of a "Queen Anne" turned foot as late as 1793.[8] The sketch of the deal bedstead helps us to date similar American examples (fig. 9). Although present understanding suggests that straight legs denote a "Chippendale" date, the piece was made in 1796. The Gillows archives also signal the reintroduction of styles and features as the nineteenth century took up the revival of earlier ideas.

The study of such records can be part of moving to smaller and smaller concerns or part of opening the field to wider artistic and cultural questions, questions that were once held to be the prerogative of

---

[8] Kirk, *American Furniture*, p. 322, fig. 1255.

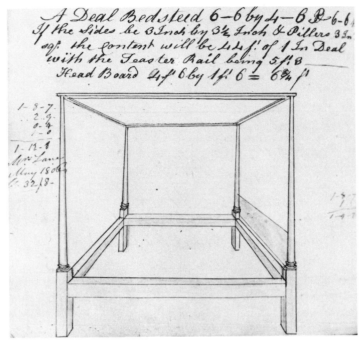

Fig. 9. Part of page showing a bedstead, Estimate Books, Gillows of Lancaster papers, dated 1796. Ink drawing on paper; H. (full page) 12½", W. 7¼". (City of Westminster Public Library, London: Photo, John T. Kirk.)

art historians: patronage, style, quality, and connoisseurship. Some scholars who deal with artifacts dismiss these areas of exploration as too aligned with elite work—excellent aesthetic achievements—which they find unique and thus too unrepresentative to demonstrate cultural significance. That aesthetic questions greatly concerned the original makers and owners of what they study is ignored. Such an easy dismissal gives credence to scholars of "high art"—academic painting and architecture—who dismiss furniture as part of the minor arts existing below any level of importance. For them, artifacts as we understand them remain outside eternal truths which they see as the property of high art. For them, paintings and not chairs have a creative power which by instruction and delight can add a dimension to the viewer. I believe that this power to increase our stature lies also in artifacts, vernacular and elite, urban and rural.[9] To understand and use American furniture significantly as art and as a cultural indicator, it is essential to consider the artistic quality of each object, the interdependence of all objects—American, European, and Oriental—made at any historical moment, and the ways in which they can be examined as cultural expressions at any point in their continued existence; that is, how they integrated into and expressed their time of creation and their role anytime thereafter when they again took an active part in the cultural context.

The quest to exploit fully *all* artifacts means an openness to valuing continuum as much as uniqueness. In the hands of many scholars, dealers, and collectors, the bold silhouette of a late seventeenth-century Boston leather chair is American and particular to Boston (fig. 10). But similar chairs were used in England, and accepting the parallel between English and American people using similar objects reveals the bridges that existed between the disparate societies.[10]

At the English court level there was another expression unlike American work. In this milieu a chair could employ a covering of expensive velvet, even to the floor (fig. 11; the velvet was probably originally purple but is now black with exotic material cut up and applied: probably Turkish embroidery executed in silver strip over what looks like leather or vellum).[11]

The separation of similar American and English furniture from English court work has been suggested before, but the unity this gave the similar English and American owners has not been sufficiently

[9] Jules David Prown in a recent guest editor's statement (*Art Journal* 44, no. 4 [Winter 1984]: 313–14) describes a shift back to art history as the base for many young scholars of American objects. After discussing how much of the work during the past decade has been by those in "American studies, literature, folklore and folklife, anthropology, and other fields," he notes: "But the younger contributors [to this issue of the *Journal*] are once more, I believe, pure art historians, suggesting the resiliency of our field as we have assimilated new approaches and methodologies to our academic programs."

[10] A comparison with English chairs with original cushions (fig. 11, for example) and their appearance in contemporary paintings and prints shows the modern cushion included in figure 10 to be overfull. It denies both the original aesthetic stance of cushions that continued the line of the seat upward and their cultural role which guaranteed warm and easy comfort.

[11] Peter Thornton to John T. Kirk, 1980. The chair is accompanied by a footstool and X-frame stools of chair-seat height; see Kirk, *American Furniture*, figs. 676–678.

Fig. 10. Chair, Boston, Mass., 1640–80. Oak and maple, leather; H. 38″, W. 23⅝″, D. 16⅜″. (Courtesy Museum of Fine Arts, Boston, William E. Nickerson Fund.)

explored.[12] If we move to an even more elaborately structured Continental culture, such as Venice, we can find a leather chair, a velvet chair, and a gold chair (fig. 12). The gold chair has the same basic units as the velvet and leather chairs—rectangular seat and back and similar posts and arms, although they are elaborately carved and gilded. Broadening the study in this way allows the Venice gold chair to be seen in relationship to the English velvet chair in much the same way that the velvet chair relates to the Boston leather chair. Such comparisons do

[12] Kirk, *American Furniture*, pp. 159–62.

Fig. 11. Chair, London, 1625–40. (Knole: Photo,
Robert Wemyss Symonds Collection of Photographs, Joseph Downs Manuscript and Microfilm Collection, Winterthur Library.)

not alter the cultural or aesthetic importance of the Boston chair; rather,
it now becomes an active contributor to understanding the cultural tex-
ture of the Western world, and through this we more fully understand
Boston. To this international regionalism should be added American
regional differences. A Pennsylvania William and Mary–style high chest
of drawers differs from a Massachusetts version in having paired pulls
on the outer drawers in the stand and spaces between the lower drawers
as though the inner legs continued between them, which they do not
(fig. 13). The Massachusetts one has single pulls and no spaces (fig. 14).
Establishing such American regional patterns contributes to understanding local cultural developments: European linkage and conscious
and unconscious changes from sources. But when such American var-

Fig. 12. Chair, Venice, 1600–1630.
Wood with gold leaf. (San Zaccaria,
Venice: Photo, John T. Kirk.)

iants are seen with similar London pieces (fig. 15), the commonality of
such American and English work is more evident than their differences.
Seeing these American and English pieces against English or Continental court work, such as an Antwerp cabinet on stand (fig. 16), enriches
their use as arbiters of ever more complex questions, thus increasing
each object's role in understanding broad cultural developments and,
by contrast, each region's personal stance.

The court level Continental piece in figure 16 *is* different from the
American experience, but its basic form, arrangement of parts, and
placement of strong horizontals are similar to those in figures 13 through

Fig. 13. High chest of drawers, Philadelphia, Pa., 1700–1735. American black walnut, Atlantic white cedar, yellow pine; H. 66″, W. 42⅔″, D. 23¾″. (Courtesy Yale University Art Gallery, the Mabel Brady Garvan Collection.)

Fig. 14. High chest of drawers, Boston, Mass., 1715–
35. Walnut, walnut veneer, burl veneer, eastern white
pine, soft maple, aspen, chestnut; H. 66″, W. 40½″, D.
21⅜″. (Courtesy Yale University Art Gallery, the Mabel
Brady Garvan Collection.)

Fig. 15. High chest of drawers, London, 1690–1715. (Photo, Robert
Wemyss Symonds Collection of Photographs, Joseph Downs Manuscript and Microfilm Collection, Winterthur Library.)

Fig. 16. Cabinet on stand, Antwerp, Flanders, 1680–90. Ebony and other woods, tortoiseshell, ivory, and ormolu; H. 77″, W. 51″, D. 19¾″. (Toledo Museum of Art, Gift of Florence Scott Libbey.)

Fig. 17. Dressing-table or high-chest leg
and foot, Boston, Mass., 1700–1735.
Maple with original brown paint; leg H.
(without tenon) 14″, foot H. (without
tenon) 4⅜″. (Private collection.)

15. On the Antwerp piece the row of ivory balusters in the cornice
creates much the same emphasis as the pulvinated cornice drawers in
figures 14 and 15. All the legs are alike in sharing a baroque styling that
desired dramatic movements from thick to thin areas and placed a force-
ful, overreaching mass three-quarters of the way up the design. The
dominance of this design attitude in the latter part of the seventeenth
century makes it possible to see the Boston turned leg in figure 17 as
sharing the outline of the Dutch gentleman in figure 18: the cape of
the man laps out and over the main shaped vertical, and his feet are

Fig. 18. Gerard Terborch (1617–81), *Portrait of a Gentleman in Black.* Netherlands, 1660–70. Oil on canvas; H. 26⅛″, W. 21⅜″. (National Gallery, London.)

arranged to a low, small, central emphasis. Thus the Boston leg is universal in idea while being, upon close inspection, discernibly Boston both in material and in the particular shaping of its silhouette; it takes part in an international arena and is particular to one American region.[13]

In these comparisons I have moved to ever richer expressions of a form. In a longer essay I would have added the dispersion of these ideas into the vernacular expressions of the interlocking societies.[14] Allowing *all* American objects to participate in an international review and asking of them *all* available questions permit each piece both to delight and to inform to the degree that they contain those properties.

[13] Forman inspected the leg and foot and pronounced them to be particular to Boston in their shaping. He noted, however, that in a Boston leg he would have expected the round tenon connecting the leg and foot to originate from the leg and go down through the now missing stretcher and the foot to terminate at the floor. In this example the tenon originates from the foot and goes up to end in the leg.

[14] For parallel British and American vernacular objects, see Kirk, *American Furniture*.

Reflections of Their World

The Furniture of the Upper St. John Valley, 1820–1930

Edwin A. Churchill and Sheila McDonald

The St. John Valley is a bilingual, a bicultural, and an international region that includes a major portion of Maine's northern borderland (fig. 1). This area is named for and bisected by the St. John River, a Maine-born waterway that empties into the Bay of Fundy at St. John, New Brunswick. The Maine, or southern, side of the St. John Valley is the focus of this study; it includes an area of approximately 394,500 acres, with a 1980 population of more than 21,000 people and the major towns of Fort Kent, Frenchville, St. Agatha, Madawaska, Grand Isle, and Van Buren (fig. 2). The people of the valley, historically and in the present day, are French-speaking, with more than 90 percent of the inhabitants on the Maine side of the valley still speaking the language.[1]

Knowing little more than that a French culture of some sort exists in the St. John Valley, the Maine State Museum staff began in 1980 to

[1] *Maine Register State Yearbook and Legislative Manual* 114, 1981–1982 (Portland: Tower Publishing Co., 1982); Guy F. Dubay, *Chez-Nous: The St. John Valley* (Augusta: Maine State Museum, 1983), p. 5; Madeline Giguere, "Sources of Quantitative Data on Franco-Americans," *Vers l'évolution d'une culture*, ed. Celeste Roberge (Orono, Maine: F.A.R.O.G. Office, 1975), pp. 89–102, as cited in Béatrice Craig, "A History of the Madawaska Settlement, 1785–1840" (draft, Ph.D. diss., University of Maine at Orono, 1982), p. 2.

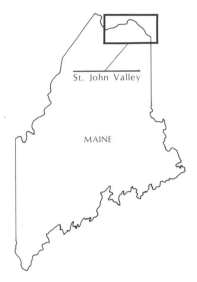

Fig. 1. Outline of Maine, showing location of St. John Valley. (Map, Sheila McDonald.)

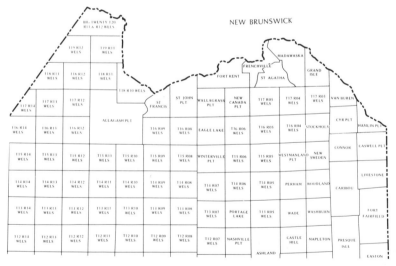

Fig. 2. St. John Valley, Maine. Hatching indicates areas represented in this study. (Map, Sheila McDonald.)

study its material expressions in preparation for an exhibition. The National Endowment for the Humanities provided funding, and after eighteen months of fieldwork, research, and planning, the exhibition opened in 1982. The exhibition and its attendant research provided the catalyst for further, more intensive investigation of St. John Valley furniture. This study focuses on furniture from two time periods. The first era begins about 1820 and spans approximately eighty years. During this period, local furniture reflected the valley's conservative culture, geographic isolation, economics, and family structure. The second period covers roughly forty years beginning about 1900. Then furniture forms, construction, and uses began to show a dialogue between tradition and change.

The St. John Valley became home for a French-centered culture in 1785 when a group of mostly Acadian people settled the river's shores. These first sixteen families were later joined by more Acadians who traveled up the St. John River from their homes in what is present-day southern New Brunswick. They, in turn, were joined by larger numbers of French Canadians who moved from the banks of the lower St. Lawrence River. These migrations created a mixed Acadian and French Canadian population that grew steadily throughout the first half of the nineteenth century (fig. 3).[2]

Acadian refers to those New World residents of Acadia (comprising present-day Nova Scotia and New Brunswick) who had migrated from France's western provinces of Poitou, Saintonge, and Brittany during the 1630s. *French Canadian* refers to the inhabitants of or descendants from the present-day province of Quebec. Some of these people had Acadian ancestry; others were progeny of Normandy, Picardy, Maine, Ile de France, and other provinces of northern France.[3]

When they moved to the St. John Valley in 1785, the Acadians were looking for a peace and stability that had eluded them during the

[2] Béatrice Craig documents important aspects of migration to the St. John Valley, especially regarding the importance of family ties to French Canada in determining which New Brunswick Acadians moved there, in "Kinship and Migration to the Upper St. John Valley [Maine–New Brunswick]" (Paper presented at Second Annual Conference of the Northeast Council for Quebec Studies, Yale University, October 1981), pp. 1–7.
[3] Thomas Albert, *The History of Madawaska*, trans. Thérèse Doucette and Francis Doucette (Madawaska, Maine: Madawaska Historical Society, 1985), p. 20.

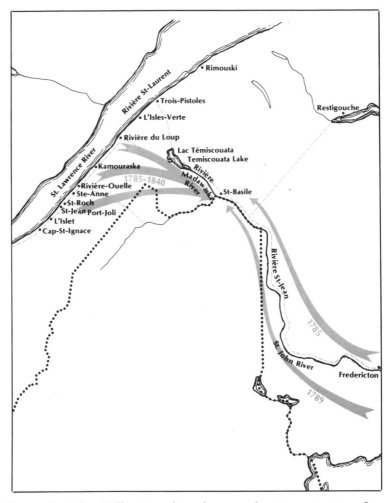

Fig. 3. St. John Valley French settlement, showing migrations from two major points. The first group of settlers came from French Acadian areas of New Brunswick (1785, 1789); the second, larger group, from the lower St. Lawrence River area of Quebec (1785–1840). From Guy F. Dubay, *Chez-Nous: The St. John Valley* (Augusta: Maine State Museum, 1983), p. 18.

battles between England and France over control of Acadia. These people and later their Quebec cousins were also attracted by the agricultural promise of the valley's fertile intervale and the opportunity, as one Acadian land petitioner described it, "to obtain such lands for their families . . . and to have the assistance of a priest in the performance of the rites and ceremonies of their religion and the superintendence of their children's education."[4]

When the first settlers arrived in the valley, they found themselves in an unsettled land save for a small Malecite Indian village at the confluence of the St. John and Madawaska rivers. It was a distant 70 miles to Rivière du Loup on the St. Lawrence and an even longer 170 miles downriver to St. John, New Brunswick—the nearest population centers. The St. John River, despite few settlers on its shores, was, however, an important travel and communication route between Quebec to the west and the eastern seaport of St. John. From a Canadian perspective, the remoteness of the upper St. John Valley was thus slightly mitigated. From an American perspective, however, the valley was simply isolated. It lay a distant 200 miles from the northern outpost of Bangor, and that distance traversed some of Maine's roughest, least-known lands and waters (fig. 4).[5]

Geographic isolation shaped St. John Valley life, as did the common language—French—and common religion—Catholicism—of all inhabitants. Thus generations of valley settlers also enjoyed and fostered a cultural isolation from the English-centered concerns surrounding them, yielding a cultural conservatism that prompted one traveler through

---

[4] Land petition of Oliver Tibodo (Thibodeau), Joseph Tarrio (Theriault), and Francis Violet (Violette), 1789, New Brunswick Provincial Archives, Fredericton, as cited in Dubay, *Chez-Nous*, pp. 89–90, 110.

[5] The importance of the St. John River to Canadians is shown in a 1783 letter to Gov. John Parr of Nova Scotia from Gov. Frederick Haldimand of Quebec in which Haldimand outlines a plan to settle the river's shores "which will contribute much to facilitate the communication so much to be desired by the two provinces" (William O. Raymond, *Winslow Papers, 1776–1826* [1901; reprint, Boston: Gregg Publishing Co., 1972], p. 149, as cited in Dubay, *Chez-Nous*, pp. 17, 105). In 1794, Park Holland was the first American to describe a trip to the St. John Valley. He describes the valley and the surrounding area as "far from any potable water, and wholly unexplored and the distance to be run uncertain." His early descriptions of the Madawaska settlement are also important, especially his observation, "They appear happy and contented though they begin to suffer from the want of edge tools, etc." (Park Holland, "Autobiography, Part III," in *William Bingham's Lands, 1790–1820*, ed. Frederick S. Allis, Jr. [Boston: Colonial Society of Massachusetts, 1954], pp. 217, 222).

Fig. 4. Geographic setting of St. John Valley. (Map, Sheila McDonald.)

the valley in 1837 to comment: "It is curious to observe how perfectly they have retained all their French peculiarities. The forms of their houses, the decorations of their apartments, dress, modes of cookery, etc. are exactly as they originally were in the land of their ancestors."[6]

[6] Charles T. Jackson, *First Report on the Geology of the Public Lands in the State of Maine* (Boston: Dutton and Wentworth, 1837), p. 30. The same observations are expressed in "A Letter from Louisbourg, 1756," *Acadiensis* 10, no. 1 (Autumn 1980): 123–24; and "An Aroostook Yankee's Anonymous Letter, ca. 1845," *Maine History News* 21, no. 3 (July 1985): 4.

St. John Valley families were unusually large and tended to settle near each other, forming extended kin networks.[7] Virtually everyone farmed, yet the valley was too remote from population centers to develop markets for agricultural produce. So markets were developed within local communities or kin networks. Production and population balanced each other, and although farms were not necessarily self-sufficient, the larger region was. The lack of diversification implicit in St. John Valley subsistence economy dominates both written observations about the area and census records throughout the nineteenth century. In 1831 John G. Deane and Edward Kavanaugh visited the valley and reported: "There are few blacksmiths and carpenters in the colony—they get their tools from the English provinces. . . . They manufacture agricultural implements which are rudely, badly made." The 1850 census does not indicate much change. Covering the entire valley population on the American side of the river, that document lists 393 farmers or farm laborers and 17 other heads of household engaged in nonfarming occupations. A sampling of the 1860 census indicates 92 percent of household heads as farmers or farm laborers, with a corresponding dearth of specialized craftspeople.[8]

The valley's economic fabric as indicated by these records has clear implications for the production and use of furniture. The subsistence life-style, supported by extended kin networks and enforced by the valley's remote location, effectively bypassed the development of craft shops where furniture was produced and sold on a full-time basis. Instead, throughout the nineteenth century, furniture production and consumption apparently remained within the conservative province of the house-

[7]Craig and Marcella Sorg have shown that, for the period 1791–1838, St. John Valley French inhabitants had a completed family size that averaged 11.3 children (Béatrice Craig and Marcella Sorg, "Family and Household in the St. John Valley French Population: 1785–1900" [Report prepared for Chez-Nous: The St. John Valley Project of Maine State Museum, March 1982], p. 17). Putting this figure in context, Craig and Sorg compare it with a completed family size of 9.5 children for Acadians from 1600 to 1755; 8.4 for French Canadians, 1700–1730; and 7.8 for other North American preindustrial groups. Craig documents spatial organization and land ownership in the valley as generally dominated by the family network, not only in the early years of settlement but at least until the 1840s (Craig, "History of the Settlement," chap. 5).

[8]Béatrice Craig, "The Pioneer Economy of the Upper St. John Valley" (Paper delivered at Acadian Adjustments to North American Environments symposium, University of Maine at Orono, September 26, 1985); "Contested Jurisdiction and Dispute Concerning the Frontiers: Deane Kavanaugh Statement, 1831," as cited by Albert, *History of Madawaska*, p. 211; Craig and Sorg, "Family and Household," tables 4, 5, 6.

Fig. 5. Joined chest, ca. 1800–1820, found in Lille, Maine. White pine; H. 24¾", W. 45", D. 22¾". (Maine State Museum.)

hold or kin network until factory-manufactured pieces became available and families were able to purchase them.

The inhabitants of the St. John Valley created traditional, French-style furniture produced with hand tools. Its construction relied on basic frame-and-panel joinery techniques brought to the New World from seventeenth-century France. Continued in French Canada and Acadia, these methods were subsequently maintained by migrants to the valley. There, joined furniture construction persisted until the late 1800s, far later than in neighboring New England and much of Canada, which had long since replaced traditional methods with later cabinetmaking techniques.

Frame-and-panel joinery construction allowed for the production of wholly suitable furniture with a small repertoire of skills and tools. These limited requirements for furniture construction were ideal for the transfer of furniture-making techniques through kin networks in the isolated, subsistence-based communities of the St. John Valley. The limited number of required tools and skills are well demonstrated by an early nineteenth-century framed chest (*coffre*) from Lille, Maine (fig. 5). Necessary tools included a marking gauge, a saw, a chisel, a brace and bits, a jack, beading and rabbet planes, a knife, a mallet, and a hammer. The single sophisticated task was that of cutting the mortises into which the tenons fit.

A side chair (*chaise*) from St. David demonstrates a second key feature of the valley's traditional furniture—its extraordinary stylistic resiliency through time (fig. 6). Valley chairs have square legs and posts, through-socket, hand-shaped, rounded stretchers and side seat rails, and through-mortise back slats, with the lower slat often resting on or nearly on the seat. The tops of the posts extend slightly above the top slat and are rounded. The overhanging plank seat rests on side rails, and the front upper stretcher is often placed high on the legs to strengthen the upper frame. Many, perhaps half, of the chairs have chamfered legs and posts. This was the traditional valley chair; there were virtually no other types. The pattern of closely repeated forms permeates the furniture of the region, being most pervasive on the less elaborate forms.[9]

The constancy of form and style resulted from several factors, not the least of which was the basic resistance to change implicit in a traditional society, a trait noted by several observers. Further forcing an adherence to traditional methods was a lack of tools to do otherwise. Local artisans probably never had the quantity or quality of tools that would facilitate fine woodworking. While an Anglo-American cabinet-maker had ripsaws, fine-tooth saws, back saws, keyhole saws, and so forth, the valley woodworker probably had simply a saw. Furthermore, it was the late 1800s before powered machinery appeared in the area. The earliest power tool found locally is a lathe, dating circa 1870–1900,

[9] The stylistic similarity of the simpler traditional forms (especially chairs) was striking. There were differences between specific objects; for example, a chair might have two or, less often, four slats rather than three; some chairs were chamfered, and others were not; and the placement of the middle and lower slats varied from chair to chair. Still, these variations all occurred within the parameters of a generally accepted stylistic and technological artifactual vocabulary, one repeatedly incorporated in traditional valley furniture. One divergent traditional chair form was the so-called Convent chair. These frequently had paired narrow slats or rungs across the center of the back rather than a single regular-size slat. That, however, was the extent of the diversity. In construction techniques and basic form, these chairs articulated the same traditions as the more standard examples. This conservative pattern persisted until new models, introduced in advertisements and imported furniture, suggested different design interpretations of specific forms. Then change came rapidly—a point covered below in a discussion of rocking chairs.

Fig. 6. Side chair, ca. 1830–
70, found in St. David,
Maine. Birch, white pine; H.
32½", W. 16", D. 16¾".
(Maine State Museum.)

in the possession of Edward Dubay of Van Buren.[10] It is not surprising
that one finds few early pieces of furniture with such features as turned
elements, dovetails, and ruled joints.

Still, change probably would have come had there been a viable
alternative. From what is known, however, there were no cabinetmakers in any of the communities from whom the settlers could have learned
basic cabinetmaking skills. Similarly, the people of the valley had few
examples of cabinet furniture in their communities before the late nineteenth century and thus had little chance to copy such pieces even if
they had wished to do so. The difficulties encountered in attempting an
unfamiliar form are exemplified in a small pine chest of drawers (*com-*

[10]The resistance to change is noted by Jackson, *First Report*; "Letter from Louisbourg"; and "Aroostook Yankee's Letter." Although the Dubay lathe is unmarked, the
castings, hardware, and other features date it no earlier than the 1870s and perhaps as
late as the early twentieth century.

Fig. 7. Small bureau, ca. 1875–1900, found in Lille, Maine. H. 36″, W. 34¾″, D. 18¼″. (Maine State Museum.)

mode) found in Lille (fig. 7). Probably locally made in the last quarter of the nineteenth century, it is the product of a traditional maker who must have seen such an object, or at least a picture of one, but never had the opportunity to examine the internal construction.

The maker approached the project in the manner of a joiner, beginning with heavy corner posts, measuring 2¾ by 2 inches at the front and 1¾ by 3 inches at the rear, and through-mortise horizontal end frames of the same size as the back posts. These held the ½-inch-thick end panels (fig. 8). More typical were the drawer dividers mortised into the front posts and the horizontal backboards rabbeted and nailed into the back posts. Up to that point the construction was a bit unorthodox but had not created any major problems.

Fig. 8. Detail of bottom of bureau in figure 7. (Maine State Museum.)

Fig. 9. Drawer construction of bureau in figure 7. (Maine State Museum.)

The drawers proved a different matter (fig. 9). Made of heavy boards (⅞-inch thick), the sides were rabbeted and nailed into the ends. The bottom boards, equally heavy and unchamfered, were set within the drawer and nailed in place from the sides. Ash veneer (¼-inch thick) was nailed to the drawer front to provide a contrasting surface. The solution for supporting each drawer was to use a single rectangular shaft at the center, mortised into the backboard and slotted into the drawer

Fig. 10. Detail of front of bureau in figure 7. (Maine State Museum.)

divider. The drawer simply rides on top of this slide, creating interesting problems when being opened and closed (fig. 10).

Furniture produced within the traditional artifactual vocabulary could also be very successful. Such is the case of a tall cupboard (*buffet*) with paired upper and lower doors, owned by the Hébert and then the Albert families in St. David (fig. 11). While the basic fabrication is quite unpretentious, the front is a masterpiece of joined construction. Applied moldings are positioned to create several horizontal recesses outlining the piece and supplementing the raised panels in the doors. More subtly, but extraordinarily effectively, the maker provided upper doors slightly narrower than the lower, and by keeping the molded decoration in the same relationship to these doors as to those below, he created a sense of upward narrowing and lightness. Obviously the red and green painted surfaces introduce an interest all their own, but these are not the earliest colors, and we are not sure what the first paint scheme was.

Valley furniture fulfilled two general roles in the lives of the inhabitants: utility and prestige. All the furniture had useful purposes, but

Fig. 11. Cupboard, possibly by Vital Albert of St. David, Maine, ca. 1840–60. White pine; H. 90", W. 36", D. 13¾". (Maine State Museum.)

specific forms, especially tables, chairs, and benches, were based on practicality and applicability. Exhibiting straightforward construction techniques, general functional simplicity, and stylistic uniformity, these pieces had little ornamentation. They also show substantial wear and replacement. Table and front chair stretchers are often worn almost through, if not missing. Many tables have replaced tops—the originals having been worn out and discarded long ago.

A second and smaller body of furniture served a secondary role, that of elevating one's self- and social esteem. Including more substantial forms such as armoires and buffets, these objects often reflect cosmopolitan features not seen in more utilitarian furniture. Usually well made, and including such elaborations as boldly shaped cornices and raised panels, these pieces have close analogues in French Canada. Significantly, they tend to be less regularized and to exhibit elements suggesting a familiarity with more recent developments in style and construction. Unlike the utilitarian furniture that was clearly the product of traditional artifactual training, the elaborate items suggest a complex heritage. The most probable design source appears to have been pieces brought into the region by early French Canadians moving into the valley. In his report to the states of Massachusetts and Maine, geologist Charles T. Jackson stated: "Families of emigrants are also continually passing over [to the St. John Valley]; we met several on the road with their loads of furniture moving from Canada."[11] The inclusion of such pieces in the cargo derived from several motivations. First, these items tended to be favorite objects; second, they would be difficult to replicate once the emigrants reached the frontier settlements; and, third, they were objects that could serve as packing containers—a handy characteristic for the moving families. It is probable that such items served as models for valley-made pieces. It is also likely that some of the more substantial items came up the St. John with Acadian immigrants; however, stylistic and technological features strongly suggest a Canadian heritage for most of these pieces.

Although most of these objects received more than a few coats of paint, and exhibit deterioration and recent abuse, many are still structurally sound, minimally worn, and essentially unaltered. The special status of such items is further suggested by their being owned not by all, but generally only by the more well-to-do.[12]

In one instance, that of dining furniture, valley examples reveal specific aspects of family makeup and behavior. Probably the most frequently encountered traditional items are small side chairs. The seat height of these chairs ranges from 14 to 15¾ inches (fig. 12), more than

[11] Charles T. Jackson, *Second Annual Report on the Geology of the Public Lands . . . of Me. and Mass.* (Boston: Dutton and Wentworth, 1838), p. 61.
[12] Interviews with Blanche Collin, St. Agatha, September 12, 1985; and Abel Corriveau, Augusta, October 8, 1985.

Fig. 12. Side chair, ca. 1860–1900, found
in St. John Valley, Maine. Birch, white
pine; H. 32½″, W. 14¾″, D. 16½″.
(Maine State Museum.)

2 inches lower than contemporary Anglo chairs.[13] Along with small
chairs, there is a substantial number of long, low benches (*bancs de
cuisine*) (fig. 13). Finally, one finds numerous valley tables similar in
form to the New England stretcher-base "tavern" table, except that they
are extraordinarily large (fig. 14).

[13] The figures are derived from three chairs in the collection of Maine State Museum
(80.123.1, 81.124.5 [fig. 12], 83.109.1), ranging from 14½ to 15¾ inches; nine chairs
in the Ste. Agathe Historical Society collection in St. Agatha, measuring between 15 and
15¾ inches; and two chairs in the Madawaska Historical Society collection in Madawaska
that were 14 and 14½ inches high respectively. It should be noted that from observations
of similar chairs in the valley, these examples seem typical.

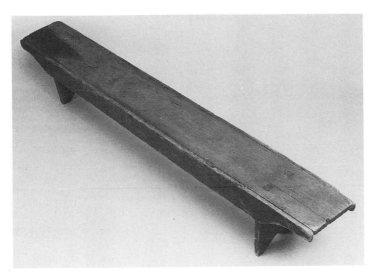

Fig. 13. Long bench, ca. 1860–1900, found in St. John Valley, Maine. White pine; H. 15¾″, W. 95¾″, D. 12½″. (Maine State Museum.)

Fig. 14. Stretcher-base dining table, ca. 1850–1900, found in St. John Valley, Maine. Birch, white pine; H. 28½″, W. 66¾″, D. 33″. (Maine State Museum.)

These pieces reflect a significant feature of valley society—extremely large family size. It is almost certainly in direct response to these large groups of children that the small chairs, long benches, and sizable tables were produced. These items continued to be used in some homes well into the twentieth century, long after other options were available, in part because of their usefulness in families with numerous offspring. Blanche Collin of St. Agatha described such a pattern in her own girlhood home. During her childhood in the 1920s and 1930s, her family was arranged around the table with her father at the head. The younger children sat on benches on one side and the end, and the smallest were put on various objects to get them up to proper height. The older children and their mother sat in chairs along the other side with mother near father, but often with the smallest child in a highchair between them. When Mrs. Collin had her family, she had benches made and copied the same seating pattern in her home.[14]

During the last third of the nineteenth century the valley was undergoing slow but steady economic development evolving from the growing lumber industry on the river and the arrival of the Canadian Pacific Railroad across the border in 1878. The upshot of the new outside influences was an increasing economic centralization and occupational diversity as the region moved toward a cash economy. Concurrently, traditional life patterns were undergoing fundamental changes as the local population adjusted to the new economic parameters. Family sizes fell, kinship bonds weakened, and the material environment changed, reflecting more and more what one could purchase rather than what was locally available.[15]

There is some evidence of these increasing outside contacts in valley furniture—most specifically in an increased number of turned-leg tables and stands. Several of these items predate the earliest known local lathes, suggesting importation—a conclusion bolstered by the scarcity of these items and their lack of similarity. There is one variety, a heavier turned-leg kitchen table, which may be indigenous (fig. 15). Several

[14] Interview with Collin.

[15] In 1878 the Canadian Pacific Railroad extended its line from Fredericton to Edmundston, across the river from Madawaska. The full benefits of this service were not realized for another twelve years, however, when the entire run was completed and the railroad was extended all the way to Quebec and thus through to Ontario (Albert, *History of Madawaska*, pp. 125–26). Dubay, *Chez-Nous*, pp. 38–51, 59–61; Craig and Sorg, "Family and Household," pp. 7–8, 10–11, 13–15, 18–19.

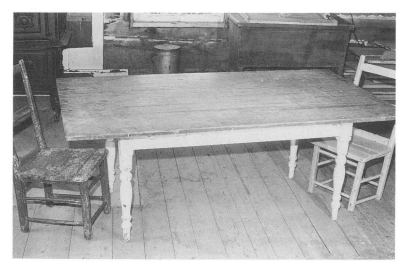

Fig. 15. Turned-leg kitchen table, ca. 1860–1900, found in Madawaska, Maine. (Madawaska Historical Society.)

examples have been found in the valley with local provenances, and, unlike the other turned pieces, they have a typological similarity. The legs on these pieces remind one of those seen on New England office furniture fabricated circa 1850–75. However, construction and hardware details suggest that the tables were made during the last quarter of the nineteenth century; thus the legs may have been turned locally on recently acquired lathes.[16]

The economic evolution of the late 1800s was galvanized and accelerated with the arrival of the Maine-based Bangor and Aroostook Railroad at Van Buren on the eastern end of the valley in 1899 and Fort Kent to the west in 1902. Lured by the potential lumbering wealth in the region, the railroad also meant that the valley's agricultural produce had access to outside markets. In fact, with the railroad's entrance to Van Buren and Fort Kent, the valley began to shift from subsistence agriculture to potatoes as a single cash crop. A potato brokerage firm opened, new machinery and larger barns appeared on the landscape,

---

[16]Two of the kitchen tables are at Madawaska Historical Society, and one is at Ste. Agathe Historical Society.

and banks in both Fort Kent and Van Buren capitalized and opened their doors.[17]

With more markets for their products of forest and field, valley residents found themselves with increased buying power and the ability to take advantage of newly introduced manufactured furniture. In 1899, the same year that the railroad arrived in Van Buren, Addis E. Keegan, a local storekeeper, set up Van Buren Furniture Company, and in 1905 fellow townsman Henry A. Gagnon established a second furniture store there. Beginning in 1890, Fort Kent, the second valley entrepôt, had at least one and sometimes two furniture firms in operation. These businesses, all short-lived, probably obtained their wares through the nearby Canadian Pacific Railroad. The first long-term successful furniture store in Fort Kent waited for the establishment of the American line. This operation, started by Cleophus Nadeau in 1905, continued well into the second quarter of the nineteenth century. A second firm, that of Michael J. Pelletier, was established in 1919.[18]

The stores were only one source for furniture. For many inhabitants, especially those not living in Fort Kent or Van Buren, mail-order catalogues provided a second option. Sears, Roebuck was a major supplier. Darius Levesque of Madawaska summed up local recollections with the assertion: "The Sears and Roebuck catalogue was the Bible." There were other competitors, though, including Spiegel's and Montgomery Ward. A particularly pervasive publication appears to have been the catalogue brought along by numerous Larkin dealers. Repeatedly informants recalled buying products from Larkin and ultimately acquiring furniture as premiums or as purchases.[19]

To enhance interest, distributors introduced modern advertising. Keegan repeatedly advertised in the *Journal du Madawaska* between

[17] Louis C. Hatch, ed., *Maine: A History*, vol. 1 (New York: American Historical Society, 1919), p. 711; Charles D. Heseltine, "A Guide to Maine Railroad History" (typescript, Maine State Museum, 1968), p. 7; Dubay, *Chez-Nous*, pp. 59–60. It should be noted that the shift from traditional to contemporary patterns occurred at varying rates in different communities, in large part in relationship to closeness to or distance from the railroad (Craig and Sorg, "Family and Household," pp. 7–8, tables 5, 6).

[18] Data developed from *Maine Registers*, 1896/97–1929/30; and *Journal du Madawaska*, 1903–5.

[19] Interviews with Darius Levesque, Madawaska, September 13, 1985; Agatha Morneault Bouchard, Old Town, September 30, 1985; Collin; Claude L. Cyr, Madawaska, September 12, 1985; and Rolande Michaud Levesque, Madawaska, September 13, 1985.

1903 and 1905 with large cuts of furniture and lists of "marked-down prices." Gagnon similarly used the journal in late 1905, advertising furniture "de toutes sortes, de toutes qualités, de tous les près, toujours à bon marché."[20]

Valley inhabitants quickly responded to these new sources, acquiring manufactured furniture as soon as they could afford to do so. Superficially, the rapid approval of a major novel category of material culture might seem at variance with the expected reactions of a strong traditionalist society. In fact, this reaction was quite reasonable. In the eyes of the inhabitants, the introduction of the new furniture did not challenge the basic tenets of the social belief system. Language, religion, family—all so important—seem unthreatened. Furthermore, the ownership of such furniture, viewed as technologically and stylistically superior to traditional products, reinforced the hierarchical socioeconomic patterns of society.[21]

It is not surprising that the first purchases were made by the wealthier inhabitants. For example, in 1915, the well-to-do Morneault family of Lille purchased the largest house in town. Upon moving in, they bought a new dining set from Gagnon. Brought to Lille by railroad, the order included a table, six chairs, a "China" cabinet, a buffet, and a serving table. This set replaced an older, manufactured one.[22]

For others, change was less rapid. Darius Levesque of Madawaska has several pieces of a bedroom set acquired by his father, Joseph, who lived in Grand Isle. Purchased in 1928 from Spiegel's, this set was the first manufactured furniture in the house. Blanche Collin remembered that her family, the Joseph C. Bossés, obtained their first manufactured furniture in the 1920s and 1930s from Larkin Company. The first item was a "buffet vitre" (china cabinet). Interestingly, this was a new form in the home, providing Mrs. Collin's mother her first opportunity to display the family's better glass and china. Other items acquired included

---

[20] *Journal du Madawaska*, August 26, 1903, January 25, April 5, December 13, 1905, and elsewhere.

[21] The interactions between traditional societies and contemporary material culture are discussed in Lawrence E. Dawson, Vera-Mae Frederickson, and Nelson H. H. Graburn, *Traditions in Transition: Culture Contact and Material Change* (Berkeley, Calif.: Lowie Museum of Anthropology, 1974).

[22] Interview with Bouchard. The Hébert/Albert home in Madawaska similarly had manufactured dining furniture by the late teens.

side chairs, an ornate pressed-back rocker, and several iron beds. Excepting the beds, all the manufactured furniture was placed in the living room.[23]

What happened to the traditional furniture when the new pieces arrived? In the Ligourie Marquis house in St. Agatha, the traditional furniture had migrated to the kitchen, upper bedroom, attic, and back shed. By 1940 most of the furniture in the Fred Albert house in St. David was manufactured; however, the kitchen and family dining room still had handmade tables and two traditional rockers. The red and green Hébert cupboard (see fig. 11) clearly illustrates the fate of traditional furniture in the early twentieth century. It had been a major item prior to the introduction of manufactured furniture; still, it had already been moved to a large, open, upstairs room above the kitchen when the Hébert home was acquired by the Albert family in 1922. There it was used for the storage of bags of dry goods. In 1932, the Albert family built a new brick house, and the cupboard was relegated to the basement where it held paints and other low-value items.[24]

In many instances, when families moved they left the traditional furniture behind. For example, when the Bossé family of St. Agatha lost their farm during the depression, they brought their new furniture with them when they moved to town, but left most of the handmade pieces back at the farm.[25]

Still, retired furniture did return to use. Newlyweds frequently received old handmade pieces with which to set up housekeeping. These stayed only until the couple could afford manufactured substitutes. Fire victims were also recipients of such furniture. One such instance was the Donat Cyr home in Lille which burned in 1938. All that was saved was a back shed in which were several pieces of traditional furniture. When a new house was built, an old armoire was set in the kitchen, and several traditional beds were put back into use. In a few years these pieces were replaced, the beds by manufactured items, the armoire by a refrigerator.[26]

Although traditional furniture remained in use after the introduc-

[23] Interviews with Darius Levesque and Collin.
[24] Floor plan and furnishings layout of the Albert house (ca. 1940) provided by Renaud Albert, September 13, 1985. Interview with Bouchard; interview with Bernette Albert of Madawaska, September 12, 1985; Renaud Albert to Edwin A. Churchill, October 8, 1985.
[25] Interview with Collin.
[26] Interviews with Bernette Albert and Cyr.

Fig. 16. China cabinet, by Joseph Levesque, Grand Isle, Maine, 1928. (Darius Levesque, Madawaska.)

tion of manufactured wares, its production virtually ended, and hand-made furniture making of any type continued only as a minor activity. A few individuals continued making items for their families and relatives. For example, Leonard Michaud of St. David made several chairs and rockers for his own home and those of several relatives, and Joseph Levesque of Grand Isle built a straight-front china cabinet in 1928, the year he acquired his new, manufactured bedroom set (fig. 16). The piece was made from furniture crates, very likely those used for shipping the bedroom set. Noting the stylistic similarity to contemporary furniture, Joseph's son Darius stated, "the idea came from one of the catalogues." As with the Bossé home in St. Agatha, this was a new form in the Levesque house and was used in the living room for the display of good glass and china. Presently the cabinet is in the basement of Darius's home where it holds paint, hardware, and similar items.[27]

By the early twentieth century the production of handmade furniture focused on one form. Paradoxically, that form, the rocking chair, was not a traditional valley type, but one introduced to the region in the late 1800s.[28] The rocker achieved rapid and widespread acceptance. In fact, today it is viewed by most inhabitants as an intrinsic part of the valley's past character and very much a French phenomenon. The swift incorporation of the rocking chair into the society could have resulted only from strongly perceived benefits. The first was probably the simplest—increased comfort. There was no traditional form of relaxed seating furniture. Thus the rocker was introduced into what was very close to a vacuum.

The rocker also fit nicely with locally held familial values. It came to the area fully freighted with a mythology tying it to family togetherness, respect for the elderly, and the nurturing role of motherhood— all values central to the valley inhabitants.[29] In a period experiencing dramatic economic change, and the increased arrival of outside people and competing ideas, the rocker seemed a material bulwark of what was felt to be good and proper. It became a key nostalgic vehicle to the region's past, an expression of earlier and simpler times when family, community, and church protected the individual and secured a stable, dignified society. Ironically, it may have better served this purpose than would some of the traditional furniture, for in the early chairs and tables could be read hardship and lack of finery—also a part of that earlier period.

Still, the rocking chair's great popularity does not, by itself, account for its domestic manufacture. That is explained, essentially, by the pressures of supply and demand. With most other forms of furniture, the

[27] Interviews with Rolande Levesque and Darius Levesque.

[28] Ellen and Bert Denker document the rocking chair as an American invention in their *Rocking Chair Book* (New York: Mayflower Books, 1979), pp. 37–39. Evidence of the rocker's rather late adoption in rural French Canada is provided in Jean Palardy, *The Early Furniture of French Canada* (Toronto: Macmillan of Canada, 1973), pp. 247–58; and Paul Louis Martin, *La Berçante Québécoise* (Montreal: Editions du Boréal Express, 1973), pp. 78–115. In the valley few traditional rockers can be found and, as is the case of an attractive example owned by Cyr, are invariably late conversions.

[29] The rocking-chair mythology is well presented in Denker and Denker, *Rocking Chair Book*, pp. 26–28, 40–41, 46, 152, 175, and passim.

inhabitants continued using traditional items until they had funds to purchase manufactured replacements; however, there were no traditional rocking chairs.

There were three ways to acquire a rocking chair: by purchasing one from a commercial supplier; by adding rockers to a traditional chair; or by having a rocking chair made locally. For many people the purchase of a rocker was too expensive for immediate consideration. Also, manufactured examples were usually placed in the living room and probably viewed as too formal to fulfill the more relaxed values attributed to the form. [30]

Only a few traditional chairs were converted to rockers. There are two probable reasons. First, not many traditional chairs had arms, and as armed rockers seem to have been most popular, there were few chairs available for conversion. Second, traditional chairs were already very low, and to cut them down further for rockers would have dropped the seat to an impractical level.

Ultimately newly handmade pieces filled the need. The makers produced two distinct varieties, the key characteristics being incorporated for the most part in the backs. One group echoed patterns seen in catalogues, advertisements, and furniture stores. A typical example, a rocker found in Van Buren, was constructed in the early twentieth century and has a crest rail similar to those found on contemporary inexpensive oak furniture (fig. 17). Other examples, though, reflect a very different approach. Freed from traditional forms, more than a few makers also attempted patterns beyond those offered by commercial sources, creating their own individual interpretations. A yellow and black rocker found in the Wallagrass region is representative of this genre (fig. 18). The shaped and pierced crest rails have no parallels in either traditional or manufactured furniture. Even more exotic is a second example attributed to a Mr. Chassé of St. Agatha (fig. 19). The shaped, curved, and pierced crest rail, back, and arm splats, as well as the bentwood arm and a sawtooth fringe around the seat, make this a unique piece of furniture.

Many of these idiosyncratic rocking chairs can be found throughout the valley, and although some are rather extravagant, many are

---

[30] Interview with Collin; Albert house floor plan. It is interesting that manufactured rockers were frequently used for posed formal pictures, whereas the handmade versions never were.

Fig. 17. Rocking chair, ca. 1890–1920, found in Van Buren, Maine. Birch, white pine; H. 34¼", W. 20", D. 32¼". (Maine State Museum.)

more reserved and can frequently be distinguished as to maker. A rocker made by Joseph O. Bossé of St. Agatha is typical (fig. 20). Conservative in design, its major departure is a laced rawhide back. Relatively characteristic of his work, this chair also reflects another craft he practiced— that of making snowshoes. Michael Rossignol of Fort Kent acquired a fairly substantial clientele for his rocking chairs. Working in the 1920s and 1930s, he made chairs with long, forward-projecting rockers which proved to be comfortable footrests. His reputation was such that several people from Stockholm, Maine, 30 miles to the south, owned examples— including the George Corriveau family. Unfortunately, their "Chaise du Michael" suffered an ignominious fate. Mrs. Corriveau, after having

Fig. 18. Rocking chair, ca. 1890–1920, found in Wallagrass, Maine. Birch, white pine; H. 32½", W. 20½", D. 30¼". (Maine State Museum.)

tripped over those projecting rockers one too many times, took her husband's saw and cut them off—much to the consternation of several other family members. [31]

The novelty vanishes when one inspects the bases of the rockers. On chair after chair, the frame, stretchers, and seat are absolutely traditional. The contrast between the backs and the bases illuminates the proclivity for and limitations of change experienced by St. John Valley makers. In seeing the numerous examples of manufactured furniture, they realized the possibility for more than one solution for a specific form. The response, reflected in the backs, was either copied or cre-

[31] Interview with Corriveau.

Fig. 19. Rocking chair, attributed to Mr. Chassé of St. Agatha, Maine, ca. 1890–1920. Birch, ash, white pine; H. 39″, W. 30½″, D. 30½″. (Maine State Museum.)

atively innovative. The self-expression was limited once the makers moved to the frame and seat, however, for much of the basic construction was done with traditional techniques. In other words, the spirit was soaring at the end of a technological tether.

The rocking chair represents a key aspect of this study. It serves as an explanatory vehicle of the dramatic shift in the material culture and life patterns of St. John Valley society; more important, it functions as a fundamental analytic tool in the revelation of those changes.

Still, the rocking chair is only one example in which the study of furniture led us directly to cultural patterns. Whether we examined a heavily painted side chair with a traditional form and round nails, identified the handmade and manufactured furniture comprising a valley

Fig. 20. Rocking chair, by Joseph O. Bossé, St. Agatha, Maine, ca. 1954. (Blanche Collins, St. Agatha.)

household of the 1920s, or interviewed a woman who recreated a traditional bench form from her girlhood for her own family in the 1950s, the furniture led us to questions and framed answers. Sometimes we found furniture forms, construction, and uses on the leading edge of change, signaling a shift in circumstances or a modification of values. At other times the furniture echoed a remarkable resiliency that survived and embodied a way of life that would never return. In any case, the entire assemblage of furniture made and used in the valley from 1820 to 1930 speaks a remarkable artifactual language tracing otherwise unarticulated cultural dynamics. In a most real way these objects served as reflections of their world.

Poor, Proud, and Primitive
Images of Appalachian Domestic Interiors

Dean Herrin

As with many other groups of people in American history, those from the Appalachian Mountains have had to face cultural stereotypes. Television programs in the past twenty years, such as "The Beverly Hillbillies" and "The Dukes of Hazzard," are only the latest examples of a process that has occurred since Appalachia was "discovered" in the nineteenth century to be a distinct region. In an article for *Scribner's* in 1929, a sympathetic observer of the Appalachian region satirized the prevailing attitudes of the general public toward Appalachian natives:

The simple southern highlanders converse among themselves in sentences compounded of "hit," "you uns" and "tote," a vocabulary which they find sufficient for all ideas. The cultivation of four rows of corn supplies all their needs and their babies cry for moonshine as soon as they are born. By day their chief occupation is to sit; by night they sleep seven in a bed, though they will promptly vacate the bed on the approach of a furriner and migrate to the floor which they prefer. They never wear nothing but sun bonnets and blue jeans. None of them has even seen a train, and in the intervals of singing ballets they ejaculate from time to time, "Yeh ain't done right by our little Nell," and immediately shoot everybody in sight with a rifle which saw service at Kings Mountain.[1]

Since the late nineteenth century, when middle- and upper-class Americans began to notice the people of the southern mountains, two

[1] Howard Mumford Jones, "The Southern Legend," *Scribner's*, May 1929, as quoted in Rupert Vance, *Human Geography of the South* (Chapel Hill: University of North Carolina Press, 1935), p. 243.

images have been dominant in America's thinking about Appalachia. The first portrays Appalachia as the epitome of poverty in America, a place where a culture of poverty has been passed down from generation to generation. The well-publicized trips of presidents John F. Kennedy and Lyndon B. Johnson to the region in the early 1960s and the subsequent establishment of the Appalachian Regional Commission have made the name *Appalachia* synonymous with *poverty* in the last twenty-five years. The second image of Appalachia is a romantic one, focusing on the pioneer traditions and the handicrafts that recall simpler times of America's past. A quilt, a dulcimer, a log cabin, a chair—these are the products of a romanticized Appalachia. These two images, of poverty and of the pioneer past, have sometimes been combined, but more commonly they represent contradictory views of Appalachian society. Recently a front-page headline in the *New York Times* proclaimed, "Despite 20 Years of Federal Aid, Poverty Still Reigns in Appalachia." On the same day another newspaper carried a story on "the glories of Appalachia," in which the author invited the reader to "meet the folks of Appalachia who are preserving our pioneer past."[2]

It is appropriate that this latter article is about a museum that preserves Appalachian artifacts, because the material culture of the region has played a prominent role in the presentation of images about Appalachia. Popular images of the interiors of Appalachian homes, from nineteenth-century magazine illustrations to twentieth-century photographs and modern television programs, have fostered and perpetuated stereotyped myths about Appalachian society, namely the myths of a culture of poverty on the one hand and of pioneer survivals on the other. Some of these views of Appalachian domestic interiors were invented; others were simply altered. Most misrepresent the diversity and reality of Appalachian life. The dominance of these views for the past century in literature, travel accounts, social analyses, and national media has resulted in the continuation of stereotypes about Appalachia, stereotypes that have taken attention away from the primary cause of poverty in Appalachia—the exploitation of natural resources by a capitalist economy.

[2] Ben A. Franklin, "Despite 20 Years of Federal Aid, Poverty Still Reigns in Appalachia," *New York Times*, August 11, 1985, p. 1; Elizabeth Gaynor, "Meet the Folks of Appalachia Who Are Preserving Our Pioneer Past," *News-Journal* (Wilmington, Del.), August 11, 1985, *Parade*, p. 12.

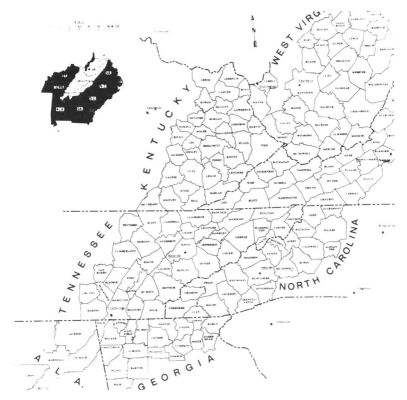

Fig. 1. Southern Appalachian region. From Thomas Ford, ed., *The Southern Appalachian Region: A Survey* (Lexington: University of Kentucky Press, 1962), fig. 1.

The Appalachia that I am identifying is composed of the mountainous areas of seven states: Alabama, Georgia, North Carolina, Tennessee, Virginia, Kentucky, and West Virginia (fig. 1). This southern highland region began to be perceived as a distinct part of the nation in the decades following the Civil War, principally through the efforts of local-color magazine writers and Protestant church representatives. Searching for "exotic little corners" of the United States in order to entertain the middle-class readers of such magazines as *Harper's*, local-color writers found in Appalachia an area and a people that seemingly had been bypassed by the emerging industrialization felt elsewhere in the late nineteenth century. Will Wallace Harney's "Strange Land and a Peculiar People," appearing in *Lippincott's Magazine* in 1873, was the first article to assert Appalachian "otherness." More than 200 sketches and short stories were published by 1890, planting firmly in the American consciousness the idea that Appalachia was "quaint" and "different" from the rest of American society. Appalachian society was treated in these stories and travel accounts much as were the picturesque and exotic lands of Africa and Asia, the resort areas in America, and other "little corners" of the world. Henry D. Shapiro, in his perceptive study of the idea of Appalachia, *Appalachia on Our Mind*, asserted that the local-color movement merely provided reinforcement for what middle-class American readers wanted to hear: that other cultures, other ways of life were indeed "quaint," thus making their familiar world normative. In attempts to explain why a vast and undeveloped region such as Appalachia existed in the very heart of America, writers by the 1890s cited both temporal and spatial isolation as the root causes. Appalachia was a geographical island on which the natives lived much as other Americans had lived 100 to 150 years earlier. The mountaineers were described as "Our Contemporary Ancestors." This appealed to many Americans in an era that also saw the founding of the Sons of the American Revolution (1889), the Daughters of the American Revolution (1890), the Colonial Dames of America (1891), and other such groups. That Appalachia also seemed to contain a vast reservoir of "pure Anglo-Saxons," in contrast to the waves of immigrants coming into the United States at this time, was another contributing factor for America's interest in Appalachia. [3]

Following closely on the heels of the local-color writers were representatives of mostly northern Protestant churches. These missionary churches turned to the mountain whites after their work with southern blacks became politically untenable in the post-Reconstruction South. Quickly establishing schools and rural versions of settlement houses in the mountains, missionaries propagated a view of Appalachia somewhat different from that of the local-color writers. Convinced by the writers'

[3] Henry Shapiro, *Appalachia on Our Mind* (Chapel Hill: University of North Carolina Press, 1978), pp. 3–4, 16, 18; William Goodell Frost, "Our Contemporary Ancestors in the Southern Mountains," *Atlantic Monthly* 83, no. 497 (March 1899): 311–19; James C. Klotter, "The Black South and White Appalachia," *Journal of American History* 66, no. 4 (March 1980): 839–40.

assertions of the "otherness" of Appalachian society, missionaries focused not on living conditions, but rather on what they perceived as an impoverished and culturally backward people. This vision of Appalachia was influential both within the region, as more than 200 church schools and settlements had been established by the 1930s, and outside the region, through the missionaries' appeals to their northern brethren for funds to continue their work. Shapiro and other historians have suggested that the missionaries' view of Appalachia was based less on actual observed conditions in the mountains and more on cultural and religious ethnocentrism, occupational self-preservation, and an ethos of "new worlds to conquer."[4] Whatever their motives, the perceptions of both the local-color writers and the church missionaries are important, for they influenced every generation of tourists, geographers, sociologists, developers, and observers of Appalachia to the present.

Residents of the Appalachian Mountains have often been depicted as not just culturally inferior but culturally degenerate as well. In 1887 one writer proclaimed that the mountaineer "is more of a genuine barbarian and closer related in instincts, habits, and morals to the Huns and Visigoths that hung on the girdle of Rome and drove arrows into the bosom of the Mother of the World, than would appear on first thought." By 1958, a writer for *Harper's Magazine* was less prosaic, simply calling the mountaineers "proud, poor, primitive, and fast with a knife."[5]

Appalachian material culture has often been portrayed in a similar derogatory fashion, examples of which can be found in every decade since the 1860s. For example, in *Atlantic Monthly* in 1864, Elizabeth Appleton presented a portrait of a fictitious domestic interior in eastern Kentucky. The house consisted of "bare uncouth walls, with their ugly, straight-backed chairs, and their frightfully painted yellow or red tables and chests-of-drawers." "Ugly, unmatched crockery" complemented the scene. The mountain heroine of the story, when confronted with the furnishings of a newcomer to the mountains, did not know what half of

[4] Shapiro, *Appalachia on Our Mind*, chap. 2; Klotter, "Black South," p. 841; David Whisnant, *All That Is Native and Fine* (Chapel Hill: University of North Carolina Press, 1983), pp. 12–13.
[5] Klotter, "Black South," p. 834; *Harper's* quoted in John S. Otto, "Reconsidering the Southern Hillbilly: Appalachia and the Ozarks," *Appalachian Journal* 12, no. 4 (Summer 1985): 328.

the objects were, much less where they should be placed in a room.[6]

Part of the problem, according to a traveler in the same region in 1886, was the mountaineers' lack of acquisitiveness. "Most of the people are abjectly poor," he wrote, "and they appear to have no sense of accumulation." He listed one native's inventory of household goods as consisting of "a string of pumpkins, a skillet without a handle, and a bed."[7]

The image of poverty was magnified by church missionaries after the turn of the century. In a mission text from 1916, the Reverend Walter C. Whitaker described an average interior:

> The family have been sleeping for many hours scattered on beds and pallets of the severest and most meagerly furnished kind . . . the faded, dirty, and musty quilts of a vintage of ten or twenty years ago thrusting the fact of their existence on the olfactories of the stranger. . . . Two wooden beds and two pallets on the floor, one or two "split-bottom" rocking chairs, and one or two straight chairs of the same construction, never painted and now grown dark and finally all but black, a short deal table, and an upturned drygoods box, flanked by a tin trunk bought many years ago for $1.50—this is the furniture.[8]

Twenty years later the poverty image was further reinforced due to the effects of the Great Depression. In the 1930s photographers for the Farm Security Administration (FSA) documented the hard times of Americans all across the nation. Their photographs informed the rest of the country about how a "submerged third" of the nation coped with rural blight and depression. The subject matter of the FSA photographers was poverty and its consequences; they were even instructed at times to find the very worst examples of poverty to photograph. Appalachia seemed as promising an area as any in which to find poverty. Ben Shahn said of both Appalachia and the South, "wherever you point your camera there is a picture." Shahn, Walker Evans, Marion Post Wolcott, and others journeyed to Appalachia, photographing people in economic hardship (fig. 2). It is not known how many of these Appalachian photographs were published in the 1930s in magazines and

---

[6] Elizabeth Appleton, "A Half-Lie and a Half a Lie," *Atlantic Monthly* 13, no. 76 (February 1864): 160, 167.

[7] James Lane Allen, "Through Cumberland Gap on Horseback," *Harper's New Monthly* 73, no. 433 (June 1886): 58–61.

[8] Reverend Walter C. Whitaker, *The Southern Highlands and Highlanders* (Hartford, Conn.: Church Missions Publishing Co., 1916), pp. 34–35.

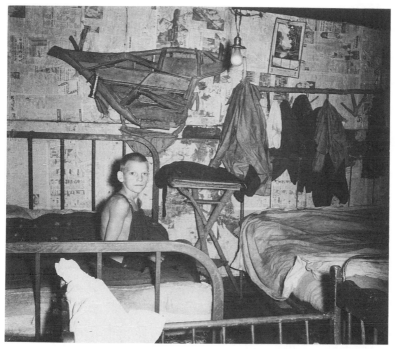

Fig. 2. Marion Post Wolcott, interior of a coal miner's house, Purs-
glove, W. Va., 1938. (Farm Security Administration Collection, Library
of Congress.)

newspapers, but the files of FSA photographs in Washington were widely
used at the time. Several of these photographs have also appeared in the
last twenty-five years in books about both the FSA photographers and
Appalachia. Russell Lee, one of the photographers, also published images
in the 1940s that reinforced the image of Appalachian poverty in the
popular consciousness (fig. 3).[9]

[9]Penelope Dixon, *Photographers of the Farm Security Administration: An Anno-
tated Bibliography, 1930–1980* (New York: Garland Publishing Co., 1983), p. xviii; Charles
Alan Watkins, "The Blurred Image: Documentary Photography and the Depression South"
(Ph.D. diss., University of Delaware, 1982), pp. 86, 198, 178, 101–3. See also *Walker
Evans, Photographs for the Farm Security Administration, 1935–1938* (New York: Da
Capo Press, 1973); and F. Jack Hurley, *Russell Lee, Photographer* (Dobbs Ferry, N.Y.:
Morgan and Morgan, 1978). United States Coal Mine Administration, *A Medical Survey
of the Bituminous Coal Industry* (Washington, D.C.: Government Printing Office, 1947).

Fig. 3. Russell Lee, interior of a house, Bell County, Ky., 1946. From F. Jack Hurley, *Russell Lee, Photographer* (Dobbs Ferry, N.Y.: Morgan and Morgan, 1978), p. 132.

By the 1960s, some natives of Appalachia were not surprised that the rest of the country focused once again on the most extreme elements of the region. One mountaineer exclaimed, "the southern mountains have been missionized, researched, studied, surveyed, romanticized, dramatized, hillbillyized, Dogpatched and povertyized again." Once more, photographs, books, and articles appeared showing a destitute Appalachia. An article in the *Saturday Evening Post* in 1960, titled "The Plight of the Hill People," proclaimed to be "the story of our most miserable citizens."[10] Television programs like "The Beverly Hillbillies" and "The Dukes of Hazzard," movies such as *Deliverance*, and even comic strips continue to perpetuate stereotypes about Appalachia

[10] Don West, "Romantic Appalachia," in David S. Walls and John B. Stephenson, *Appalachia in the Sixties: Decade of Reawakening* (Lexington: University Press of Kentucky, 1972), p. 212; *Saturday Evening Post* 232, no. 49 (June 4, 1960): 43.

Fig. 4. Fred Laswell, "Snuffy Smith," comic strip. From *News-Journal* (Wilmington, Del.), June 18, 1985.

(fig. 4). Recall the line from "The Beverly Hillbillies" theme—"poor mountaineer barely kept his family fed."

What is wrong with these images? Poverty, after all, did exist (and still exists) in Appalachia. But there are at least three criticisms that can be leveled not at the idea of poverty in Appalachia, but at the stereotype of Appalachian poverty propagated in part by images of domestic interiors.

First, writers and photographers have been selective in their efforts to find images representative of Appalachia. A mountaineer complained to a church official in 1916 about those outsiders who portrayed all of Appalachia as isolated, backward, and poor: "You missionary people do not treat us right. You come with your cameras and photograph our worst homes and our lowest people and then throw them on the screens to be seen. You never tell of our good people nor of the substantial things of the community. But I reckon you have to do that in order to get money out of your members."[11]

Principally due to the development of the coal industry in Appalachia beginning in the 1870s, people native to the region were tied into the national economic system to a much greater degree than most people realize. By 1900 four major railroads had run lines into the central Appalachian area of West Virginia, eastern Kentucky, and southwestern Virginia. As the coal industry attracted more and more people, all of Appalachia experienced a phenomenal growth in population. Between 1900 and 1933, the population in the region increased 56 percent. In one study of a coal community in southwestern Virginia, it has been found that as early as the 1890s both the miners in the town as well as

---

[11] Quoted in Vance, *Human Geography*, p. 244.

other local residents had the option of purchasing furniture from mountain peddlers, from a nearby store, from a Sears, Roebuck catalogue, or from the company store, which stocked furniture from such places as New York, Louisville, Cincinnati, and Chattanooga. It is significant and indicative of the power of stereotypes that a study of coal mining families in 1980 felt compelled to declare, "miners' homes . . . are apt to be furnished with the same appliances and amenities as other American homes."[12] As in any region of the country, there existed in Appalachia extremes of poverty and wealth, located in diverse geographical settings, in various-size hamlets and towns, and at various distances from larger and more commercial areas. The material conditions of farm families, of mining-camp residents, of townspeople, and of the more isolated hollow and ridge folk were not identical, not to mention the differences between the various ethnic and racial groups brought into the mountains by the coal industry. Some authors and photographers admitted that they were only interested in the poor or the picturesque. The author of an article that appeared in the *Overland Monthly* in 1888 admitted his biases in a note printed in small type at the end of his article:

The territory of the Southern mountaineer stretches from Alabama to Virginia, and is here and there more and more intersected by railroads, or enlivened by the building up of towns and the development of new industries. These descriptions and strictures [given in his article] do not apply so much to districts thus more or less modernized, as to more secluded belts scattered irregularly over this broad mountain domain, where life still moves on in pretty much the same groove it occupied sixty years ago.[13]

Most interpreters of Appalachian society neglected to provide such a disclaimer, even though their work was also selective in scope.

A second criticism of the poverty stereotype concerns the definition of what constitutes poverty. By any definition, there were people in Appalachia at the turn of the century, or in the depression, or in the 1960s who were hungry, who were without adequate shelter and health care. But that the majority of Appalachian residents were so impover-

[12] Ronald D. Eller, *Miners, Millhands, and Mountaineers* (Knoxville: University of Tennessee Press, 1982), pp. 225–26; Dean Herrin, "From Cabin to Camp: Southern Mountaineers and the Coal Town of Stonega, Virginia" (M.A. thesis, University of Delaware, 1984); President's Commission on Coal, *The American Coal Miner* (Washington, D.C.: Government Printing Office, 1980), p. 26.

[13] William Perry Brown, "A Peculiar People," *Overland Monthly*, 2d ser., 12, no. 71 (November 1888): 508.

Fig. 5. Russell Lee, interior of a house, Bell County, Ky., 1946. From F. Jack Hurley, *Russell Lee, Photographer* (Dobbs Ferry, N.Y.: Morgan and Morgan, 1978), p. 131.

ished, as popular images of Appalachia have implied, is questionable. It is now a cliché, but poverty is relative.[14] Besides the issue of selective evidence, the behavior, furnishing patterns, and interior decoration that have been portrayed since the nineteenth century as evidence of impoverishment may in fact have been misunderstood by outsiders.

Homes that used newspapers, magazines, and other printed matter as wallpaper have consistently been portrayed in a negative light (fig. 5). Charles Martin, a folklorist who has studied traditional housing in eastern Kentucky, has found that newspapered walls were actually part of a very orderly and conscious decorative aesthetic in many Appalachian homes. A decorative technique prevalent mainly in the period from 1900 to the 1940s, when wallpaper first became readily available

[14] See Walter Precourt, "The Image of Appalachian Poverty," in *Appalachia and America: Autonomy and Regional Dependence*, ed. Allen Batteau (Lexington: University Press of Kentucky, 1983).

in eastern Kentucky, newspapers provided a less expensive alternative to paint. Using photographs and oral history testimony, Martin has revealed that there was a system to how the newspaper was applied to the wall. Some families liked the print always to be right-side-up, others interspersed photographs in the papers at appropriate intervals, and still others segregated the photographs by subject matter, placing, for example, all photographs of food on the walls where the family ate. Magazine illustrations were favorites for some—one mother pasted Norman Rockwell covers from the *Saturday Evening Post* on her walls, since they told little stories that her small children could enjoy. Others who grew up in homes with newspapered interiors remembered first learning to read from looking at their walls. However newspaper and magazine pages were used in Appalachian homes, the common assumption that they were symbols of poverty and neglect is a relative assertion.[15]

The second example of cultural relativism concerns the use of space in Appalachian houses.One-room log cabins and their meager furnishings were often exhibited as examples of Appalachian poverty, their simplicity evidence of scarcity. In a study of traditional homes in western North Carolina, Michael Ann Williams uses oral history to modify our assumptions. Interiors of these homes were more complex than they have been portrayed. In the absence of walled partitions, furniture, particularly beds, was used to divide space and signify the function of a particular area in the room. In one example, a hallway, a living room, and a kitchen were conceptually formed through the placement of furniture. George McDaniel, in *Hearth and Home*, also has found this conception of space used in farm tenant housing in Maryland and Virginia. Furniture itself was used to designate personal space, as each member of the family may have had his or her own chair or bed, located in a defined place in the room. In other words, descriptions of these homes as examples of unordered and simplistic communal living, often symbolic of poverty, were not necessarily accurate.[16]

The third and final criticism of the poverty stereotype concerns the

[15] Charles Martin, "Appalachian House Beautiful," *Natural History* 91, no. 2 (February 1982): 4–16.

[16] Michael Ann Williams, "The Little 'Big House'—The Use and Meaning of the Single-Pen Dwelling," in *Perspectives in Vernacular Architecture II*, ed. Camille Wells (Columbia: University of Missouri Press for the Vernacular Architecture Forum, 1986), pp. 130–36; George McDaniel, *Hearth and Home: Preserving a People's Culture* (Philadelphia: Temple University Press, 1982), pp. 175–84.

long-term effects of such a stereotype. In an article from 1947, Lionel Trilling cautioned us about good intentions: "Some paradox in our nature leads us, once we have made our fellow men the objects of our enlightened interest, to go on to make them the objects of our pity, then of our wisdom, ultimately of our coercion."[17]

Many of the missionaries who established church schools in the first few decades of this century seem to have been genuinely concerned about what they perceived as poverty in the mountains. They also thought, however, that their middle-class culture was better than what they found in Appalachia, and through such teaching devices as "model homes," they were determined to "elevate and uplift" the mountain population. When one of the largest and most important church schools, Hindman Settlement School, was started in eastern Kentucky about 1900, the missionaries first lived in tents that were used to instruct by example (fig. 6). One of these missionaries reported that the tents were made "as clean and attractive as possible . . . with flags, Japanese lanterns, and photographs of the best pictures." She continued, "one who has seen the dirt, poverty, and desolate lack of beauty in the interior of a mountain cabin, can realize what a revelation this camp was to all who visited it." Model furnished houses were also suggested for Appalachian coal camps, even though one coal company felt that the mere presence of good furniture was not enough and that price tags and accompanying cards with suggestions for furniture placement were necessary to achieve the desired results. Furniture actually made in Appalachia was not considered appropriate to emulate. In the same letter to her family in which she mentions a local craftsman, one school worker asked to be sent photographs of "good old-fashioned bureaus and little tables." "We may as well have good lines," she explains. In *All That Is Native and Fine*, David Whisnant mentions these and many other examples of cultural imperialism in Appalachia. Model gardens, model farms, model kitchens, model laundries, model homes, and even model privies have been favorite tools to teach people in Appalachia how to live.[18]

[17] Trilling quoted in David J. Rothman, "The State as Parent," in *Conflict and Consensus in Modern American History*, ed. Allen F. Davis and Harold D. Woodman (Lexington, Mass.: D.C. Heath, 1984), pp. 280–81.

[18] Missionary quoted in Shapiro, *Appalachia on Our Mind*, pp. 147–48. Joseph White, *Houses for Mining Towns*, United States Bureau of Mines, Bulletin no. 87 (Washington, D.C.: Government Printing Office, 1914), p. 32. Whisnant, *All That Is Native*, pp. 29, 169; Shapiro, *Appalachia on Our Mind*, p. 149.

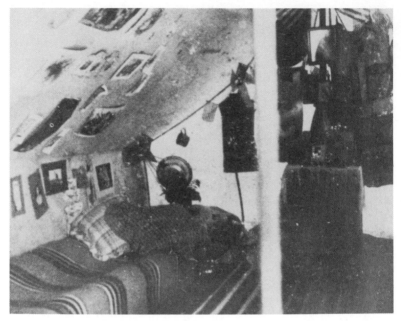

Fig. 6. Interior of a settlement worker's tent, Hindman, Ky. From David E. Whisnant, *All That Is Native and Fine: The Politics of Culture in an American Region* (Chapel Hill: University of North Carolina Press, 1983), fig. 1–3.

The image of Appalachia as an impoverished region has been accompanied by a second major stereotype which romanticizes Appalachia and its material culture. Numerous magazine articles have indicated this viewpoint simply through their titles, such as "Our Contemporary Ancestors in the Southern Mountains" (1899), "Where the Frontier Lingers" (1935), and "Yesterday's People" (1965). As recently as 1974 one scholar portrayed Appalachia "as a vanishing frontier and its people as frontiersmen, suspended and isolated, while the rest of the country moves across the twentieth century." The seeming simplicity of Appalachian life has served for almost a century as a form of escapism for other Americans harried by modern society. Dramatist Percy MacKaye described this feeling in 1924: "Over there in the mountains are men who do not live in cages; a million Americans, who do not chase the

Fig. 7. "A Mountaineer's Home." From Margaret W. Morley, *The Carolina Mountains* (Boston: Houghton Mifflin Co., 1913), p. 182.

dollar, who do not time-serve machines, who do not learn their manners from the movies or their culture from the beauty parlors."[19]

This vision of Appalachia has used traditional ballads, dulcimers, quilts, furniture, log cabins, and quaint speech as symbols of some sort of cultural "purity" (fig. 7). One author claimed in 1896 that if George Washington could return to America, he would have said of Appalachia: "At last here I find a part of the world as I left it." If so, Washington might have met William Shakespeare, for the speech of the mountaineers inspired another writer to claim that if the Bard "could revisit the earth today, he would feel more at home among our Mountain People than anywhere else."[20]

[19] Ronald D. Eller, "Toward a New History of the Appalachian South," *Appalachian Journal* 5, no. 1 (Autumn 1977): 75. MacKaye quoted in Shapiro, *Appalachia on Our Mind*, p. 261.

[20] Klotter, "Black South," pp. 838–39.

Fig. 8. Depiction of a mountain home parlor. From William Aspenwall Bradley, "Song Ballets and Devil's Ditties," *Harper's New Monthly*
130, no. 780 (May 1915): 909.

Romantic images of Appalachian interiors are usually centered
around the fireplace and prominently show such stock items as handmade chairs, musical instruments, spinning wheels, and rifles over the
fireplace mantle (fig. 8). Several of the images appear to have been
copied from one another.[21] Hearth scenes, spinning wheels, and looms
were favorites of photographers and illustrators, as they were particularly
symbolic of bygone days.

Unfortunately these views of Appalachia were just as selective as
the views of Appalachian poverty. That the coal industry was rapidly
transforming Appalachian society even before the turn of the century

[21] Compare, for example, the illustrations in William Aspenwall Bradley, "Song
Ballets and Devil's Ditties," *Harper's New Monthly* 130, no. 780 (May 1915): 909, with
those in Laura Spencer Porter, "In Search of Local Color," *Harper's New Monthly* 145,
nos. 867, 868 (August, September 1922): 283.

Fig. 9. A mountain home and family. From Margaret W. Morley, *The Carolina Mountains* (Boston: Houghton Mifflin Co., 1913), p. 142.

was conveniently overlooked by the perpetrators of the romantic image. Some even ignored evidence in their own photographs, as one can spot in a romantic-style photograph from 1913 a sewing machine in the shadows behind the spinning wheel (fig. 9). Others posed their subjects. The caption for a photograph by Doris Ulmann, used in Allen Eaton's *Handicrafts of the Southern Highlands* (1937), does not tell the reader that Ulmann had her subject dress in her grandmother's clothes, using antiques as props (fig. 10).[22]

Further romanticization of Appalachia has involved the handicrafts of the mountains. Traditional crafts such as furniture making were encouraged by the early settlement and church schools as both a pioneer survival and a means of making money for the mountaineer. Unfortu-

[22] Allen Eaton, *Handicrafts of the Southern Highlands* (New York: Russell Sage Foundation, 1937), pp. 68, 258.

Fig. 10. "Survival" of a mountain handicraft, Pine Mountain, Ky., 1934. From David Featherstone, *Doris Ulmann, American Portraits* (Albuquerque: University of New Mexico Press, 1985), p. 177.

nately most of the crafts instructors employed by the schools were not native to the region, but were instead from northern urban centers, trained in the prevailing arts and crafts revival movement. Some of the furniture they taught mountaineers to make was indeed traditional to the region, such as split-bottom chairs, but much was of the Roycroft–William Morris design, having little to do with local craft traditions. Appalachian museums and recent studies of Appalachian chairmakers, such as Michael Owen Jones's *Hand Made Object and Its Maker*, have concentrated more on local designs and influences. But even here there is a tendency to highlight the unusual or the unique, such as a bookcase rocker in Jones's book, or a polka-dot chair featured at one Appalachian museum in eastern Tennessee. Even with so-called typical furniture, there is the danger of isolating the object from its context. Jones has rightly observed that an individual object tells us absolutely nothing about the values embodied in that object. French historian Fernand Braudel noted, "However characteristic it may be, one piece of furniture does not reveal a whole picture; and the whole picture is all that matters."[23]

In conclusion, images of Appalachian interiors have aided the propagation of two dominant stereotypes about Appalachia: the first is the image of impoverished Appalachia; the second is the romantic image of Appalachia. There is some truth to each image, but neither accurately portrays the nuances, complexities, variances, and actual history of the Appalachian region. By treating a million people in parts of seven states as one homogeneous whole, observers of the region have ignored the diversity of social conditions that have existed in Appalachia and have often misunderstood and misrepresented the social conditions that they have examined. There are photographs, surviving objects, and oral histories that can help us to recover the material history of Appalachian homes, but the effort will be to no avail if conducted within the framework of stereotypes. Finally, a lasting effect of these stereotypes has been to distract attention from one of the principal reasons that real poverty exists at all in Appalachia—the exploitation of natural resources. By concentrating on the perceived results of impoverishment, or on Appalachia as an idyllic land of pioneer traits, one overlooks that such poverty as does exist is more the *result* of modernizing influences than a product of a lack of those influences. In a recent study, 13 million acres of land were sampled in eighty Appalachian counties spanning six states. More than 70 percent of that land was controlled by absentee owners, principally those concerned with timber and minerals.[24] If Washington and Shakespeare could go to Appalachia, they would probably have to be renters. Our study of furniture, our study of material culture must be placed within larger social and economic contexts. As Braudel said, the whole picture is all that matters.

[23] Whisnant, *All That Is Native*, pp. 61, 63; Michael Owen Jones, *The Hand Made Object and Its Maker* (Berkeley: University of California Press, 1975), p. 4; Gaynor, "Meet the Folks of Appalachia," p. 13; Michael Owen Jones, "The Useful and the Useless in Folk Art," *Journal of Popular Culture* 6, no. 4 (1973): 801; Fernand Braudel, *Capitalism and Material Life, 1400–1800* (New York: Harper and Row, 1973), p. 222.

[24] Eller, "Toward a New History," pp. xxiii–xxiv; Appalachian Land Ownership Task Force, *Who Owns Appalachia? Landownership and Its Impact* (Lexington: University Press of Kentucky, 1983), pp. 14, 150.

The Study of American Furniture from the Perspective of the Maker

Edward S. Cooke, Jr.

For some time social historians have pointed out the disproportionate amount of attention devoted to the Puritan settlers of New England. But even considering the number of studies in relation to the total number of Puritans, it is remarkable how much we still do not know about this segment of early American society. Another group of Americans about whom much is written but little really known are those who made or make furniture. In spite of a voluminous record of names, biographical data, and photographic images of products, we know very little about these craftsmen as full human beings—their values, shop-floor activities, and relations with clients. Instead, studies of these artisans and their works are beleaguered by temporal fragmentation and incomplete analysis.[1]

Each specific temporal setting—preindustrial, industrial, reform, and twentieth-century—possesses its own scholarly tradition. Studies of preindustrial cabinetmakers are dominated by object-oriented, descrip-

[1] The most recent scholar to comment on the overemphasis on New England Puritans is Gary Nash, "Social Development," in *Colonial British America: Essays in the New History of the Early Modern Era*, ed. Jack Greene and J. R. Pole (Baltimore: Johns Hopkins University Press, 1984), pp. 233–38. Other important references include Darrett Rutman, *American Puritanism* (New York: W. W. Norton, 1977), pp. vii–xi; and Edmund Morgan, "The Historians of Early New England," in *The Reinterpretation of Early American History*, ed. Ray Allen Billington (New York: W. W. Norton, 1968), pp. 41–43. The shortcomings of past studies of artisans are discussed more fully in Edward S. Cooke, Jr.'s, chapter on craftsmen in *Decorative Arts and Household Furnishings Used in America, 1650–1920: An Annotated Bibliography*, ed. Kenneth L. Ames and Gerald W. R. Ward (forthcoming).

tive biographies and by long lists of craftsmen with skeletal genealogical information. These works also favor master craftsmen, who have remained more visible in historical records, surviving accounts, or labels. Scholars interested in furniture craftsmen of the nineteenth century reflect a similar concern with the accumulation of names and dates of firms, the data for which can be gathered from labeled examples, advertisements, and directories. A few recent scholars, following the lead of labor historians, have examined the human components of these firms but have made little attempt to go beyond gross quantification or to incorporate the products of these skilled workers into the analysis. In short, industrial studies are either studies of furniture made in one factory or quantified analyses of faceless workers.[2]

Studies of craftsmen who made furniture in the late nineteenth and early twentieth centuries also reflect a keen interest in the identification of craftsmen. These lists of furniture makers, however, have been compiled and superficially interpreted with the assistance of the self-conscious promotional literature that distinguished this period. The writers of these tracts—such people as Gustav Stickley and Oscar Lowell Triggs—sought to evoke certain standards of craftsmanship. The plentiful examples of this romantic genre have generated far greater interest in furniture producers guided by the philosophy of the arts and crafts movement rather than in the producers guided by other facets of the reform impulse during the same period. Few studies of late nineteenth- and early twentieth-century furniture have taken into consideration the rise of scientific management or the fight for workers' control. Studies of arts and crafts furniture makers accept the rhetoric of promotional tracts at face value and seldom search for its impetus, its relation to the actual product, or its relationship to other small-shop or factory production. We therefore know little about the full range of the furniture industry and the details of furniture production at this time.[3]

[2] Good examples of works featuring master craftsmen include E. Milby Burton, *Charleston Furniture, 1700–1825* (Columbia: University of South Carolina Press, 1970); William Voss Elder III and Lu Bartlett, *John Shaw, Cabinetmaker of Annapolis* (Baltimore: Baltimore Museum of Art, 1983); and Ethel Hall Bjerkoe, *The Cabinetmakers of America* (Garden City, N.Y.: Doubleday, 1957). Examples of industrial studies are Mary Jean Madigan, ed., *Nineteenth Century Furniture: Innovation, Revival and Reform* (New York: Art and Antiques, 1982); and Eileen Dubrow and Richard Dubrow, *American Furniture of the Nineteenth Century, 1840–1880* (Exton, Pa.: Schiffer Publishing, 1983).

[3] For examples of the romantic tradition, see Robert Judson Clark, ed., *The Arts and Crafts Movement in America, 1876–1916* (Princeton, N.J.: Princeton University Press, 1972); and David Cathers, *Furniture of the American Arts and Crafts Movement: Stickley*

Similarly, publications on twentieth-century furniture-making artisans provide a skewed, incomplete picture. An emphasis on designers and a fascination with new materials and processes preclude a sense of the whole industry and of the technical continuum within the furniture trade. Even the study of contemporary studio craftsmen, the artisanal descendants of the small-shop masters of the eighteenth century, is misguided. Instead of following the example of folklorists who write interpretive studies based on interviews and fieldwork, scholars examining contemporary furniture makers depend on "artists' statements" which are often either postfacto justifications or rhetorical flourishes designed to link the maker to a cosmic plan and therefore command critical attention. Studies of these living craftsmen make no attempt to explain the relationships or discrepancies between ideas, rhetoric, process, product, or market.[4]

The reasons for this fragmented, incomplete view of furniture makers are many, but can be grouped into three major headings. The consistent interest in compiling lists of craftsmen reflects an obsession with the identification of a piece of furniture and the attribution of it to a known maker. Since the early twentieth century, furniture has been increasingly recognized as a decorative art. As a result, the study of it and its makers has become subject to the vagaries and demands of the collecting market. Interest in the names and genealogies of cabinetmakers only sprang up in the early 1920s, in conjunction with the rapid growth of antique collecting at that time. Primary among a collector's demands is the identification of the maker, date, and origin of an object. This typological exercise fulfills a collector's nostalgic needs, builds his self-assurance and security, and increases the market value of the object. While identification of a craftsman is certainly an important step in the understanding of an object, it should not become an end unto itself. Canonization, whether of Thomas Dennis, William Savery, Duncan

---

and Roycroft Mission Oak (New York: New American Library, 1981). On scientific management, see Hugh G. J. Aitken, *Taylorism at Watertown Arsenal: Scientific Management in Action, 1908–1915* (Cambridge, Mass.: Harvard University Press, 1960); on workers' control, see David Montgomery, *Workers' Control in America* (New York: Cambridge University Press, 1979).

[4]Representative of these studies are David Hanks, *Innovative Furniture in America from 1800 to the Present* (New York: Horizon Press, 1981); Philippe Garner, *Twentieth-Century Furniture* (New York: Van Nostrand Reinhold Co., 1980); Katy Kline, *Furniture by Architects: Contemporary Chairs, Tables, and Lamps* (Cambridge, Mass.: Hayden Gallery of MIT, 1981); and *Woodenforms* (Brockton, Mass.: Brockton Art Museum, 1981).

Phyfe, John Henry Belter, Gustav Stickley, Eero Saarinen, or Sam Maloof, permits little understanding of the individual's relation to other furniture makers or to his society.[5]

A second explanation for the uneven analysis of furniture makers is the difficulty of understanding the process. Too often scholars have restricted themselves to a static view of furniture making. Books from the seventeenth century to the present have identified tools and other utensils of the crafts, but have not considered their interrelationships. These publications devote considerable attention to geometric principles and describe and illustrate certain tools; they do not consider the assemblage of tools, weigh the various choices of tools or techniques, analyze the appropriateness or sequence of use, explain the favoring of a tool or convention, or extrapolate the routines of production. These encyclopedias provide little information about the vocabulary of production and the sequence of steps. As a result, our understanding of process is largely intuitive or romantic. The broader aspects of the technical process are crucial to the analysis of an artisan. Often a craftsman defines himself by his kit of tools, individual adaptation of a tool, or development of special jigs for specific situations he confronts. Surprisingly, there have been few attempts to use the best source material—the furniture itself—for information regarding the practices of a particular shop. From an examination of materials, constructional details, and tool marks, one can often infer what a shop's practices were.[6]

---

[5] Although his tone is a bit strident, Michael Ettema makes some astute observations about the need to identify artworks in Michael J. Ettema, "History, Nostalgia, and American Furniture," *Winterthur Portfolio* 17, nos. 2/3 (Summer/Autumn 1982): 135–44. The early studies of furniture craftsmen include Walter Dyer, *Early American Craftsmen* (New York: Century Co., 1915); R. T. H. Halsey, "William Savery, the Colonial Cabinetmaker and His Furniture," *Bulletin of the Metropolitan Museum of Art* 13, no. 12 (December 1918): 254–67; Walter Dyer, "John Goddard and His Block Fronts," *Antiques* 1, no. 5 (May 1922): 203–8; Walter Dyer, "Collector's Biographical Dictionary," *Antiques* 2, no. 3 (September 1922): 136–38, 2, no. 4 (October 1922): 183–84, and 2, no. 6 (December 1922): 285–91; Charles O. Cornelius, *Furniture Masterpieces of Duncan Phyfe* (Garden City, N.Y.: Doubleday, Page, 1922); Charles O. Cornelius, "Goddard, Savery and Phyfe," *Arts* 4, no. 1 (July 1923): 33–44; Mrs. Guion Thompson, "Hitchcock of Hitchcocksville," *Antiques* 4, no. 2 (August 1923): 74–77; and Clarence Wilson Brazer, "Jonathan Gostelowe, Philadelphia Chair and Cabinetmaker," *Antiques* 9, no. 6 (June 1926): 385–92, and 10, no. 2 (August 1926): 125–32.

[6] Jonathan Fairbanks makes the strongest case for the difficulty of studying artisanal process in Jonathan L. Fairbanks, "Craft Processes and Images: Visual Sources for the Study of the Craftsman," in *The Craftsman in Early America*, ed. Ian M. G. Quimby

A third explanation for the present inadequacy of craftsmen studies is the artifactual pool on which the studies focus. Largely because of the market influence, examinations to date have focused primarily on older, more aesthetically pleasing (as determined by our own taste) examples of furniture or on professionally designed "name" furniture. Moreover, writers have often considered each object on an individual basis; they have made little effort to look at a series of objects made in one shop or in a region. Such an approach undermines any attempt to understand the economic concerns of a cabinetmaker. It prevents a more accurate assessment of a craftsman's range or line of products and his differing levels of workmanship.[7]

In general the literature on furniture makers and furniture making demonstrates little conceptual sophistication. The studies lack any sort of interpretive paradigm or broader perspective such as that which characterizes the scholarly literature on furniture ownership and use. Instead,

---

(New York: W. W. Norton, 1984), pp. 299–330. Books that present individual tools and only hint at some of the processes involved in the making of furniture include Joseph Moxon, *Mechanick Exercises* (London, 1703; reprint, New York: Praeger Publishers, 1970); Peter Nicholson, *Carpenter and Joiners Companion* (London: J. Taylor, 1826); G. Lister Sutcliffe, ed., *The Modern Carpenter Joiner and Cabinet-Maker*, 8 vols. (London: Gresham Publishing Co., 1902–4); and Charles F. Hummel, *With Hammer in Hand: The Dominy Craftsmen of East Hampton, New York* (Charlottesville: University Press of Virginia, 1968). These encyclopedic volumes nevertheless provide an important foundation for additional analysis. Sources that describe certain recent approaches to making furniture include *Popular Mechanics*, addressed to the layman, the videotapes currently produced by *Fine Woodworking*, and John Alexander, Jr., *Make a Chair from a Tree: An Introduction to Working Green Wood* (Newtown, Conn.: Taunton Press, 1978). These sources may prove useful, but one should be careful not to project certain conventions back to older furniture. Philip Zimmerman emphasizes the importance of rigorous artifactual analysis in "Workmanship as Evidence: A Model for Object Study," *Winterthur Portfolio* 16, no. 4 (Winter 1981): 283–307. Helpful recent studies that use the objects as source material to understand better the craft process and use of tools include Edward S. Cooke, Jr., "Rural Artisanal Culture: The Preindustrial Joiners of Newtown and Woodbury, Connecticut, 1760–1820" (Ph.D. diss., Boston University, 1984); and Barbara McLean Ward, "The Craftsman in a Changing Society: Boston Goldsmiths, 1690–1730" (Ph.D. diss., Boston University, 1983).

[7]Recent exceptions to this include Robert F. Trent, *Hearts and Crowns: Folk Chairs of the Connecticut Coast, 1720–1840* (New Haven: New Haven Colony Historical Society, 1977); and Benno M. Forman, "Delaware Valley 'Crookt Foot' and Slat-Black Chairs: The Fussell-Savery Connection," *Winterthur Portfolio* 15, no. 1 (Spring 1980): 41–64. See also Michael J. Ettema, "Technological Innovation and Design Economics in Furniture Manufacture," *Winterthur Portfolio* 16, nos. 2/3 (Summer/Autumn 1981): 197–223.

studies of furniture and its makers remain mired down in data accumulation, uncritical acceptance of promotional literature, preoccupation with the identification of design sources, and a sense of linear industrialization. Underlying much work on the process of furniture making is the assumption that there has been an inexorable evolution of the means of production from craft to industry to art. Such a simplistic, ahistorical perspective ignores the dynamism of the trade. The growth of mass-production capitalism and the emergence of the art furniture market are two of the diverse developmental sequences in American furniture making.[8]

From the seventeenth century to the present, there have been a number of possible modes of furniture production. They range from amateur or expedient do-it-yourself work, to domestic piecework for other craftsmen or firms, to small shops run by part-time (not part-skilled) craftsmen who fit furniture making in among other tasks, to shops that specialize in certain forms, to larger production-oriented outfits. The greatest change has occurred at the latter end of the spectrum: There are now many large-scale factories that make use of the latest labor-saving jigs and tools. But, to judge from the shops of seventeenth-century chairmakers in Charlestown, Massachusetts, and those of Solomon Fussell in Philadelphia and Peter Scott in Williamsburg, much of this growth has been a change in degree rather than in kind. Ever since the second quarter of the nineteenth century, as demand for fur-

---

[8] Studies on furniture as nonverbal communication include Robert Blair St. George, " 'Set Thine House in Order': The Domestication of the Yoemanry in Seventeenth-Century New England," in Jonathan L. Fairbanks and Robert F. Trent, *New England Begins: The Seventeenth Century*, 3 vols. (Boston: Museum of Fine Arts, 1982), 2:159–88; Kevin M. Sweeney, "Furniture and the Domestic Environment in Wethersfield, Connecticut, 1639–1800," *Connecticut Antiquarian* 36, no. 2 (December 1984): 10–39; Edward S. Cooke, Jr., "Domestic Space in the Federal-Period Inventories of Salem Merchants," *Essex Institute Historical Collections* 116, no. 4 (April 1980): 248–64; Lizabeth A. Cohen, "Embellishing a Life of Labor: An Interpretation of the Material Culture of Working-Class Homes, 1885–1915," *Journal of American Culture* 3, no. 4 (Winter 1980): 752–75; and Kenneth L. Ames, "Meaning in Artifacts: Hall Furnishings in Victorian America," *Journal of Interdisciplinary History* 9, no. 1 (Summer 1978): 19–46. The linear perspective is explicitly stated in Kathleen Catalano, "Cabinetmaking in Philadelphia, 1820–1840: Transition from Craft to Industry," *American Furniture and Its Makers: Winterthur Portfolio 13*, ed. Ian M. G. Quimby (Chicago: University of Chicago Press, 1979), pp. 81–138; and Sharon Darling, *Chicago Furniture: Art, Craft, and Industry, 1833–1983* (New York: W. W. Norton, 1984). A well-argued attack against the linearity of classical developmental economic theory is Charles Sabel and Jonathan Zeitlin, "Historical Alternatives to Mass Production," *Past and Present* 108 (August 1985): 133–76.

niture and other consumer products grew due to the establishment of a wage-based economy and the increasing sophistication of marketing techniques, the large-scale furniture producers drew on and exploited the existing patterns of labor indebtedness, outwork, and technology to expand. Conversely, small shops have often introduced and exploited special-purpose machinery. Small-shop and part-time traditions, labor-intensive customwork, and low-technology nailed or turned construction have never disappeared. Instead, each of the productive modes has had its own viability over the past three and a half centuries, depending on the cultural and economic conditions of particular times and locations. For example, chronic underemployment in crowded towns of eighteenth-century New England supported a viable small-shop tradition, but in Boston and Newport a burgeoning coastal trade necessitated special flexible types of large-scale production. Family-run chair shops with three to seven benches or merchant-orchestrated cooperative arrangements among several smaller shops producing tables and case furniture provided a sufficient quantity of objects for the local market and for export. Later, in the early twentieth century, the rhetoric of the arts and crafts movement heightened the validity of amateur work.[9]

The distinguishing change over time in the furniture trade is the greater number of options available to the craftsman. Whether working alone or in a factory, cabinetmakers have enjoyed an increasing number of choices—new methods of learning skills, additional types of woods, new materials besides wood, a greater range of tools, a variety of power sources and speeds, new adhesives, new finishes, and wider markets. Yet none of these new possibilities has automatically subsumed earlier preferences; rather, they coexist with the more traditional ones.

We should be careful, however, not to dismiss categorically all the

[9]Fairbanks and Trent, *New England Begins*, 2:216–17; Forman, "Delaware Valley Chairs"; and Wallace Gusler, *Furniture of Williamsburg and Eastern Virginia, 1710–1790* (Richmond: Virginia Museum of Fine Arts, 1979). The importance of particular context is stressed by Sabel and Zeitlin, "Historical Alternatives"; and Mark Duginske, "Thoughts on a Working System," *Wood News* 15 (Spring 1985): 8–9. On eighteenth-century New England, see Cooke, "Rural Artisanal Culture"; Brock Jobe, "Urban Craftsmen and Design," in Brock Jobe and Myrna Kaye, *New England Furniture: The Colonial Era* (Boston: Houghton Mifflin Co., 1984), pp. 3–46; and Jeanne Vibert Sloan, "John Cahoone and the Newport Furniture Industry," *Old-Time New England* 72, no. 259 (1987). The increased interest in amateur work at the beginning of this century is evident in such works as *Popular Mechanics*; and H. H. Windsor, *Mission Furniture: How to Make It* (1909; reprint, Santa Barbara, Calif.: Peregrine Smith, 1976).

existing work on furniture makers. Future research should bring a different set of questions to bear on the data and derive additional information from all varieties of source material. In order to correct the shortcomings of current studies and establish the agenda for future work, we should draw inspiration from folklorists who study living craftsmen and develop rich analytical biographies of their subjects. One folklorist, Michael Owen Jones, has compiled extremely comprehensive questions that analyze the craftsman's own makeup, his processes, and his relationships with people around him. Even if it is not possible to interview craftsmen directly, one can study their behavioral patterns and, in combination with solid contextual research, reconstruct the "measurable social reality" of an artisan's life.[10]

The importance of contextual analysis, to explore and explain changes in experiences or patterns of behavior, underscores the need for more sophisticated record and artifactual linkage. Account books can be an especially valuable source for information about work rhythms and the craftsman's socioeconomic relations. Craftsmen appear frequently in the public records of their time, but scholars have made limited use of these primary sources. Writers have drawn from these documents more to establish the existence, location, or date range of a craftsman than to construct an insightful explication of his world. Furthermore, scholars have made greater use of probate inventories, newspaper advertisements, and directories than the more difficult sources like court and census records. Private records are even more problematic. Few past cabinetmakers have left memoirs or played important enough roles that their possessions or writings were preserved. These artisans simply made things. Consequently their products may be the most important source material for craft scholars. Yet these three-dimensional records cannot be "read" easily. We need to cut through subjective judgment and preconceived notions to examine carefully what an object says. This is where contextual knowledge is so important.

For all past and present cabinetmakers, we must not be content with a descriptive profile of a maker or his product. We must strive for

---

[10] Michael Owen Jones, "The Study of Traditional Furniture: Review and Preview," *Keystone Folklore Quarterly* 12, no. 4 (Winter 1967): 233–45. For the results of his approach, see Michael Owen Jones, *The Hand Made Object and Its Maker* (Berkeley: University of California Press, 1975). Quoted phrase from Robert Malcomson, *Life and Labor in England, 1700–1780* (New York: St. Martin's Press, 1981).

a richer, more comprehensive understanding of the craftsman and his world. To accomplish this we need to cast our net wider and use all sorts of records in a more sophisticated and interconnected manner. The analysis of artifacts, account books, inventories, wills, court records, tax lists, town and church records, land deeds, census records, newspaper articles, advertisements, photographs, surviving tools, surviving work environments (including archaeological investigation), and other sorts of material will enable us to explore the connectedness between different facets of culture, technology, and society. We need to understand the full complexity and broader context involved in making furniture, what labor historian Philip Scranton has called the "matrix" of production. Scranton's dynamic model, which examines the interrelationship between material, sociocultural, and external factors and the effects of decisions based on these factors on future directions, is invaluable because it demonstrates there was and is no single ideal type of productive system. Rather, there have been and always are multiple correct solutions, each arising from a specific set of circumstances. Our task is, therefore, to unlock, reconstruct, and interpret the various layers of a furniture maker's experiences.[11]

The importance of artifactual evidence demands a more complex model of examination to replace the current simplistic studies of cabinetmakers. A promising model involves a complex series of interlocking spheres of analysis that focuses on composition, process, and performance (fig. 1). The investigation of one area does not precede the other, but rather should be conducted in association with the others. Information gathered under the auspices of each informs the range of questions applied to the others. This synergistic approach, the applicability and workability of which is suggested by several existing scholarly works, should contribute to a deeper analytic level.[12]

The most essential and yet most difficult and slippery area is composition. Commonly called design, composition is often thought of as a cosmic or spiritual sort of endeavor. Yet composition possesses a less

[11] Philip Scranton, *Proprietary Capitalism: The Textile Manufacture at Philadelphia, 1800–1885* (New York: Cambridge University Press, 1983).
[12] Although the references cited for each of the three analytical thrusts are often pertinent to the other two, they have been cited for particular strength regarding that concept. Several works are even cited for more than one sphere of analysis. This overlapping and the Venn diagram demonstrate the connectedness within the process of conceiving and making furniture.

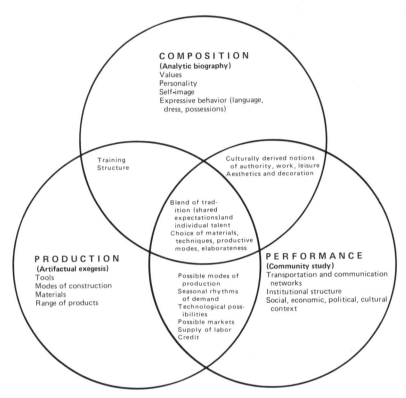

Fig. 1. Venn diagram showing interlocking mode of analysis for the study of the craftsman. Within each circle are the Category (research strategy) and Issues. The overlapping zones contain issues explored through several strategies.

abstract quality that is grounded in social reality, whether it is the artisan's training, the influence of a printed design, or the development of new forms through the reorganization of older parts or through the adoption of new materials or tools. Composition is the process by which a craftsman draws from experience and observation a structural, technical, and decorative solution to the question of creation. From a range of alternatives derived from his particular physical and social environment and from his own expectations and needs, the craftsman picks the appropriate rules that will satisfy the needs, resources, and fancy of the client.[13]

Accepting this socially based definition of conception, it is important to assess the maker's values and environment. If the artisan was an individual or a household productive unit, one can draw on account books, diaries, and interviews or compare demographic patterns to those of similar individuals from the same time and place. If the productive unit was larger than the household, the scholar must then look at each type of smaller unit within the larger whole and understand the influence each unit exerted on each step of the process and on the final product. It is important to separate the different attitudes, experiences, and tasks of the capitalist owners, designers, foremen, various skilled workers, and various semiskilled workers. To a varying extent, depending on the setup, each group had a say in the derivation and production of furniture. Frequently the professional designer drew up the proposed form and included general instructions to the various craftsmen, each of whom—whether framer, carver, finisher, or some other specialist— would interpret the plans based on his own intuitive knowledge, experience, and skill.[14]

The second analytical thrust in future work should be a reexami-

[13] This definition of composition is derived from Henry Glassie, *Folk Housing in Middle Virginia* (Knoxville: University of Tennessee Press, 1975), esp. chaps. 3, 4, 7.

[14] Exemplary studies of individuals and small-shop production include Alan Macfarlane, *The Family Life of Ralph Josselin* (New York: W. W. Norton, 1970); R. Gerald Alvey, *Dulcimer Maker: The Craft of Homer Ledford* (Lexington: University Press of Kentucky, 1984); Jones, *Hand Made Object*; and Robert Blair St. George, "Fathers, Sons, and Identity: Woodworking Artisans in Southeastern New England, 1620–1700," in Quimby, *Craftsman in Early America*, pp. 89–125. Macfarlane's study uses diaries and account books to reconstruct the life and values of a seventeenth-century English minister. Alvey and Jones draw heavily on interviews and fieldwork in their monographs on contemporary craftsmen. St. George's work uses aggregate demographic data to draw generalizations about changes in mobility and craft occupations and explains the attitudes and opportunities that influenced these patterns. For suggestive studies of larger productive units, see Scranton, *Proprietary Capitalism*; Thomas Dublin, *Women at Work* (New York: Columbia University Press, 1979); Joan Wallach Scott, *The Glassworkers of Carmaux* (Cambridge, Mass.: Harvard University Press, 1974); and Anthony F. C. Wallace, *Rockdale: The Growth of an American Village in the Early Industrial Revolution* (New York: W. W. Norton, 1980). Although these studies focus on different sorts of industries, they provide helpful insights into research strategies that uncover group values and valuable explications of the web of socioeconomic relations that influence the process and product. A more specific work which addresses the relationship between designer and craftsmen is Charles H. Carpenter, Jr., *Gorham Silver, 1831–1981* (New York: Dodd, Mead, 1982).

nation of production. We need to shift our concerns from a static view of the individual tools that does not take into consideration the social and economic factors of production. Instead we should focus more on what labor historians call shop-floor history to understand the interrelationship of the technical and social dynamics in furniture manufacture. To move in this direction, we should take into consideration the wide number of options available to the cabinetmaker. Each craftsman has always been able to draw from a wide selection of preparatory, joinery, decorative, and finishing options. Each of these options had its own economic viability or social acceptance. Therefore, we need to look at certain features of the manufacturing environment such as its physical setup (size, ownership, location, arrangement of shop), technical makeup (variety of tools, relationship to equipment of other shops, source of power, relationships with other shops), and daily and seasonal rhythms. Comparative analysis of a shop's full production can help to reveal the role of design economics and technical preferences; that is, the relationship between style, materials, and technology. In addition, we need to upgrade the quality of our artifactual exegeses so that we recognize not only what tool or process was used in the preparation, joining, and decoration of each part but why that particular tool or process was chosen.[15]

The social basis of furniture production is equally important. We need to probe thoroughly into who contributed their time and skill to the production of furniture: the origins of the workers, their particular

[15] For an example of the classic literature on process, see Charles F. Hummel, "The Business of Woodworking, 1700 to 1840," in *Tools and Technologies: America's Wooden Age*, ed. Paul Kebabian and William Lipke (Burlington: University of Vermont, 1979), pp. 43–63. The *Chronicle of the Early American Industries Association* is the major periodical that espouses the tool-centered view of technology. Montgomery's *Workers' Control* is a good example of shop-floor history with a broader perspective. The best monograph on the social economy of the craft process is John Burrison, *Brothers in Clay: The Story of Georgia Folk Pottery* (Athens: University of Georgia Press, 1983). Useful works on individual craftsmen include George Sturt, *The Wheelwright's Shop* (1923; reprint, Cambridge: At the University Press, 1963); and John M. Vlach, *Charleston Blacksmith: The Work of Philip Simmons* (Athens: University of Georgia Press, 1981). The influence of design economics and alternative technologies is discussed in Ettema, "Technological Innovation"; Jeannette Lasansky, *To Draw, Upset, and Weld: The World of the Pennsylvania Rural Blacksmith, 1742–1935* (Lewisburg, Pa.: Oral Traditions Project of the Union County Historical Society, 1980); and Bob Reckman, "Carpentry: The Craft and the Trade," in *Case Studies on the Labor Process*, ed. Andrew Zimbalist (New York: Monthly Review Press, 1979), pp. 73–102. The last is an important work that distinguishes between complementary and competitive technologies and demonstrates that craft production and new technologies are not mutually exclusive.

tasks and how they related to others, the nonwork relationships among workers in the workplace, the workers' residences, how workers spent their leisure time, and what cultural ties linked each worker to the larger social units of neighborhood or town. This line of investigation will reveal the human hierarchy within the shop—division of tasks, relationships of activities to age or status, the learning environment—and help to shed light on the preference for certain technologies, the look of the final product, or the origin of a design.[16]

The importance of the social context to the process of furniture making leads naturally to the third sphere of analysis: performance. A consideration of performance has to be more than our own judgment of the final product in relation to an ideal academic archetype. As a form of material culture, furniture embodies and manifests the shared values and experiences of its maker and user. Therefore, performance, or the actualization of composition, is rooted within the social, economic, and cultural context in which the furniture maker lived and worked. The contextual study of the craftsman's environment permits the full understanding of such production issues as local labor conventions, technical possibilities, capital formation, and material sources. A community study would also help to answer questions regarding distribution—what was the ratio between customwork and stockwork, how were commissions initiated, and who marketed the final result and how.[17]

Whereas it is important to recognize the craftsman's ultimate control over a piece of furniture's structural makeup, his clients often exerted a greater influence on the parameters of form and decoration. Hank Gilpin, a contemporary small-shop cabinetmaker, criticizes many of his peers for taking the unsocial stance of producing whatever they want, "and the public be damned." Disagreeing with the connection between business success and creative loss, Gilpin believes it best "to do what

[16]On the relationship between life cycle and task orientation, see Edward Fix, "A Long Island Carpenter at Work: A Quantitative Inquiry into the Account Book of Jedidiah Williamson," *Chronicle of the Early American Industries Association* 32, no. 4 (December 1979): 61–63, and 33, no. 1 (March 1980): 4–8. Hummel, *With Hammer in Hand*; Forman, "Delaware Valley Chairs"; and Gusler, *Furniture of Williamsburg*, touch on various aspects of the social structure in furniture shops. Much is still implicit or overlooked in their discussions.

[17]The importance of local social structures on process is stressed in Cooke, "Rural Artisanal Culture"; Jonathan Prude, *The Coming of Industrial Order: Town and Factory Life in Rural Massachusetts, 1810–1860* (New York: Cambridge University Press, 1983); and Merritt Roe Smith, *Harpers Ferry Armory and the New Technology* (Ithaca, N.Y.: Cornell University Press, 1977).

somebody else wants your way." The interface of craftsman's conventions and client's desires is the essence of the furniture-making trade. Therefore, the study of performance has to take into consideration the demand for and use of furniture from that particular place and time. To accomplish this, we need to examine a shop's product in relation to others made by that shop, made by other craftsmen, or even owned within the community. Surviving objects, account books, probate records, and interior photographs all shed light on the ownership of furniture within a particular community. Pertinent questions include the types of furniture owned, the demand for furniture, and the relationship between furniture ownership and the production and consumption of other domestic artifacts. This permits the linking of the material world to the values and behavior of clients. After all, the craftsman's ultimate success or failure is determined by his clients' acceptance or disapproval. By investigating the social, cultural, and economic situation for which a craftsman made furniture, it is also possible to discern certain motivations—conscious conservatism, economic conservatism, selective adaptation, aspiring innovation, supply-driven innovation. The well-rounded community-based analysis, in conjunction with the other types, will better enable the scholar to weigh the full range of possibilities associated with making furniture.[18]

Rigorous record and artifactual linkage and more analytical frameworks that synthesize greater varieties of material will permit greater understanding of the historical development of furniture making rather than of furniture forms. Yet, at the same time, we should be realistic enough to recognize that not every study will seek or be able to explore all possible avenues. But if we can upgrade the analytical framework of those attempting a smaller slice of the pie that constitutes the cabinetmaker's world, we can then start collaborating and putting together some of the smaller pieces to form greater portions. Our common goal should be an understanding of one of our nation's oldest industries.

[18]Gilpin quoted by Roger Holmes in "Survivors," *Fine Woodworking*, no. 55 (November/December 1985): 97. Historical examples of craftsmen making the same sorts of concessions include Catherine W. Bishir, "Jacob W. Holt: An American Builder," *Winterthur Portfolio* 16, no. 1 (Spring 1981): 1–31; Burrison, *Brothers in Clay*; Dell Upton, "Toward a Performance Theory of Vernacular Architecture: Early Tidewater Virginia as a Case Study," *Folklore Forum* 12, nos. 2/3 (1979): 133–96; and Philip Zea, "Clockmaking and Society at the River and the Bay: Jedediah and Jabez Baldwin, 1790–1820," in *The Bay and the River: 1600–1900*, Annual Proceedings of the Dublin Seminar for New England Folklife 6 (1981), ed. Peter M. Benes (Boston: Boston University, 1982), pp. 43–59.

Timothy Loomis and the Economy of Joinery in Windsor, Connecticut, 1740–1786

William N. Hosley, Jr.

Although the products of urban cabinetmakers from coastal cities such as Boston, Philadelphia, and Newport dominate the literature on eighteenth-century American furniture, it is the diversified joiner who serviced agrarian regions in New England and the Middle Colonies that best represents predominant modes of manufacturing and prevailing tastes. To understand furniture making better in the context of a largely agrarian society, I have examined a rich body of objects and documents representing the leading woodworking dynasty in one of inland New England's oldest and most prosperous farming communities. For more than four generations the Loomis family dominated the joiner's trade in Windsor, Connecticut. Although more than a dozen members of this family have been documented as practicing joiners in the Windsor area during the seventeenth and eighteenth centuries, it is Timothy Loomis III (1724–86) who left the most informative record of his career, a career that spanned forty years. Six account books exist documenting his labors as well as those of six members of his immediate family and Zebulon Hoskins (1728–68), a neighboring joiner, contemporary, and occasional partner. Loomis's own record is the most complete, including a practice book kept by him during his education and apprenticeship, a daybook kept during the second half of his career, and the ledger he maintained through most of his working years. Together these documents furnish an accurate picture of the woodworking industry in an agrarian Connecticut River valley town during the mid eighteenth century.[1]

Timothy Loomis III was one of Joseph Loomis's fifth-generation descendants. Joseph Loomis, a woolen-cloth maker from County Essex, England, who arrived in Windsor in 1639, three years after the English commenced settlement there, died with a small estate in 1658. Two of his five sons, Joseph (1616–89) and John (1622–88), remained in Windsor, while their brothers settled on the east side of the Connecticut River at East Windsor and Bolton. Joseph and John Loomis both acquired land near their father's plot at the confluence of the Farmington and Connecticut rivers and achieved a modest level of prosperity by raising grain and livestock. The brothers between them sired seventeen children who lived to adulthood. Of 277 heads of household on the Windsor tax list of 1686, 11 (4 percent) were named Loomis, significantly more than any other family in town. Unable to provide all their children with land, John and Joseph each trained several sons to practice trades: weaving, blacksmithing, and joinery. Four of John's sons, Joseph II, Timothy, Sr., Nathaniel II, and Samuel, became joiners. Timothy, Sr., accumulated the largest estate of the four brothers and was the first of a direct line of Loomises who would dominate the joiner's trade in

[1] Patricia E. Kane, "The Joiners of Seventeenth-Century Hartford County," *Connecticut Historical Society Bulletin* 35, no. 3 (July 1970): 65–85. Kane documented Nathaniel Loomis I (1657–1733) and Nathaniel Loomis II (1663–1732) as joiners. To their number can be added Joseph II (1651–99), Sgt. Daniel (1657–1740), Timothy, Sr. (1661–1710), Samuel (1666–1754), Stephen (1668–1711), Moses (1671–1742), Daniel II (1682–1752), Capt. Joseph IV (1684–1748), Timothy, Jr. (1691–1740), Odiah (1705–94), Isaac (b. 1719) of Farmington, Joseph (1725–86), Luke (1736–1811) of East Windsor, Maj. Watson (1747–1800), Timothy IV (1750–1832), George (1753–1804), Simeon (1767–1865) of East Windsor, and Reubin (1773–1860) of Windsor and Suffield. These men were identified as joiners on the basis of the tools recorded in their estate inventories or by references to their work in account books (Connecticut Valley Archive, Wadsworth Atheneum, Hartford). The six documents are (1) practice book/diary, Timothy Loomis III, Windsor, 1738–83 (Loomis Chaffee School, Windsor); (2) daybook, Timothy Loomis III, Windsor, 1766–86, and George Loomis, 1787–1804 (Loomis Chaffee School); (3) ledger, Thomas Cooke, Windsor, 1689–1724, and Odiah Loomis, 1725–48, and Ozias Loomis, 1748–60s (Loomis Chaffee School); (4) ledger, Reubin Loomis, Windsor and Suffield, 1796–1836 (Connecticut Historical Society, Hartford [hereafter cited as CHS]); (5) ledger, Timothy Loomis, Jr., Windsor, 1731–40, Timothy Loomis III, 1745–86, and George Loomis, 1786–1804 (CHS); and (6) ledger, Zebulon Hoskins, Windsor, 1749–68, and Alson Hoskins, 1768–1808 (CHS). The most useful of these was the ledger Timothy Loomis III maintained 1745–86 (hereafter cited as Loomis III ledger). On several pages he referred to an "old book," which indicates that the 1745–86 ledger was a second volume, and most entries are posted from the 1760s and 1770s. His earlier ledger is lost.

Windsor during the next four generations, from the late seventeenth century until the death of his great-grandson George in 1804.[2] Where and by whom these four men were trained is unknown. In the case of Timothy, Sr., a clue is furnished by his marriage to Rebecca Porter (1666–1750) of Windsor, whose father, John Porter (d. 1688), and several first cousins were joiners. Her first cousin Hezekiah Porter (1665–1752) was a joiner in Hartford where he owned the largest inventory of tools documented among any of his Hartford contemporaries.[3] During his brief life of forty-nine years, Timothy, Sr., prospered, accumulating an estate valued at some £400, 80 percent of which was comprised of land and livestock.

Like father, like son. Timothy, Sr., prepared two of his four sons for the joiner's trade. His premature death in 1710 left his nineteen-year-old son, Timothy, Jr., with an inheritance that included a house, land, and a full set of joiner's tools. Young Loomis thus began adulthood with advantages shared by few of his Windsor contemporaries. These were put to good use, and Timothy, Jr.'s, wealth and stature grew rapidly. In 1731, at the age of thirty, he began keeping the ledger later used by his son Timothy III and grandson George. His transactions document a man with diverse skills and cultivated talents. He made chests, tables, spinning wheels, and beds; built and repaired houses and barns; raised grain, livestock, and tobacco; spun wool and flax; and kept bees. Although the value of his shop tools, appraised after his death at more than £10, was probably greater than any of his Windsor contemporaries, joinery was only a part-time seasonal occupation for Loomis. A greater part of his income and the largest part of his prestige came from his role as Windsor's town clerk, an office he held for almost

[2] Henry R. Stiles, *The History and Genealogies of Ancient Windsor, Connecticut*, vol. 2 (Hartford: Case, Lockwood, and Brainard, 1892), pp. 432–34; estate inventory, Joseph Loomis, Windsor, 1658, Hartford District Probate Court Records, Connecticut State Library, Hartford (hereafter cited as HPR); tax list, Windsor, 1686, microfilm, CHS; estate inventories, Joseph Loomis II, Windsor, 1699, no. 3437, Timothy Loomis, Windsor, 1710, no. 3469, Nathaniel Loomis, Bolton, 1732, no. 3449, and Samuel Loomis, Colchester, 1754, HPR.

[3] Stiles, *History of Windsor*, 2:620–21; estate inventory, John Porter, Windsor, 1688, HPR. John's brother Samuel Porter was a joiner in Hadley, Mass. (*The Great River: Art and Society of the Connecticut Valley, 1635–1820* [Hartford: Wadsworth Atheneum, 1985], cat. 75). His son Hezekiah owned more than £12 in joiner's tools when his estate was probated in 1754 and is documented as making unusually expensive chairs for East Windsor's minister in 1729 (estate inventory, Hezekiah Porter, Hartford, 1752, no. 4346, HPR).

twenty years. As town clerk his duties were similar to those performed by lawyers. He wrote deeds, indentures, and bonds, assisted in organizing account books, and took inventories of estates. After merchants, ministers, and physicians, the town clerk was the next most learned occupation. Unlike most of his Windsor contemporaries, few of whom owned more than a Bible and a psalm book, Timothy Loomis, Jr.'s, library of about a dozen divinity books was complemented by a dictionary, a spelling book, a guide on record keeping, and several history books.[4]

Unlike most of his Windsor contemporaries, who married locally, Loomis sought a wife beyond the boundaries of town. By marrying Hannah Phelps in 1722, Timothy, Jr., further penetrated the network of Hartford's leading joiners. Already related by his mother to Hartford joiner Hezekiah Porter, his new brother-in-law, Timothy Phelps (1702–56), was an accomplished furniture maker.[5]

Timothy Loomis III was born into this relatively privileged and cosmopolitan environment in 1724. Sixteen years later the cycle of premature death reasserted itself, and Timothy Loomis, Jr., the town clerk, was dead at age forty-nine. During his short adult life, he had tripled the family inheritance, leaving an estate valued at almost £1,100. One thing was different, however; where Timothy, Sr.'s, estate was divided among seven heirs, Timothy III and his sister Esther were their father's only heirs, and thus each received a much larger share of an estate already swollen by hard work and careful management. The effect of this inheritance was to place Timothy III immediately among Windsor's wealthiest men. In addition to land and an impressive array of agricultural and joiner's tools, young Loomis inherited a house, a shop with unfinished stock, an account book that placed a significant number of neighbors in his debt, his father's best clothes, and, in all likelihood, his reputation.[6]

Timothy III's formal education had begun two years earlier when, at the age of fourteen, he began keeping a practice book in which he

---

[4] Stiles, *History of Windsor*, 2:437; estate inventory, Timothy Loomis, Jr., Windsor, 1740, no. 3470, HPR.

[5] Robert F. Trent, "Wheels within Wheels: The Genealogies of Some Major Connecticut River Valley Woodworking Artisans" (typescript, CHS, 1984). This study was the first to explore genealogical connections between the Loomis and Phelps families of joiners.

[6] Loomis, Jr., estate inventory.

Fig. 1. Handwriting sample, Timothy Loomis III, practice book/diary, 1738. Ink on paper. (Loomis Chaffee School, Windsor: Photo, William N. Hosley, Jr.)

entered extensive notations on a wide range of subjects. The practice book is a curious document that served several functions. Although his name and dates appear throughout the book, the chronology of notations does not follow sequentially from one page to the next. Many of the most pertinent references are undated, making it difficult to reconstruct the sequence of his learnings. Nonetheless, the book is a fascinating document that furnishes a perspective on the training and world view of one of Connecticut valley's leading mid eighteenth-century woodworkers.[7]

The book contains handwriting samples (fig. 1), rules of grammar and punctuation, vocabulary definitions, multiplication tables, genealogical notations, sample transcriptions of public documents undertaken with his father's supervision, his own poetic compositions, and computations of the distances between various Windsor landmarks. The

[7] Loomis III practice book/diary.

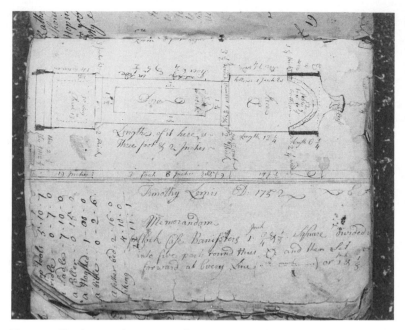

Fig. 2. Clock-case diagram and notes, Timothy Loomis III, practice book/diary, ca. 1752. Ink on paper. (Loomis Chaffee School, Windsor: Photo, William N. Hosley, Jr.)

book also contains several pages of notes pertaining to Loomis's training as a joiner. These include some of the earliest known proportional diagrams by a New England furniture maker and instructions for measuring and cutting the parts for several furniture forms including a chest of drawers, a dressing table, a clock case, a staircase, and a corner cupboard. The sketch of the clock case, in particular, was carefully prepared and closely resembles a style of "pagoda top" clock case that was popular in the Connecticut valley during the mid eighteenth century (fig. 2).

From Loomis's book we also learn that in 1746 Timothy III sliced open his leg with an ax while cutting timber to build his house and that in 1748 he helped to build a sloop for nine Windsor speculators. In the first season managing the farm Loomis noted, "I planted corn the first time and it did not come up well." Abandoning his agricultural pursuits, he spent the following autumn and winter helping his "Uncle Bull" build a new meetinghouse in neighboring Simsbury. Young Loomis was then seventeen years old. Unfortunately, this is the only mention of his training in the book. Although no primary kinship with an Uncle Bull has been determined, he was probably either John Bull or Isaac Bull, two joiners who spent part of 1739 working in Hartford on one of the Connecticut valley's first baroque-style meetinghouses. In all likelihood, young Loomis began his apprenticeship with his father and worked periodically with his Uncle Bull before completing his education in Hartford under the tutelage of his other uncle, Timothy Phelps. There he would have met and perhaps worked with his first cousin of the same age, Timothy Phelps, Jr. (1725–84), who was destined to become Hartford's leading furniture maker. Both Loomis and Phelps would become instrumental in developing and popularizing a style of cabinetwork that remained fashionable until the eve of the Revolution. Although Loomis's training in Hartford is conjectural, he undoubtedly spent enough time there to meet and court Sarah Talcott, granddaughter of a Connecticut governor and member of a high-ranking Hartford family. They were married in 1743 and returned to Windsor where Loomis practiced his trade and managed his interests for the next forty-three years.[8]

Loomis's prosperity was clearly reflected in his increasingly elevated position on the Windsor tax rolls. Yet neither lofty family connections nor wealth prevented him from immersing himself in his trade and reintegrating himself into the dynamics of Windsor's culture and economy. Lacking his father's sideline occupation as town clerk, Timothy III became more intensively occupied as a joiner than any of his ancestors. In spite of the broad opportunities presented by his wealth and superior training, Loomis concluded his apprenticeship by settling back into the timeless rhythm of the agricultural year, tending the farm during planting and harvest and fitting joinery into the off-season hours. He shared with other Connecticut valley joiners of his generation a multioccupational existence, dominated by labor exchange and long-term mutual indebtedness with a bewildering array of cousins, in-laws,

[8] Loomis III practice book/diary. First Ecclesiastical Society of Hartford, Miscellaneous Papers, 1739, CHS. Neither Isaac Bull's nor John Bull's probate files contain an estate inventory, making it difficult to ascertain the extent of their involvement in the joiner's trade. The prestigious Hartford meetinghouse would have attracted many of the area's most skillful woodworkers. Stiles, History of Windsor, 2:441.

and neighbors. Although Loomis's own apprentices eventually emerged as professionals and specialists, he applied his learning in more traditional ways. The ledger maintained by Loomis from 1745 until his death in 1786 provides a comprehensive perspective on his occupation and relations. Because of the primitive accounting methods employed by virtually all colonial tradesmen, it is impossible to quantify accurately the extent and range of their labors; income cannot be computed with accuracy. Numerous transactions took place off the books. In spite of these shortcomings, a tradesman's ledger is still the most valuable document of his industry. From it economic relationships can be understood, and, if not in exact proportion, impressions of the kinds of labor and even the seasonal patterns of labor can be determined. Loomis's ledger is especially valuable because, in addition to his accounts, it contains a record of his annual tax assessment from 1749 until his death, extensive genealogical information, early population statistics for Connecticut, a record of his inheritance, and price lists for his cabinetwork dated 1759 and 1760 (Appendix 1), the earliest documented attempt by a Connecticut valley joiner to regulate his prices.[9]

Loomis's labor was divided into a dozen basic categories. Unlike his father, who devoted most of his time to his farm and clerking for the town of Windsor, Timothy III was as close to a professional tradesman as any rural joiner in his time. This is not to say that he was a specialist, and indeed, although he made cabinetwork, he did not consider himself a "cabinetmaker." Most of his time was devoted to building, repairing, and remodeling houses, barns, and outbuildings. Builders worked in crews; unfortunately, the composition of these crews and the division of labor within them is rarely determinable from reading the ledger of a single builder. Although they labored together, they were paid separately by their mutual client who usually acted as his own contractor. This was especially true with Loomis's clients. In the construction of the parsonage for the Reverend William Russell, built between 1753 and 1755 at a cost of £395, Loomis acted as both a laborer and a contractor (figs. 3, 4). He and at least two unidentified "apprentices" were also the principal builders of the town meetinghouse in 1757.[10] These

---

[9] Loomis III ledger, pp. 97, 99.

[10] Loomis III ledger, pp. 102, 100. Unfortunately, the specific tasks involved in building the parsonage were not itemized in Loomis's accounts. After 1755 he returned periodi-

Fig. 3. Timothy Loomis III, Zebulon Hoskins, and others, William Russell house, Windsor, Conn., 1753–55. (Courtesy the Reverend and Mrs. Van Parker: Photo, William N. Hosley, Jr.)

were prestigious contracts that demonstrate Loomis's highly esteemed reputation among his neighbors.

With the construction of the Russell house, Loomis introduced the first "Connecticut valley doorway" to Windsor. These ostentatious, baroque-style doorways symbolized the taste of the valley's gentry elite which included the region's leading merchants, ministers, and military leaders. The earliest documented example of this style was built only two years previously in East Hartford for a colleague of Russell's, the Reverend Eliphalet Williams. Although the central-chimney floor plan of the Russell house was not innovative and its ornament unelaborated, it was as stylistically advanced and monumental as any house then

---

cally to add window shutters (1757), build a bookcase (1763), and "finish" the parlor (1772). Loomis debited the First Society for £30 of labor in "working at the new Meeting house" and was also paid for "boarding" himself and "apprentices." John Grant (1721–1802) was another prominent joiner in Windsor and was paid for helping to frame the meetinghouse. Several other joiners would undoubtedly have been involved as well. Loomis labored with apprentices for almost 200 days and likely was the master builder.

standing in Windsor. As befitting the dignity of the minister's office, Russell furnished the house with luxuries that were second to none among Loomis's patrons. Loomis and Russell maintained accounts for twenty-three years, until the minister's death in 1775. Although almost 93 percent of the debts posted to Russell's account were for architectural work, Loomis also made furniture and coffins for Russell and occasionally traded agricultural produce and the labor of his apprentices. These goods and services were exchanged for lumber and credits with local merchants and, most important, were applied toward Loomis's payment of the tax assessed for the support of the minister's salary.[11]

Loomis exchanged different goods and services with each of his 108 patrons. While most accounts were maintained for many years, from single transactions valued at a few shillings to several dozen transactions valued at £20 and more, Loomis rendered service according to the needs of each client. Since Loomis was characteristically sloppy in posting credits to his accounts, it is not always possible to ascertain why he worked more at joinery for some individuals while trading agricultural labor and produce with others. Jonathan Beamon, a joiner who worked frequently with Loomis, was debited mostly in agricultural produce. Barter was always preferable to paying scarce currency, and Loomis supplied most of his family's needs by establishing accounts with neighbors who could supply their wants; dry-goods merchants, physicians, blacksmiths, tanners, weavers, hatmakers, clockmakers, dentists, and fishermen were among those who traded goods and services with Loomis. Yet it was not always possible for Loomis to use his skills as barter to supply his family's needs; Jerijah Barber, a shoemaker on whom Loomis depended, required mostly cash payments, preferring to purchase most of his furniture from someone else.[12]

Loomis performed inexpensive renovations and repairs more often than he completed large building contracts. He built bookcases and cupboards, repaired mills, stills, fences, and barns, laid flooring in gar-

[11] *Great River*, cat. 7; Kevin M. Sweeney, "Mansion People: Kinship, Class, and Architecture in Western Massachusetts in the Mid Eighteenth Century," *Winterthur Portfolio* 19, no. 4 (Winter 1984): 239–40; Amelia F. Miller, *Connecticut Valley Doorways: An Eighteenth-Century Flowering* (Boston: Boston University for the Dublin Seminar for New England Folklife, 1983); Loomis III ledger, p. 102.

[12] Loomis III ledger, pp. 54, 134. Loomis paid Beamon in produce on thirty-one occasions, more than for any other individual. He was credited with "sundrys," "sash stuff," and other evidence of joinery (estate inventory, Jerijah Barber, Windsor, 1792, no. 300, HPR).

rets, built hog pens and staircases, cased rooms, and clapboarded exteriors.[13] Much of his time was devoted to making and repairing relatively inexpensive forms. In spite of the frequency of such mundane chores, Loomis was capable of molding an edge or carving a shell equal to the best of his contemporaries, when called to do so. A remarkable characteristic of rural workmanship is the joiner's ability to produce an aesthetically and technically competent product at irregular intervals. Timothy Loomis's wares fit that pattern.

Among Loomis's larger accounts was that maintained with the town physician, Alexander Wolcott (1712–95), a Yale-educated son of the colonial governor, Roger Wolcott. Loomis posted seventy-five transactions with Wolcott, from the time their accounts were opened in 1754 until Loomis's death in 1786. Loomis debited Wolcott's account for more than £26, divided among furniture making (49.6 percent), architectural repairs and renovations (17.3 percent), agricultural produce (14.5 percent), labor by sons and apprentices (14.5 percent), miscellaneous services (5.8 percent) such as farm labor and presenting evidence at court, repairing furniture (2.3 percent), and trading lumber and domestic produce (2 percent). In 1774 Loomis was paid 90s. for a "crown case [of] draws, you found . . . the brace [brasses] & locks." In 1762 Loomis helped to modernize the parlor in Wolcott's then twenty-year-old house (fig. 5).[14] This room and its handsomely finished buffet, or corner cupboard, was elaborately finished with raised-panel work, fluted pilasters, cased summer beams, and wainscoting, comparable in style and ornament to the best cabinetwork. It shares with the interior of the Russell house hallmarks of the region's prevailing high-style taste: an asymmetric composition of paneling and boldly articulated framing members, with a nod to classicism reflected in the use of fluted pilasters. Although hardly innovative by the standards of classical design, this room clearly communicated its owner's willingness to reach deep into his pockets for the resources required to embrace fashion. In the context of Windsor society, style was measured as much by the amount of labor that went into it as by the product of that labor.

During the span of Loomis's career, Connecticut valley joiners were almost uniformly compensated at a rate of 3s. per day. In 1783 Loomis charged his neighbor Phineas Wilson 110s. for a "case of draws,"

---

[13] Loomis III ledger; Loomis III daybook, 1766–86.
[14] Stiles, *History of Windsor*, 2:810; Loomis III ledger, p. 110.

Fig. 4. Parlor, William Russell house, Windsor, Conn. (Photo, William N. Hosley, Jr.)

Fig. 5. Timothy Loomis III, parlor, Dr. Alexander Wolcott house, Windsor, Conn., 1762. (Courtesy Mr. and Mrs. Warren Ball: Photo, William N. Hosley, Jr.)

presumably a scroll-top high chest. This was the single most expensive furniture form recorded in his ledger. Assuming that the materials comprised 25 percent of the chest's value, Loomis still invested twenty-two days of labor in making it. This must have been an extraordinary piece of furniture, all the more so when compared with Windsor-made examples of what Loomis described in his 1760 price list as a "cherry case of nine draws with a shell at the bottom." These he priced at 54s., less than half the rate of his most expensive product. An example compatible with this description was donated to the Wadsworth Atheneum by a descendant of Jabez Haskell's (1746–1816) of Windsor, who was allegedly its first owner (fig. 6). Although Haskell is not listed among Loomis's patrons, this chest, which retains its original hardware, represents a cheaper version of work that is attributed to him. In addition to his cheapest high chests, several Windsor-made examples of the thirteen-drawer variant, described as a "case of drawers" in his account book, are known. One of these bears the date "A.D. 1760" inscribed in chalk and descended in his immediate family (fig. 7). It is undoubtedly an example of his work and was among the group of Loomis family heirlooms that included Timothy III's ledger. These are the furnishings of the Loomis Chaffee School's Loomis Homestead, which belonged to Timothy III's grandfather Timothy, Sr., and later to his uncle Odiah Loomis and first cousin Ozias (1746–96). Timothy III reputedly remodeled the parlor of this house about 1750 and undoubtedly supplied most of the new furniture that his uncle and cousin bought during their occupancy.[15] The lower case retains its original hardware, recently reproduced during restoration of the upper case. The diminutive character of the brasses on this and the preceding chest reflect an economy of design typical of Connecticut valley furniture at midcentury.

The most expensive offering in Loomis's price list is described as a "scroll topped case of drawer" priced at 80s. Allowing 25 percent for materials, this represents twenty days of labor. Although no examples with Windsor histories are presently known, these must have closely resembled the many examples documented throughout the Connecti-

[15] Numerous account book citations for "day work" by the Connecticut valley's eighteenth-century woodworkers document the standard rate of payment during the era (Connecticut Valley Archive). Between 1700 and the 1780s, when wage rates finally increased, no instances of a valley joiner being paid more than 3½s. or less than 2½s. per day have been recorded. Prices were highly stable in the valley. Loomis III ledger, p. 141; Stiles, *History of Windsor*, 2:368; Wadsworth Atheneum, acquisition file, 1980.8; *The Loomis Homestead* (Windsor: Loomis Chaffee School, n.d.).

Fig. 6. High chest of drawers, possibly Timothy
Loomis III, Windsor, Conn., ca. 1780. Cherry and
pine; H. 70⅛″, W. 40½″, D. 21¼″. (Wadsworth
Atheneum: Photo, John Giammatteo.)

cut valley from Middletown to Northampton.¹⁶ The basic components
of this regional style of cabinetwork are surprisingly homogeneous. The
work of one joiner's shop was much like another. It is difficult to differ-

¹⁶Just a few of the many recorded examples are documented in *Great River*, cats.
93–99.

Fig. 7. High chest of drawers, Timothy Loomis III, Windsor, Conn., 1760. Cherry and pine; H. 73″, W. 40½″, D. 20½″. (Loomis Chaffee School, Windsor: Photo, William N. Hosley, Jr.)

entiate between cabinetwork produced in one town and the next and virtually impossible to identify the work of specific shops. Histories of ownership, particularly since most furniture was bought locally, thus provide an indispensible clue to identifying the place where a particular object was made.

Fig. 8. Tea table, probably Timothy
Loomis III, Windsor, Conn., ca. 1780.
Cherry; H. 27½", diam. (top) 33⅛".
(Loomis Chaffee School, Windsor:
Photo, William N. Hosley, Jr.)

Loomis's price list includes twenty furniture forms, about half the
number described in his accounts (Appendix 2). These include plain
chests, dressing tables, tea tables, coffins, bedsteads, and cradles. A tea
table attributed to Loomis descended through the same branch of the
Loomis family as the preceding high chest (fig. 8). Its pedestal and construction are nearly identical to a pedestal sketch and corresponding
walnut tea table attributed to Thomas Hayden (1745–1817), Loomis's
apprentice.[17]

Absent from the price list and accounts are complex or expensive
examples of turned work such as the ubiquitous crown chairs that his

[17] *Great River*, cat. 105.

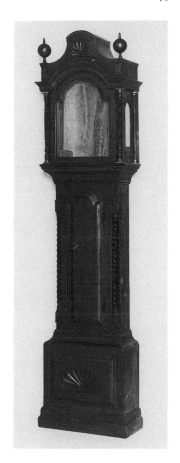

Fig. 9. Clock case, proably Timothy
Loomis III, Windsor, Conn., ca. 1760.
Cherry and yellow pine; H. 84″, W.
18½″, D. 9¼″. (Private collection:
Photo, John Giammatteo.)

clients purchased elsewhere. One of Loomis's specialties was making
stylish clock cases which he undoubtedly supplied to the customers of
his neighbor Seth Youngs (1711–61), the Connecticut valley's first
clockmaker, who set up shop in Windsor in 1745. Timothy Loomis
was, in all likelihood, the only joiner who made clock cases in the
Windsor area prior to the Revolution. An example attributed to him is
decorated with deeply carved shells and represents his top-of-the-line
work (fig. 9). This case and its clock (now lost) entered the Grant family
of East Windsor through the marriage of Flavia Wolcott (1754–1827)
to Roswell Grant in 1783. It was probably made for Flavia's father,

Gen. Erastus Wolcott (1722–96), one of the wealthiest and most influential men in eighteenth-century East Windsor.[18]

The tradition of joinery persisted among furniture makers into the mid eighteenth century and explains the use of architectural methods of construction and ornament in Connecticut valley furniture, long after such methods had been abandoned by "cabinetmakers" working in the city. Loomis's furniture is characteristically overbuilt; lumber is far thicker than was needed to do the job, joints are reinforced with numerous pins, and drawers are built of half-inch-thick pine stock, dressed and assembled in the joiner's manner. What little carving is employed is executed in coarse large features as suitable to decorating a cupboard or a chimney breast as a drawer front or a scroll.

In addition to woodworking, Loomis's ledger cites numerous transactions unrelated to his trade. In 1772, he acquired an interest in a sawmill and thereafter began selling finished boards and slitwork for window frames. He maintained an inventory of building stock, paint, and glass and frequently supplied other joiners with these goods. Loomis also operated a farm that grew to include almost 100 acres. There he raised sheep, cattle, and hogs. His numerous agricultural transactions document the sale of fish, turnips, tobacco, potatoes, corn, and grains. From the home, he and his wife sold woven goods, candles, butter, and beeswax. Loomis also labored occasionally at preparing documents, as his father had trained him, butchering a neighbor's animals, renting his horses, appraising estates, or charging for his sons to labor in the fields at harvesttime. Loomis occasionally paid cash for services rendered. Yet most of his accounts were maintained by labor exchanges that transpired during the course of decades. Indeed, at the time of his death, most of his lifelong accounts remained open, and his bookful of obligations represented a significant portion of his son's inheritance.

In an economy based on labor exchange, individuals frequently worked off their debts by transferring obligations from one party to another. Loomis's accounts record at least a dozen individuals who labored at

---

[18] The rarity of clocks in Windsor's colonial households makes it plausible that Timothy Loomis was the only joiner in town who made stylish clock cases. Neighboring joiners like Zebulon Hoskins turned to Loomis when their own patrons sought clock cases. During the 1750s Hoskins debited Jonathan Ellsworth and Samuel Chapman for clock cases made by Timothy Loomis (Hoskins ledger, pp. 10, 19). For information on Seth Youngs, see *Great River*, cat. 230. Stiles, *History of Windsor*, 2:811–12.

joinery on his behalf. Among them, only three, notably Loomis's sons George and Timothy IV and Thomas Hayden, were of apprenticeship age. The rest were neighboring joiners and carpenters who exchanged labor as a regular part of their occupation. These men were not journeymen as usually understood. They served a local clientele and worked with, rather than for, Loomis, and then only periodically. One of these trade partners was Zebulon Hoskins, who worked alongside Timothy Loomis on numerous occasions between 1749 and 1755. During the construction of the Russell house in 1753, Loomis was paid for Hoskins's labor. The same year Hoskins received payment from Jonathan Ellsworth of Windsor for a "clock case by Tim Loomis."[19]

Loomis occasionally accepted furniture in payment for debts by fellow joiners, suggesting an economy based on fluid exchange relations and widespread interdependency. In spite of the prevalence of labor exchange and barter, Windsor's joiners limited competition by cultivating separate rosters of clients. Remarkably, Hoskins's ledger also survives and provides a vehicle for comparing the products and clientele of two men of similar age and training.[20] Hoskins's ledger records transactions with 110 individuals, almost exactly the number recorded in Loomis's ledger. Although working at the same time and place for a primarily local clientele, Loomis and Hoskins held only 17 percent of their trading partners in common. They developed separate rosters of exchange partners, perhaps in conscious deference to one another. Yet the composition of their clientele was relatively similar, as were the kinds of tasks they performed. Both labored at agriculture, building, and furniture making.

To provide a perspective on his exchange relations, biographical profiles of Loomis's clients have been assembled from vital statistics, tax

---

[19] The individuals who worked with Loomis on building projects or who were credited in the Loomis III ledger for joinery or joiner's work were: Zebulon Hoskins, 1755 and 1749, p. 102; Mathew [?], 1749, p. 118; Joseph [?], 1753 and 1755, pp. 107, 118; David [?], 1753, p. 107; John [Grant?], 1755–58, p. 118; M. Holcomb, 1758, p. 118; Elisha Moore (1739–1819), 1760–83, p. 93; Jabez Gillet (d. 1815), 1761–62, pp. 113, 119, 131; Thomas Hayden, 1761–65 and 1777, pp. 104, 108, 130, 131, 135; Ebenezer Loomis, 1765, p. 123; Timothy Loomis IV, 1767–69, pp. 108, 115; Jonathan Beamon, 1769–74, pp. 54, 134; George Loomis, 1773–77, pp. 108, 12, 143; Fitch Loomis, 1778, p. 149. For Hoskins's labor and payment, see Loomis III ledger, p. 102; and Hoskins ledger, p. 10 (special thanks to Christopher Bickford for calling this recent acquisition by CHS to my attention).

[20] Stiles, *History of Windsor*, 2:406.

lists, and, whenever possible, individual estate inventories. The most conspicuous characteristic of Loomis's clientele was its geographic concentration in Windsor; 93 percent of his 108 patrons resided in Windsor, and most of his patrons beyond Windsor were either relatives or fellow joiners. In Hartford he traded with his wife's brother and with his father-in-law, Capt. John Talcott. Loomis's patrons were an entrenched, immobile group of landowners; 83 percent were born and died in Windsor. Occupation and wealth were determined for 69 percent of Loomis's male patrons, those individuals whose estates were probated. Like Loomis himself, most were multioccupational landowners. Only two individuals, Reubin Ellsworth and Isaac Chandler, had no apparent involvement with agriculture. Ellsworth's estate, appraised near the median for Loomis's clients at £797, contained tools for blacksmithing, clockmaking, tanning, and saddlery.[21] Although almost all Windsor residents contributed in some way to the economy of commercial agriculture, the balance between raising livestock and grain varied considerably, as did the extent of land holdings. Land and livestock were the basic currency of Windsor's economy, and few people invested more than 20 percent of their wealth in housing and furnishings. Despite occupational similarities, wealth in Windsor was unevenly distributed with almost half of the total value of probated assets belonging to the upper 10 percent of Loomis's clients. The poorest half of his clients owned only 9 percent of the probated assets. Such inequality is reflected in the consumption of luxury goods which Loomis manufactured. On the eve of the Revolution, less than 5 percent of Loomis's clients owned silver goods, about 10 percent owned clocks, and 3 percent owned slaves, including the Reverend William Russell and a local blacksmith.[22] While

[21] Joseph Loomis of East Windsor was a cousin and joiner; Capt. John Talcott (d. 1771) of Hartford was Timothy Loomis's father-in-law; Daniel Wadsworth (1720–62) of Hartford was married to Talcott's sister Eunice; Capt. Samuel Wells (1728–69) of East Hartford married Loomis's sister Esther; Ebenezer Bissell (1718–1804) of East Windsor was a joiner. Among his clients only Moses Butler (d. 1802), a Hartford taverner, and Aaron Bissell (1722–87), a wealthy East Windsor landowner, cannot be explained on the basis of occupational or kinship connections with Loomis. Stiles, *History of Windsor*, 2:passim; Lucius Barnes Barbour, *Families of Early Hartford, Connecticut* (Baltimore: Genealogical Publishing Co., 1977), pp. 596, 619, 621; estate inventory, Lt. Reubin Ellsworth, Windsor, 1785, no. 1881, HPR.

[22] The assumption that a colonial family's household goods and furniture represented "a much greater proportion of personal net worth than . . . today" is frequently suggested, most recently in Morrison H. Heckscher, *American Furniture in the Metropolitan Museum*

almost half of his clients owned a piece of cabinetwork valued at a pound or more, only 13 percent owned two or more such luxuries. Even in the most expensively furnished homes, relatively cheap turned crown chairs were the norm rather than joined or upholstered chairs. While almost everyone owned a Bible and a psalm book, less than 8 percent owned four or more titles on subjects other than divinity.

Although not poor, Loomis's landowning Windsor patrons were conservative and immobile, far more so than the tradesmen who were a more transient element of Windsor society. The years following Loomis's death in 1786 brought great change to the region, altering the way furniture was made, marketed, and used. The emergence of urban commercial centers at Hartford, Springfield, and elsewhere disrupted the traditional relations between Connecticut valley towns. Divisions between urban and rural, manufacturing and agriculture, cosmopolitan and provincial articulated the changing roles of cities and surrounding towns. City-based cabinetmaking emporiums absorbed much of the regional market for stylish luxury goods. The woodworking tradesmen who continued servicing agricultural towns like Windsor witnessed an erosion in the demand for their high end offerings as patrons turned increasingly toward the city where stylish luxuries were more cheaply and abundantly supplied.[23]

Timothy Loomis's apprentices adapted to changes in the woodworking industry in revealing ways. His son George remained in Windsor and assumed the declining practice after his father's death. Although his skills were probably equal to his father's, his work was confined to more rudimentary commissions, and he devoted a greater share of his time to furniture and building maintenance and farming. George Loomis worked almost exclusively for family and neighbors and did not participate in the emerging specialization of his trade. Another Loomis

---

of Art, vol. 2, *The Late Colonial Period: Queen Anne and Chippendale Styles*, ed. Mary-Alice Rogers (New York: Metropolitan Museum of Art and Random House, 1985), p. 17. Indeed, the opposite was true with investment in land and real estate being far more significant than today. It was the rare household in which furnishings and related consumer goods represented even 20 percent of the entire value of an estate. That part represented by furniture rarely exceeded 5 percent. The percentages of clients owning luxury goods increased among patrons who lived into the 1790s, and, especially among those who lived into the nineteenth century, clock ownership increased dramatically. Most of the silver owned by Loomis's patrons was flatware, and rarely did it comprise more than a miniscule portion of an estate.

[23] Philip Zea, "Furniture," in *Great River*, pp. 185–91.

apprentice, Thomas Hayden, took a different course by improving his skills and seeking patronage both in and beyond Windsor. Although he first appears during the early 1760s assisting Loomis in architectural renovations, Hayden traveled widely as an officer in the Revolution and thus was open to a wider range of influences and innovations. He supervised the construction of a fort near Boston, Massachusetts, where he undoubtedly interacted with other commissioned cabinetmakers and builders stationed there from throughout the northeast. Wide travels and exposure to Boston trade practices bolstered his career, for he later returned to Windsor prepared to cultivate a regional as opposed to a strictly local clientele. Hayden's renderings of molding profiles and furniture represent the earliest documented efforts by a Connecticut joiner to embrace the "science" of architecture. During the 1780s, Hayden emerged as one of the most sought-after builders in the Hartford area, benefiting from the patronage of wealthy and aggressively fashion-conscious individuals like Oliver Phelps of Suffield, John Watson of East Windsor Hill, and Oliver Ellsworth of Windsor.[24] Hayden's designs were among the earliest examples of country Palladianism, a style unfamiliar to Loomis and his patrons before the Revolution. Although trained by Loomis, the Revolution became Hayden's most valued teacher.

Hayden's apprentices went on to even greater glories, playing key roles in the emerging architectural profession. Three of his sons became specialized master builders, and his most accomplished apprentice, Asher Benjamin (1773–1845), went on to become the first American author of an architectural builder's guide and a prolific architect in nineteenth-century Boston. Theirs was an obvious but nonetheless impressive solution to the problem of eroding patronage among the valley's rural joiners. A third alternative was to move to the city and try to establish

[24]Stiles, *History of Windsor,* 2:444. George Loomis died possessed of an estate valued at $4,477, including an expensive "crowned case with drawers" that he probably made for himself. The value of his "old tools" was less than $7, and it is clear that his farm was a far more vital operation. Several of his children migrated to Attica, New York, and there is no evidence that any were involved in woodworking (estate inventory, George Loomis, Windsor, 1804, HPR). Although no apprenticeship indentures have been found, Hayden was cited in Loomis's ledger throughout his teenage years (Loomis III ledger, pp. 104, 108, 130, 131, 135). Stiles, *History of Windsor,* 2:372. Hayden was one of the first master builders to advertise for apprentices in the Hartford area newspaper (*Connecticut Courant,* August 8, 1795). His work on the Phelps, Watson, and Ellsworth houses is documented by a signed plinth from a parlor pilaster at the Phelps house (Antiquarian and Landmarks Society of Connecticut, Hartford) and by a set of architectural drawings which have been preserved by his descendants (*Great River,* cats. 24, 26).

oneself at "cabinetmaking," a route apparently followed by Timothy Loomis IV, who became a "cabinetmaker" in Torrington, Connecticut.[25] The changing demand for woodworking services led to a more rigid division of labor and thus a declining need for generalists able to make fashionable goods. Such work was increasingly left to the specialists, while generalists mopped up the local demand for carpentry and repairwork, making and fixing plain furniture and tools. The increasing dominance of specialists in the production of fashionable furniture and houses coincided with the emergence of the "cabinetmaker" and the "housewright" as distinct trades. What had been a reality in colonial cities for several generations became a necessity in the Connecticut valley as well.

Loomis was part of the old order. He was one of many Connecticut valley joiners who made regional-style goods for a local clientele. Loomis was part of a network of joiners, bonded together by similar training and frequently by marriage or blood. While these men occasionally worked together, they relied primarily on separate markets. Competition between them was limited, thus lessening the need to differentiate their products. The strong tendency toward interlocking kinship and training produced a system of manufacturing that provided fertile ground for the development of a regional style. Loomis's products and work methods were like those of fellow joiners both in Windsor and elsewhere in the Connecticut valley, reflecting the operational mechanics of an industry that was regionally based. As the traditional structure of the woodworking industry disintegrated after the Revolution, furniture became less an expression of regional outlook and more a product of modern methods of marketing and manufacturing adopted by a new generation of cabinetmakers working in cities like Hartford. Timothy Loomis died, symbolically, on the eve of a new era. With him died the tradition of regional industry based on local self-sufficiency and kinship training.

[25] Hayden's sons Horace (b. 1769), Chauncey (b. 1771), and Chester (b. 1777) all "learned the trade of builder and architect." Chester abandoned the trade for dentistry in Baltimore, and Chauncey migrated to Randolph, Vermont, where he practiced as a builder. Although Benjamin's apprenticeship under Hayden is not documented by indenture, his earliest known employment was under Hayden's direction, and Hayden's own mastery of architectural drafting and his possession of English builder's guides provide a plausible foundation for the education of someone with Benjamin's skills. Few if any of Hayden's Hartford-area contemporaries could have offered Benjamin a more substantial education in the art and science of building and architecture. *Great River*, cats. 26, 27; Stiles, *History of Windsor*, 2:373, 441.

APPENDIX 1

Timothy Loomis's List of Prices

The names of furniture forms have been modernized.

	1759 £ s d	1760 £ s d
Scroll top case of drawers	4. 0.0	4.18.0
Cherry case of 9 drawers with a shell at the bottom	2.14.0	3. 0.0
Maple case of 9 drawers	2. 9.0	—
Best cherry round table	1. 3.0	1. 4.0
Maple round table	15.6	1. 0.0
Chest of drawers	17.0	1. 0.0
Low case of drawers	1. 5.0	1.10.0
Plain chest not colored	7.0	8.0
Chest with one drawer, colored	10.6	12.0
Plain table	8.0	8.6
Dressing table	8.0	—
Cherry dressing table	1. 5.0	1. 7.0
Plain maple desk, plain riggings	2. 5.6	—
Cherry tea table	12.0	14.0
Round cherry stand table	8.0	8.0
Small round table	9.0	—
Coffin	6.0	7.0
Bedsteads not colored	6.9	8.0
Cradles with head, colored	8.0	—
Stands	1.6	—
Plain case of drawers with plain handles	2. 0.0	—
Kneading troughs	2.6	—
Window frames	1.9	—
Sashes per square	2.5	—

APPENDIX 2

Furniture Forms Listed in Timothy Loomis's Ledger

Several prices are indicated when significant variations in the valuation of furniture forms were observed. Names have been modernized.

	£ s d
Tables	
Small round table	1. 2.6; 0.10.0
Square table with leaves	1. 4.0
2 fly table	1. 8.0
Swing table	0. 4.0
Best cherry round table	1. 3.0
Tea table	0.15.0
Square table	3. 5.0
Dining table	1. 8.0
Stand tea table	0. 8.0
Miscellaneous forms	
Buffet (corner cupboard)	1. 1.6
Library case	3. 1.9
Coffin	0. 8.0
Child's coffin	0. 4.6
Clock case	3. 0.0; 2.17.0
Framing a looking glass	0. 6.0
Couch	0.15.0
Bedsteads and cradles	
Cradle	0. 8.0
"Very good" bedstead	0.11.0
Trundle bedstead	0.10.0
Bedstead & feather frame	0.10.6
Cases of drawers, dressing tables, and desks	
Desk	2.17.0
Plain maple desk	2. 5.6
Crown case of drawers	4.10.6; 5. 0.0
Case of ten drawers	2.13.0
Case of drawers	5.10.0; 3.10.0; 2.17.0
Maple case of nine drawers	2. 9.0
Scroll top case of drawers	4. 0.0
Cherry case of drawers with a shell at the bottom	2.14.0
Chest	0. 9.0
Chest with one drawer	0.13.0
Plain chest	0. 9.0
Chest of drawers	1. 5.0
Dressing table	0. 8.0
Cherry dressing table	1. 5.0

American Painted Seating Furniture
Marketing the Product, 1750–1840

Nancy Goyne Evans

It was not enough that a craftsman possessed sufficient skill to produce quality work in his line or that he was aware of current design trends; if he were to prove successful, he had to be able to market his product. And there were more than a few roadblocks in the path of success.

One of the first hurdles facing craftsman and customer alike was how to pay for purchases and services. Until the early nineteenth century general circulation of coin and paper money was limited. Even in postrevolutionary Philadelphia, cabinetmaker David Evans noted in his accounts the occasional sale of a piece of furniture "for Cash," emphasizing even then the limited occurrence of such transactions. Credit and barter were the mainstays of business at all levels of society, whether the medium of exchange was skilled services, day labor, manufactured goods, cottage products, or produce. During the early 1800s New London County, Connecticut, woodworker Amos Denison Allen exchanged chairs for shoes and tanned leather from one neighborhood specialist and ironwork for home, farm, and business from another. His father-in-law, Ebenezer Tracy, Sr., best known of the New England Windsor-chair makers, acquired an eight-day timepiece from Nathaniel Shipman, Jr., in the mid 1790s by providing the clockmaker with two sets of "green" chairs. Individuals without a specialized trade, such as farmers, might pay for furniture through general labor. A Wallingford, Connecticut, customer of Titus Preston's *earned* his Windsor chair by "threshing oats." Providing pasture for the chairmaker's cow or horse was another form of remuneration. Indeed, the chairmaker might acquire his horse by negotiating a "deal," such as that worked out in 1765 by William Barker, a rush-bottom-chair maker of Providence, Rhode Island: "by one horse to Be paid in chares." Timber in the log or further reduced to chair stock or cordwood was a popular medium of exchange among chairmakers. Many craftsmen, among them William Rowzee of Salisbury, North Carolina, even advertised their willingness to accept "Lumber suitable for the Business . . . in payment for Work." Allan Holcomb of central New York State described a special exchange with one Nathan Brown in September 1825: "to 6 Dining Chairs for which he is to Deliver at my Shop 7 [and] three quarters Bunches of Shingles," apparently for building repairs.[1]

A chairmaker might acquire manufactured goods by direct exchange with merchants, shopkeepers, and others. Early nineteenth-century records of chairmaker Thomas Boynton of Boston and, later, Windsor, Vermont, describe commodities he acquired in this manner, including woodworking tools, paint pigments, furniture hardware, "a silver english watch," and even "a masonic Jewell." At Deerfield, New Hampshire, John Fisk supplied chairmaker True Currier with 2,000 bricks in return for "six kitchen chair frames painted and five Dollars." Spinsters and widows often exchanged "cottage" products or services for household furnishings. Appropriately, Sally Munger acquired a sewing chair from Silas Cheney at Litchfield, Connecticut, in 1817 by making the craftsman a pair of pantaloons and a shirt. Across the state Patty Parrish exchanged tow cloth for chairs at Allen's Windham, Connecticut, shop. Produce exchanges ran the gamut from flour and grains to fruits, vegetables, and flesh. Allan Holcomb of Otsego County, New York, nego-

[1] David Evans account book, 1774–82, Historical Society of Pennsylvania, Philadelphia (hereafter cited as HSP); Wait Stoddard account book, 1798–1810, Andrew Frink and Jonathan Chester account book, 1806–17, Windham Historical Society, Willimantic, Conn.; Nathaniel Shipman, Jr., account book, 1785–1812, Leffingwell Inn, Norwich, Conn.; Titus Shipman account book, 1795–1817, Sterling Memorial Library, Yale University, New Haven, Conn.; William Barker account book, 1763–67, Rhode Island Historical Society, Providence; *Carolina Watchman* (Salisbury, N.C.), March 29, 1834, as quoted in James H. Craig, comp., *The Arts and Crafts in North Carolina* (Winston-Salem: Museum of Early Southern Decorative Arts, 1965), p. 234; Allan Holcomb account book, 1809–28, Metropolitan Museum of Art, New York.

tiated a rather involved agreement with one customer in 1825 who paid
for a set of chairs with "1 Barel of Cider and 2 Bushel of aples, 2½ of
wheat, 3½ bushels of oats & 1 Dollar in Cash." Unusual among commodity exchanges were the five pounds of eels traded to Cheney in
1812.[2]

Occasionally customer and supplier could find no suitable means
of coming to terms, and a third party became involved in the transac-
tion. One day in August 1841 Ransom Cook of Saratoga, New York,
received a note from a neighbor containing the following directive: "Pleas
let the bearer . . . have a half dosen Chares & I wil pay you in wood
plank or other lumber this fall as you & I shall agree." A variation of
this arrangement found Jeduthern Avery, cabinetmaker, and Daniel W.
Badger, chairmaker, residents of the Hartford area, exchanging products and woodworking materials. Avery disposed of most chairs received
in trade by retailing them to his own customers, frequently for still other
bartered goods. Often individuals who exchanged services and products
on a regular basis carried running accounts in their respective ledgers
for years before settling up. To complicate business further, the nation
adopted a new monetary system following the Revolution, substituting
dollars and cents for pounds and pence. Progressive individuals were
quick to adopt the new calculation, but records identify many conservative holdouts. Seth Pomeroy of Northampton, Massachusetts, boldly
wrote in his book of accounts on April 1, 1796, "I began my a Count
in Dollars & Cents," although more frequently than not he reverted to
the old method or a combination of the two, a practice that was
widespread.[3]

Regardless of payment method, direct sales dominated the seating
market before 1840. Generally the customer ordered, or "bespoke," his
furniture in person at the chairmaker's shop. If he lived at a distance,

[2] Thomas Boynton account books, 1811–47, Dartmouth College, Hanover, N.H.;
True Currier account book, 1815–49, Joseph Downs Manuscript and Microfilm Collection, Winterthur Library (hereafter cited as DMMC); Silas E. Cheney account book,
1799–1817, Litchfield Historical Society, Litchfield, Conn.; Amos Denison Allen memorandum book, 1796–1803, Connecticut Historical Society, Hartford (hereafter cited as
CHS); Holcomb account book.
[3] Ransom Cook papers, as quoted in Margaret Coffin, "Ransom Cook, Saratoga
Chairmaker (1794–1881)," *Decorator* (Journal of the Historical Society of Early American Decoration) 31, no. 2 (Spring 1977): 21; Jeduthern Avery account book, 1811–55,
CHS; Seth Pomeroy account book, 1794–1801, Northampton Historical Society, Northampton, Mass.

he might send a written order. By the 1820s a retail facility known as a chair or furniture wareroom, forerunner of today's furniture store, was gaining prominence. Here customers could make selections from finished stock on hand, often acquired from several sources. Increasingly, the wareroom owner was not the manufacturer, and cash or short credit was the terms.

By the early nineteenth century distribution of goods on consignment for commission sales supplemented direct merchandising by the chairmaker. The export trade to the southern states operated principally along these lines, the consignee being the ship's captain or a known retailer in a southern community. The shipper might be the chairmaker himself, but more frequently it was a merchant middleman. Closer to home there were opportunities to place consignment merchandise advantageously with a storekeeper. Ebenezer Rose of Trenton, New Jersey, supplied two such outlets in 1807, one in the town of Burlington on the Delaware River and the other at a small settlement called Rowley's Mills 10 miles away on the turnpike road, a center of some little activity. This was a small operation, however, compared with that of Lambert Hitchcock in western Connecticut two decades later. The entrepreneur distributed his chairs to consignees in Litchfield, New Haven, and Hartford. Isaac Wright described the business arrangement at Hartford in 1834: "Received of L. Hitchcock to be sold on commission 24 wood seat chairs at 92. cents each at 10 per cent commission."[4] If Wright sold a dozen such chairs a week, his commission was just shy of an average workingman's wages for one day.

Agents distributed seating furniture, receiving a fee, commission, or both, their area of activity sometimes extending beyond the local region. Thomas Howard, Jr., of Providence, agent for Tunis and Nutman of Newark, New Jersey, shipped chairs as far afield as Africa. Howard's published notice of January 1, 1823, describes the substantial relationship that existed between the two firms: "4000 fancy and Windsor chairs of superior quality with handsome patterns 50¢ to 5 dollars."[5] The auction served several purposes. The southern trade could

[4] *Trenton Federalist* (New Jersey), November 30, 1807; John Tarrant Kenney, *The Hitchcock Chair* (New York: Clarkson N. Potter, 1971), pp. 101–2; Isaac Wright account book, 1834–37, Connecticut State Library, Hartford.
[5] Eleanore Bradford Monahon, "Providence Cabinetmakers," *Rhode Island History* 23, no. 1 (January 1964): 12–17, 19.

handle large quantities of imported seating this way, although the results were disappointing at times and the market easily glutted. The same sales technique might serve to introduce a product. Washington G. Henning of Lewisburg, West Virginia, a newcomer in business, chose this method to launch his enterprise, carefully selecting the date to coincide with the first day of May court when many rural householders came to town. And the auction could effectively dispose of stock when a chairmaker curtailed or closed his business. Upon leaving Greenfield, Massachusetts, for Troy, New York, Holcomb chose an auction, or vendue, as "the quickest and best manner" to disperse his stock.[6]

Peddling constituted a limited method of disposing of chairs, its scope never approaching that realized by the clock industry. Josiah Prescott Wilder, a chairmaker of New Ipswich, New Hampshire, sponsored one such trip in 1838. The peddler was out two nights and sold 51 chairs, including 5 rockers; but such records are rare. Nor were relationships between chairmakers and peddlers always as amicable or profitable as that recorded by Wilder. Allen, in his only advertisement of record, defended himself in 1813 against the fraudulent claims of certain peddlers who hawked inferior chairs, which they represented as his, "in the streets."[7] In retrospect this actually was a compliment to Allen, who set a standard of excellence, although it did little for his reputation or business at the time.

Promotion of a chairmaker's product occurred in several ways. Word of mouth could be a positive force. Upon opening a new business or experiencing keen competition, the chairmaker might advertise (fig. 1). Nor were such notices limited to newspapers. Jonathan Mullen and neighbors promoted their Cincinnati businesses in the 1840 edition of the city directory, while William Buttre of New York advertised with a printed billhead.[8] A natural extension of this practice was the placement of printed labels on chair bottoms and interior framing. Chairmakers'

[6]*Lewisburg Chronicle* (West Virginia), February 24, 1853 (reference courtesy Anne C. Golovin); Holcomb account book.
[7]Josiah Prescott Wilder account book, 1837–61, private collection (typescript, Decorative Arts Photographic Collection, Winterthur Library); *Windham Herald* (Connecticut), April 15, 1813, as quoted in Phyllis Kihn, ed., "Connecticut Cabinetmakers, Part I," *Connecticut Historical Society Bulletin* 32, no. 4 (October 1967): 103.
[8]David Henry Shaffer, *The Cincinnati, Covington, Newport and Fulton Directory for 1840* (Cincinnati: J. B. and R. P. Donogh, 1840), facing p. 296; William Buttre billhead, inscribed December 8, 1810, CHS.

Warranted Green Windsor
C H A I R S.

THE subscriber informs his friends and
customers, that he has removed from the shop on
Moore's wharf, to a shop next below the Draw-Bridge,
in Fore-Street ; where may be had, Green Windsor
Chairs, of all kind, and Cabinet Work, of all sorts,
equal to any imported. Chairs taken in and painted.
                                    EBENEZER STONE.
   N. B. English and West-India Goods taken in payment.

Fig. 1. Advertisment of Ebenezer Stone. From *Massachusetts Gazette* (Boston), September 11, 1787.
(Winterthur Library.)

brands impressed into the wood (fig. 2) and stencils in black paint or
gilt letters served the same purpose in briefer format.

If the craftsman wanted to expand his merchandising potential significantly, he had to extend his sights beyond the local market. In 1750
production of seating furniture for domestic use was largely localized,
rush-bottom patterns prevailing among cheaper forms. By the Revolution, however, Windsor construction had become a force to be reck-
oned with in the Delaware River valley, New York, and Rhode Island.
During the postwar years this form steadily replaced other popular seating throughout New England, in the South, and along the expanding
western frontier. Before the turn of the century fancy ornamented seat-

Fig. 2. Brand on Windsor armchair, Amos Denison Allen, South Windham, Conn., 1797–98. (Winterthur Museum.)

ing was another option. Limited overland thoroughfares, such as the Great Wagon Road west from Philadelphia, served initially to distribute goods beyond the local area. But with the rise of the turnpike road at the end of the eighteenth century, chairmakers in all regions became active solicitors of country patronage. William Challen, for example, stated at the end of his notice at Lexington, Kentucky, dating to 1809, that he stood ready to pack and send furniture to any part of the state.[9]

The success of other chairmakers was closely linked to the inland water system—the Delaware, Chesapeake, and Hudson or rivers for shallow draft boats, like the Susquehanna and Connecticut. The first great boon to inland water distribution was development of the steamboat. Economic and territorial growth in the West was inextricably linked to the rise of steam-powered vessels on the regional waterways. As early as 1813 *Cramer's Pittsburgh Almanac* identified "the steamboat business as an establishment of the first importance." A few statistics will suggest the growth of opportunity for the enterprising chairmaker. At the beginning of the nineteenth century the upriver return of a keelboat laboriously poled by its crew against the Mississippi current over the 1,350-mile course from New Orleans to Louisville required three months or longer. The best of the early steamboats more than cut this time in half, and by midcentury the *Eclipse* covered the same distance in about four and a half days.[10]

[9] *Kentucky Gazette and General Advertiser* (Lexington), May 9, 1809.
[10] [Zadok Cramer], *Cramer's Pittsburgh Almanac for . . .* 1813 (Pittsburgh: Cramer, Spear, and Eichbaum, ca. 1812), p. 49; Marshall B. Davidson, *Life in America*, vol. 2 (Boston: Houghton Mifflin Co., 1951), pp. 232, 235.

Hard on the heels of early steamboat success came the drive to build canals. The Erie, linking East and West, was completed in 1825, the event marked by a grand celebration in New York. Theoretically, chairs manufactured in the city now could travel as far afield as Mackinaw in the upper Great Lakes, the destination of chairs shipped from Erie, Pennsylvania, in 1819. The entire route of the canal hummed with activity as freight and people moved westward. Residents of one town on the waterway counted 19,000 passing boats during the second year of operation. The rise of communities and industry in the region was phenomenal. Mrs. Basil Hall's description of Rochester had broad application: "It is impossible to describe the appearance of the outskirts of this town. To me it looks as if a box of houses had been sent from New York, the lid opened, and the houses tumbled down in the midst of the blackened stumps." Chairmakers, like James C. Gilbert of Utica, New York, capitalized on their situation to keep abreast of the latest patterns manufactured at New York, to obtain city workmen and an adequate supply of raw materials, and to distribute their products by retail or wholesale over a vast territory.[11]

Railroad development came late in the period and, in the words of Victor S. Clark, proved to be the great emancipator of American society "from typography and climate." Roadbeds penetrated new regions, oblivious to hills and chasms, winter freezes and spring mud, and all but the most substantial snowfalls. When the Athenaeum at Portsmouth, New Hampshire, refurbished its building in the 1850s, the institution sent to Boston suppliers Blake, Ware, and Company for new seating. The firm acquired a dozen armchairs from chairmaker William O. Haskell and shipped them north via the Eastern Railroad.[12]

A second broad option available to the ambitious chairmaker was the waterborne trade. Philadelphia, birthplace of the American Windsor during the 1740s, exported wooden-bottom chairs to the Caribbean as early as 1752. Two vessels sailing from the Delaware River during the autumn bound for Barbados carried between them 15 Windsors,

---

[11] George Landon account book, 1813–32, DMMC; Davidson, *Life in America*, 2:218; Una Pope-Hennessy, ed., *The Aristocratic Journey* (New York: G. P. Putnam's Sons, 1931), p. 54; William Richards, comp., *The Utica Directory: 1842–'43* (Utica, N.Y.: John P. Bush, 1842), p. 133.

[12] Victor S. Clark, *History of Manufactures in the United States*, vol. 1 (New York: Peter Smith, 1949), p. 351; Blake, Ware, and Company bill to J. M. Tredick, October 18, 1855, Eastern Railroad Corporation bill to Tredick, October 31, 1855, Portsmouth Athenaeum, Portsmouth, N.H.

Fig. 3. High-back Windsor armchair, Philadelphia,
1755–65. Yellow poplar, oak, maple, probably
hickory; H. 44¾″, W. 24¾″, D. 17⅛″. (Private
collection.)

probably made in the fashionable high-back style (fig. 3). Prior to the
Revolution members of the Philadelphia merchant community, many
of them Quakers, had deposited Windsor seating throughout the region
in ports at Haiti, St. Kitts, Montserrat, and Jamaica. The ship *Industry*
voyaging to Barbados in 1767 carried 25 "Chair Bottoms" and "Two

barrels [of] Chair Work"—that is, turned and sawed parts. This is the earliest reference to identify a shipment of unassembled Windsors, frequently called "knockdowns" or "shaken chairs." Rhode Island merchants actively traded Windsors in the Caribbean as well. Vessels belonging to Aaron Lopez, a Sephardic Jew and one of the founders of the Touro Synagogue in Newport, carried several cargoes of record during the 1760s and landed both straw- and wooden-bottom chairs at the Dutch colony of Surinam on the South American coast before 1770.[13]

Postrevolutionary decades saw the heyday of Windsor traffic to the Caribbean, actual destinations subject to the state of political affairs among European powers at any given date. Philadelphia, which continued to lead the way, counted the Windsor among its eighty top exports in 1810. Square-back styles with simulated bamboo work prevailed (fig. 4). Following in importance in this trade were New York, Baltimore, and Rhode Island, with related commerce from Boston and Connecticut falling into last position. The most substantial Caribbean market from about 1784 to almost 1800 was the island of Hispaniola, comprising Haiti and Santo Domingo, and that despite the civil turbulence there during the 1790s. For the most part, Spanish markets in the Caribbean were closed to American shipping until the late 1790s. It was the Cuban market, principally the port of Havana, that witnessed a veritable explosion of activity. Between 1798 and 1801, for example, Philadelphia alone exported more than 9,000 chairs just to Cuba, and this tabulation derives only from available shipping documents. Some cargoes were of substantial size. The brig *George* carried 40 dozen chairs and 5 settees to the island in December 1798.[14]

The Guianas on the South American coast saw activity during the late eighteenth century. Other markets on that continent gradually opened during the decades that followed, given impetus by the continuing

---

[13] Shipping returns for Barbados, 1728–53, and Jamaica, 1760–69, Colonial Office, Public Record Office, London; William Bishop, Thomas Riche, et al. bills of lading, 1716–72, Philadelphia, HSP; Customhouse Papers, Philadelphia, vols. 6, 7, 10, HSP; Aaron Lopez outward bound invoice book, 1763–68, shipping book, 1771–73, and letter book, 1767, Newport Historical Society, Newport, R.I.

[14] Tench Coxe, *A Statement of the Arts and Manufactures of the United States of America, for the Year 1810* (Philadelphia: A. Cornman, Jr., 1814), p. xiv. Tabulation of chairs derived from Philadelphia Outward Foreign Manifests, 1798–1801, U.S. Customhouse Records, including French Spoliation Claims, National Archives, Washington, D.C.; Brig *George* cargo, December 3, 1798, Philadelphia Outward Manifests, U.S. Customhouse Records, French Spoliation Claims, National Archives.

Fig. 4. Square-back Windsor side chair, by Jared
Chesnut, Wilmington, Del., 1804–10. Yellow
poplar, black walnut, maple, oak, hickory; H. 34″,
W. 18¼″, D. 20⁷⁄₁₆″. (Winterthur Museum.)

Napoleonic Wars in Europe. These included Brazil, Venezuela,
Argentina, and, eventually, destinations around the Horn on the western coast. Chairs painted in "high colours" were deemed particularly
suitable for the South American market. When Stephen Girard's *Mont-
esque* left Philadelphia in December 1810 bound for China, she carried

cabinetware and almost 11 dozen fancy and Windsor chairs for delivery in Valparaiso, Chile. This being a first voyage to that port, the captain and supercargo shrewdly made a present to the governor of four boxes of furniture, including 2 dozen fancy chairs.[15] At one time or another the wide-ranging overseas trade in American painted seating also included ports on the African coast, in the islands of the eastern Atlantic, principally Madeira, and in the East Indies.

In the coastal trade Philadelphia Windsor seating enjoyed a good foothold before the Revolution. Early markets included New York and the Chesapeake Bay region. Boston saw the importation of Philadelphia green chairs for almost two decades before there was a resident Windsor-chair maker in the city. Southern coastal and river communities proved excellent customers, Charleston commanding first place from the early 1760s onward. After the war it became increasingly common for Philadelphia chairmakers to seek their own consignees in the city and thus retain the merchant-shipper's profit for themselves. Some enterprising craftsmen even traveled to Charleston with a quantity of prepared chair stuff to assemble, paint, and sell on location, either independently or in partnership with another who could keep the supply of parts flowing from Philadelphia.

New York and Rhode Island entered the coastal trade in Windsor seating before the Revolution, but the rest of New England had little activity before the end of the century. The northern chairmakers' best markets lay in other areas of New England and the Canadian maritime provinces. A few Baltimore chairmakers mobilized for competition before the end of the century. Caleb Hannah's 1799 advertisement in the *Baltimore Daily Advertiser* describes the proportions of the new trade: "Merchants and captains of vessels may be supplied for shipping to the amount of one hundred dozen more or less."[16]

Joining Charleston as principal markets during the early nineteenth century were the Virginia communities of Norfolk, Richmond, Petersburg, and Alexandria. Savannah, Georgia, was second only to Charleston in consumption of painted seating in this period. By 1800

---

[15] Shipping memorandum, ca. 1822–25, Miscellaneous Shipping Records, Waters Family Papers, Essex Institute, Salem, Mass.; Stephen Girard invoice books, 1802–11, 1811–24, Girard Papers, Girard College, Philadelphia (microfilm, American Philosophical Society, Philadelphia).

[16] *Federal Gazette and Baltimore Daily Advertiser* (Maryland), December 2, 1799.

New Orleans was becoming an active market. Writing from the city in 1804 where he was visiting his daughter, John Pintard noted, "The furniture in general is very plain—But American manufactured chairs & tea tables are getting into vogue."[17] Victor S. Clark in his *History of Manufactures* identified the factors encouraging industrial development and trade in colonial and federal America as a "rapid expansion of [the] domestic market through [the] extension of settlement and growth of population." In postrevolutionary years new frontier states were settled in the time formerly required to clear and populate a county. The number of American consumers in 1800 was double that at the time of the Revolution and doubled again within one decade.[18] Physiography, climate, resources, and technical advances in transportation and manufacturing all contributed substantially to productivity.

The revolutionary war was the first major event to cast a shadow over the chair industry. At Philadelphia several Windsor designs fell short of achieving their fullest development or realizing their distribution potential. The fan-back side chair is missing from New York production, and the first Windsor-chair maker's advertisement in Boston dates only to 1786. French and British interference with American shipping during the 1790s and later caused new problems in some quarters, but not until Jefferson's Embargo of 1807 was there widespread hardship in the chair industry. Insolvencies were common, and within three years the country was at war again with England. The euphoria of the immediate postwar years was followed closely by a recession of national scope. Many a chairmaker described the depressed state of his affairs in the pages of the 1820 Census of Manufactures. Allen commented that his business had diminished by more than a third within two years.[19] The national economy was shaken again in 1837 by a financial crisis of even greater proportions.

To insure that products arrived at scheduled destinations safely and quickly, careful thought needed to be given to packaging and transpor-

[17] David Lee Sterling, ed., "New Orleans, 1801: An Account by John Pintard," *Louisiana Historical Quarterly* 34 (July 1951): 224–25, as quoted in "Clues and Footnotes," *Antiques* 104, no. 5 (November 1973): 887.
[18] Clark, *History of Manufactures*, 1:354.
[19] *Independent Chronicle* (Boston), April 13, 1786; Schedules of the 1820 Census of Manufactures, Connecticut, National Archives (microfilm, DMMC).

tation. Seating furniture traveled more economically by water than land, the means of conveyance varying from a small, hand-paddled boat, like the long canoe found aground in the Chesapeake in 1762 with 14 rush-bottom chairs lying in the bottom, to a sailing vessel ranging in size from the small sloop to the three-masted ship, or the powerful steamboat. Fully assembled chairs generally were put up in bundles, one chair inverted on another, the seats touching, and wrapped around with woven mats tied in place. When Captain Randall of Portsmouth, New Hampshire, purchased two sets of Windsors in the New York shop of William Ash in 1802, the chairmaker wrapped the chairs as described and charged the captain 16s. for the service, or 9 percent of the total bill. Freight rates varied, depending on region, vessel, and distance. In 1830 calculations on the steamboat *General Sheldon* of New Haven were based upon weight and bulk. The charge to send 22 chairs up the Connecticut River to Chester was $2.25, or the price of one well-ornamented Windsor or fancy chair. Shipping a settee about the same distance cost $1.00. [20] Special furniture might be placed in wooden cases, and the shipper could elect to insure the merchandise.

For reasons of economy, chairs shipped overseas or in quantity often went unassembled, small parts filling barrels and hogsheads, the seats sometimes stacked and tied in bundles. Occasionally paint and glue accompanied the shipment, and a workman might be sent to set up the chairs at their destination. Use of mats, cases, and hogsheads was a substantial improvement over early shipping methods described in a letter of 1772 from Boston to a merchant factor in Philadelphia: "If you have not ship'd the chairs before this comes to hand, should be glad you'd desire the people on board to take good care of 'em, as the others were much defaced, one with the bottom splitt, and the other being tar'd & ye paint wore off by being lashd over ther stern, if they could be brot in the cabbin it would be best."[21]

From shop to wharf, loose chairs, bundles, and packages were conveyed in flat-bed carts (fig. 5). Where warranted, the cartman placed

[20] *Maryland Gazette* (Annapolis), January 21, 1762, as quoted in Alfred Coxe Prime, comp., *The Arts and Crafts in Philadelphia, Maryland, and South Carolina* (Philadelphia: Walpole Society, 1929), p. 188; William Ash bill to Captain Randall, July 3, 1802, Baker Library, Harvard University, Cambridge, Mass.; account book of freight, 1830–31, CHS.

[21] John Andrews to William Barrell, June 22, 1772, Andrews-Eliot Papers, Massachusetts Historical Society, Boston.

Fig. 5. Peter Maverick and Asher B. Durand, trade card of Thomas Ash II, New York, 1818–19. Engraving; H. 3¼″, W. 5⁵⁄₁₆″ (trimmed). (Winterthur Library.)

stakes around the load. The cart served for local deliveries to private customers as well. For longer trips where water carriage was unavailable, the wagon was the business vehicle. Some are specifically identified in records as chair wagons or "chair racks," their ownership documented from the South to New England. As the industry expanded in the nineteenth century, larger wagons, sometimes drawn by as many as six horses, were not an unfamiliar sight, especially in northern Worcester County, Massachusetts, where natural waterpower stimulated a successful industry and Boston was an important commercial outlet two days' drive away. Along the route hotels built large barns to accommodate the chair racks.[22]

Stacked high on wagons, chairs required protection during the trip

[22] *A Completed Century, 1826–1926: The Story of the Heywood-Wakefield Company* (Boston, 1926), p. 7.

against such damage as bruising and rubbed paint. Wrapping vulnerable surfaces with a cheap commodity like straw was practiced in both England and America. A London bill of 1792 for Windsor seating specifically itemizes charges for "Haybands & Packing." Later evidence from the New Haven accounts of Levi Stillman describes the process as "Winding & Packing."[23]

A fitting tribute to the industry and enterprise of the American chairmaker occurs in the description of a grand federal procession held in 1788 at New York City to celebrate pending ratification of the federal Constitution. Among the 5,000 marchers were representatives from fifty-eight professions and trades, the chairmakers sixty men strong with green and red cockades in their hats. The spirit of the marchers was patriotically optimistic; the standard they bore, prophetic: the field, resplendent with a representation of "a large manufactory shop" attended by workmen; "in front of the Shop a view of the river, several vessels bound to different ports, taking in chairs, [and] boys carrying them to the wharves"; the "American Union" in one corner, the chairmakers' arms in another. The motto: Free Trade. The Federal States in Union Bound, O'er All the World Our Chairs Are Found.[24]

---

[23] D. Watson and Son bill to James Duff, May 17, 1792, Trade Card Collection, Guildhall Library, London; Levi Stillman account book, 1815–34, Sterling Memorial Library.

[24] *The Impartial Gazetter* (New York), August 9, 1788, as quoted in Rita Susswein Gottesman, comp., *The Arts and Crafts in New York, 1777–99* (New York: New-York Historical Society, 1954), p. 109.

My Life as an Upholsterer, 1927–1986

Andrew Passeri

Since his retirement from commercial upholstering in 1974, Andrew Passeri has worked on museum upholstery for many museums and historical organizations. He is acknowledged to be the best historical upholsterer in the United States, and his work has been recognized in Europe as well. The text of this autobiography is based on taped interviews of Andrew Passeri by Robert F. Trent, conducted between May and September 1985. The tapes and a transcription of the complete series of interviews are available at the library of the Connecticut Historical Society. The present text is a shorter version of the transcript, restructured in chronological order. The glossary of technical terms found in the text was prepared by Trent. The material in brackets and the footnotes were prepared by Trent and the editor.

My name is Andrew Passeri. I was born in Trevi Nel Lazio, Roma (now Frosinone), Italy, on February 6, 1909. I came to this country in 1913. I graduated from Samuel Adams Grammar School in East Boston in 1922 when I was thirteen years old. Then I went to Brighton High School for one year, and then I was fourteen years old. At fourteen, I had to go to work, and one of my first jobs was working at Engel-Cohen, a shoe factory in East Boston (I still have the scar on my hand from hand cutting liners there). From there I went to a macaroni factory. Then I went to work at the Statler Hotel construction site in downtown Boston [fig. 1], where my father was the working foreman of the Italian

Fig. 1. Andrew Passeri *(left)*, Jerry Mori, and Joseph Colantuone at the Statler Hotel construction site in Boston about 1926. Tintype. (Andrew Passeri.)

Fig. 2. Sully Gangi (1904–84) about 1937.
(Photo, courtesy the Gangi family.)

laborers, and I worked as a common laborer from the beginning of the structure until it was completed in the spring of 1927. After that I had another laboring job in Charlestown until the summer.

Then I met Sully Gangi at the street corner, where working boys used to hang around [fig. 2]. He became my friend and my mentor, my teacher, my financial adviser, and my father confessor. He brought me as his apprentice to work at Harry Archer's, at the corner of Tremont and Appleton streets. Sully's father was a cabinetmaker who worked with Sal Barile, who had been the head upholsterer at the Doughton and Dutton Desk Company. When Barile left Doughton and Dutton to found his own company, Sully's father went with him, and Sully himself served his apprenticeship under Barile. Barile had a large plant, with probably 150 people, making all new furniture, and he had a section designated for upholsterers and their apprentices.

Then Sully went to work for Harry Archer, who had been the head salesman at Barile's. Arthur Flynn was his working foreman. So I began my apprenticeship there under Sully Gangi. Later, the firm moved to Chardon Street. Mr. Archer had a large showroom; if I could take a guess, it was at least 125 feet back to front. This was a brick building with a freight elevator, Barile had his showroom on the fourth floor, and we were on the fifth. The floor was divided in half, one-half was showroom, the other half was the workroom. The showroom contained about one-half case goods, and the other half was upholstered furniture that we manufactured. We bought the frames, some of which came from local firms, others from Grand Rapids.

The chores of an apprentice were filling the water cooler, sweeping the floor, filling down cushions in a screened-in area we called the "Chicken Coop," stuffing spring cushions, assembling and finishing knocked-down frames in the finishing shop, and building shipping crates with the shipper. And then you might run across the street to Andrew Dutton's, the supply house, for stock if they were running short. It happened every so often that they needed some gimp to match a certain piece of furniture, or they ran out of ticking, and so forth.

And of course the theory was, the longer you stayed on those chores, the less time you had to work at the bench and to learn. I would get through my chores as quickly as possible. The more you became valuable at the bench the fewer chores would fall on you. I have always taken the work seriously. At that time, I started to make notes, and I made myself a diary to remember what I was doing from day to day. I kept the diary until I retired in 1974. Then, thinking it was of no value to anyone, I discarded it. Naturally, I wish I had it now.

In the workshop, there were ten upholsterers and four apprentices. Each upholsterer had his own pair of horses with well tops to contain the legs of the furniture [figs. 3, 4]. I had to get tools, and the joke of the tools was, before Sully brought me in, he asked me if I had a big pair of shears. I said, "Yeah, I've got a big pair of shears, you can cut tin with them." "Oh, no, no!" he says, "no, those are tin scissors, don't take them in!" I'd have been the laughing stock till today if I'd ever walked in with them. But I didn't know what the hell kind of shears. He said, "No, no, no, I'll get some shears, and you can use

Fig. 3. Upholstery shop at Paine Furniture Co., Boston, about 1927. (Photo, courtesy Paine Furniture Co.)

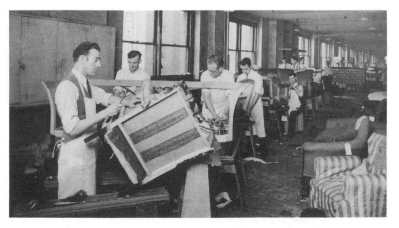

Fig. 4. Upholstery shop at Paine Furniture Co., Boston, about 1927. (Photo, courtesy Paine Furniture Co.)

Fig. 5. Upholstery tools. *Clockwise from upper left*: shears, ripping mallet, ripping chisel, regulator, webbing stretcher, curved needles, and hammer. L. (mallet) 12″. (Photo, courtesy The Connecticut Historical Society.)

my tools for a while." He had an extra pair of shears, and then his father made me a webbing stretcher, and that's the same one I have today. So then shortly I bought a hammer of my own and a mallet. That's what we needed: hammer, shears, and regulator. And you had to buy curved needles, because each man at Archer's did his own hand sewing [fig. 5].

So I worked right aside of Sully, and he always made sure that I was doing my work correctly. If I gave him a certain time within which I had completed something, bragging about it, he would see that I was going too fast, and his theory was, "Learn how to do it correctly, and then speed will come." I've carried that technique through life. And another theory he had was, "Keep your eyes and ears open, your mouth shut, and your hands at your side." You must remember, I came from the Italian ghetto, where we always had to battle for our protection and for our rights, and, you know, we were pretty free with our hands. But in the shop, you had to discipline yourself in order to learn and to compete.

When you first began, you had to learn *position*. You need to be able to observe what you're doing, your arms are only so long, and you have to put things in position so that you can reach them comfortably. If you're stitching an edge, you have to be at the height where you can feel comfortably and see how that edge is coming along. If you're tying springs, you have to stand and face right into it and reach into the object. Generally we used three or four different heights of stools to sit on and boxes to stand on, when we weren't actually tilting the furniture over on its side.

And another thing you started to learn immediately was molding and shaping. This was the shop term both for picking horsehair stuffing and for stitching edges. Here was where the regulator came in. We often said, "It feels like a sack of potatoes." That meant that when a person picked the hair over springs or in making a stitched seat, he made a bad job of it, it was lumpy. But we have the regulator, which we use to adjust the hair under the undercovers or the burlap that contains it. No human hands can make something perfect. Of course, picking hair over an object is time-consuming, it's not very dramatic, you just pick, pick, pick, and you feel, feel, feel, and you go by feeling, and by feeling, pick. Your fingers have to be sensitive to it, to try and make it as smooth as you can. And Sully would say to me, "Feel of that, you mold it and shape it, get that shape, get that feel in your hands."

Now, all my time at Archer's, where I started, there was no reupholstery. It was all new furniture. We didn't have too many slip seats there, because we didn't carry dining room chairs. The showroom was all overstuffed furniture. The simplest was the Tuxedo chair and the Tuxedo sofa [fig. 6]. These had straight arms and a straight back, the arms flared out slightly. It has straight legs, almost like a federal style. And they're quite high, both the arms and the back, and they were thin, not heavily stuffed. And we had ottomans to go with them, a regular square stool, not like a tuffet. The first thing I did was probably a little footstool. I started by tacking my webbing on a footstool. It would be the equivalent of a slip seat. And you were tying springs right off the

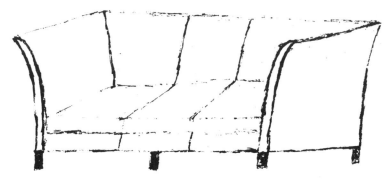

Fig. 6. Tuxedo sofa. (Sketch, Andrew Passeri, 1986.)

bat. Except for a footstool, Archer didn't carry any dead seats. Even the benches had springs in them. And you'd get all kinds of hangnails because your fingers weren't used to getting into all those pokey places reaching for the springs.

You could get nine springs in the little Tuxedo chair, three by three. And they made a lot of those chairs, they were sort of their lead product. A lot of them had flounces to the floor, a lot of them were made in chintz. And Paine's made a lot of them in a sort of black denim. The idea was, make it in a bland textile, and the wealthy people would have summer slipcovers and winter covers. The flounces were blind tacked on, right below a welt. They used a black denim cover, and another was black with a red diamond—they used thousands of yards of that. You had to be careful with it, because you could easily put the wrong side out. In a hurry, you know, *production, production!* Whisk, whisk, put it on. And this cover was used in the jacket, there was no undercovers, because slipcovers were expected.

Then you went to the Martha Washingtons, what you call a lolling chair. You got an upholstered seat. You got your springs *and* your stitched cake or foundation. You see, the Tuxedos had cushion seats, but Martha Washingtons had a stitched seat. You got your first indoctrination in feeling the molding, getting the feel of the edge. You had to quilt it on three sides and make your edge on three sides. But Martha Washingtons still had dead backs, no springs, but you had wooden arms, and *then* you had to learn how to make those cuts around the stumps and the arms. You've got to study them because if you make the cut wrong, there's gaps, there's spaces, there's no way of bringing it back. You used the regulator to find where the openings are at the tuckaways. You make sure your threads are running straight, and you cut to the point of the regulator. Later on I learned from Al Mitchell how to bring the regulator in from the *back* and then through the cover, which made an accurate mark.

Then came the more difficult ones, like wing chairs, what you call an easy chair. You had to cut two separate parts for the wing and arm. They all had a big horizontal arm roll. First you made the roll of the arm, and then you made your separate pad. In other words, you stuffed the arm in two layers, a first layer and then a second layer for the pad. Now, you realize a lot of them didn't have a wooden front panel on the roll. They just had a flat piece, and *you* would make the roll by using a side-to-side stitch all around the roll. You'd cut the burlap on the bias, because you can mold and shape it better that way. You would fold it and tack it along the edge of that little stump, and then you'd use two or three rows of stitching to form the panel in the front. We called these heavy, overstuffed pieces English. That arm was supposed to give, to be luxurious, that's not a piece of wood. But it was McLauren, another firm, that pioneered cutting a piece of wood in the shape of the roll and just putting a fox edge around it, to eliminate stitching that 3-, 3½-inch edge. Those things took you two hours to make.

I learned these things quick. I was hungry. I learned. I didn't fool around. I mean, I was *there* to learn. From 1927 until 1930, I learned to do this work very competently. That's why, in 1930, when the bottom dropped out of the business, Archer let everybody else go and kept me on. He didn't keep me on because he liked me. They kept me because I knew what the hell I was doing and I was working hard. And I wasn't getting the same money that the others like Sully and Johnny Murphy and Fred Truman were. They were older and more experienced, but I was still worth the investment.

Before 1930, the shop foreman, Arthur Flynn—God bless his soul, he was a remarkable person—he did all the cutting. He had a workbook, with all the models in it, and he did all the cutting. They were making things in bulk, so he would cut them. You didn't do any machine sewing, either. Paine's and Barile's and Irving and Casson's, they all used shop books for their standard lines. It was expedient and the right thing to do. And in Archer's we did all our finish sewing.

The most difficult thing was the spring edge. That's the kind with a wire edge lashed to the head coils of the springs. You tie the springs differently on those, with the lead twine from the top of the seat rail, not from the bottom of the rail. And I found later when I was ripping old furniture that it was always the lead twines that would snap, so I've improved that by having two or three lead twines, but in production, you can't afford to do that. If they expect you to do that piece in twenty hours, and you spend twenty-four hours, you're hurting yourself, you're hurting them. That's how everything is measured, itemized right down to the penny. At Archer's, they gave you a work tag. And on that tag the boss would mark the date and the time you started.

Now, you found out about the other upholstery shops from people who came from one shop to another. The competition was fierce, and they would hire people who would come in if they could do the work reasonably. This happened especially during the Christmas rush, when you had surplus work. Afterwards, they would be let go. Of course, if they weren't competent at all, they didn't last four hours. You would find out the rumors about how things were done at this shop and that shop.

Well, actually we had two types of furniture being made in the city of Boston. We had many, many wholesale shops, they were down by Haymarket and North Station. The rents were cheap, and naturally that's where they went. The wholesalers made cheap furniture. It was stuffed with moss, Spanish moss, and most of their springs weren't hand tied, they were unit springs on bars with chains. They would just pack the stuff into the furniture, there was no picking of hair, none of the nice details that you'd find in a true custom shop. It was mass production.

But there wasn't a shop, no matter what junk they made, that didn't call itself a custom upholstery shop. They used the term very, very loosely. They had no scruples whatsoever. At that time, the beef wagons came into the butchers' stalls in Faneuil Hall, and the beef came wrapped in burlap, and the wholesale shops thought nothing of going into the meat market and buying that used burlap and putting it in their furniture. If you went into a house with that kind of furniture on a hot, humid day, it would almost knock your hat off, the odor was that terrific. They had no scruples. They'd pick things off the floor, whether it was orange peels, banana peels, and threw it into the furniture, just packed a hole there, stuffed it here.

So, you learned about these shops from different workmen who were trying to escape from that environment and better themselves.

They would come into a custom shop like ours, hoping that they could click, make it. Because those bad conditions did *not* exist in the good shops. And I mean like Paine Furniture was the ultimate, Irving and Casson, Davenport, Barile—they were the ultimate in quality and workmanship. And Archer's had the same quality, only on a smaller scale. We had all new frames, all new materials, and the workshop was clean.

Many, many of the wholesale shops had a union, but in custom shops, very few had a union, and the upholsterers that were in the union from custom shops, those people walked on water. They talked to nobody, and they were pretty snobbish. They didn't solicit for the union in other custom shops. Back in the depression, Arthur Flynn, that fine man who was my first working foreman, was laid off, and he went to Irving and Casson looking for a part-time job, and one of the things they interrogated him about was, "Why didn't you have your shop join the union?" His answer was, "Nobody ever asked me to join the union." Well, Arthur Flynn didn't work there very long. He finally ended up working as an instructor of upholstery at the state prison in Charlestown, and then went to the prison at Walpole, and then retired from the state prison. Arthur was a wonderful man.

Regarding materials, before 1936, there were no law labels stating what the materials in the furniture were. You know, like the law labels on a mattress. But when [James Michael] Curley was governor [1935–37], the understanding I have is that a man was appointed as the first upholstery inspector. And it was his duty to go around to the different shops and enforce the use of labels identifying the contents, whether it was hair, or moss, or batting, or down, and so forth. And that man received the appointment because he was both an upholsterer and an artist, and he made a portrait of Curley, and as a result he got appointed the first inspector.

Now, on my training, the reason Sully told me to keep my eyes open was because these people weren't going to show you how it was done. You always had to keep your eyes open, and while you were working you would always take glances at people when they were using certain techniques. You would actually have to steal it with your eyes and then try to figure it out. Truthfully, I was one of the lucky ones, because Sully was aside of me, and he was number two man in the shop, so I was very, very fortunate to have someone giving me the fundamentals and making corrections as he saw fit. Ordinarily, training apprentices would have been the chore of the working foreman, Arthur Flynn, but he knew I was in good hands. Later on, I learned how to bast with skewers instead of tacks from Fred Sullivan. In furniture, it's not one-two-three, you quickly flip, and so on. You mold and you shape, and if it isn't right, you go back. Usually this was done by bast tacking, but you can get into trouble on silks. So I learned by watching Fred Sullivan to use skewers instead.

Others weren't free to teach you. Nobody would teach you anything. Whatever was done, however it was done, every one of these birds would try to keep it a military secret. Johnny Murphy, the number one man at Archer's, was one of two apprentices at Paine's that were selected to stay on as journeymen after completing their apprenticeships, something that was unheard of. He was capable. Now, next to him was Sully as number two, and next to Sully was Joe O'Donnell. Murphy and O'Donnell, as Irishmen, were buddies, needless to say. But in terms of workmanship, the difference between them was like night and day. Murphy was first class, and O'Donnell was—well, we used to say, he's a butcher. He's a man who does extremely poor work and very careless and produces a poor piece of workmanship. And although O'Donnell was already a trained workman, he wasn't in my league as an apprentice. He had already gone through the veteran's training program after World War I, not through Paine's. But although he and Murphy were friends, not *once* in all that time they were working there, from '27 until '30, not *once* in that period did I ever see Murphy go over to O'Donnell and say, "Hey, Joe, do it this way, you'll find it a little better." Not *once*. And they were friends. With friends like that, you don't need enemies.

So, they didn't help one another. They were sad. Like I said, some of the people we worked with didn't have too many scruples. If you were fussy about how you picked your hair, and how you got things fine and smooth, well, then, somebody who wanted to put you in a bad light would come along with the back of his hand, punching the object, trying to create a hole. And once the indentation is there, there's nothing you can do but open it up and fix it, because the hair has been compressed. Sully and I never stayed in at lunchtime. Our technique was to eat our lunch and go take a walk. And we walked our lunchtime and came back. Well, one day, we were coming back up the stairs, and people couldn't hear us coming up the stairs. Sully's bench was the second set of horses from the door, and we found David Motherway banging on an arm on Sully's chair. Well, that's when your hands didn't stay at your side, you know. Those things happened.

And I learned many different shop expressions, slang terms nobody else would know. One term was, *skin it*. In short, do as little as you can on an object. Fake it, don't put in the required amount of work. It takes too much time to do it correctly. Then fake it, don't put in that work. "Skin it! Skin it! I'm losing money!" Of course, you're working, and you've got to do what you're told. You may not like it, so when you skin it, you've got to skin it so that the object looks good. But it hasn't got the amount of work that you would like to put in.

And another term was, when you tied your springs too quickly, and you didn't put the work into the lashings, one of the other workmen would walk by and say, "Boy, those are hot springs!" In other words, you did it so quickly that the springs are steaming hot, they can't possibly be tied correctly.

One last thing about Archer's. We had only one tufted piece that was made there, called a Sleepy Hollow chair, I suppose because Washington Irving owned one. And of all the workmen in the shop, only one man, Fred Truman, knew how to make tufted furniture [fig. 7]. In all those years, he never showed anyone how to make that chair. This was to guarantee his job. And nobody asked him to show someone else how to do it. He would refuse. And oftentimes he would go on a binge. He would be off booze for so long, and then he would go on a drunk for two or three weeks. And another man I'd like to talk about was Jack Spinelli. Even though I was an apprentice, I learned fast, and we had these low stools that had a high stitched edge. To stitch an edge that high and not have it flopping all over was already a tricky job. Well, Spinelli was one of the part-time workers that came in during the rush each year, and then he would get laid off and go back to selling vegetables on Tremont Street. He would marvel at how I could make this edge correctly, and here he was, probably twenty years older than I was. But he wasn't trained right, and he didn't learn.

Now, as I said earlier, when the depression came, everyone was let go in the shop except for me and a younger apprentice. I would work two days and get paid for one, or three days and get paid for two, then one day and get paid for two, and so forth. Mr. Archer didn't have any

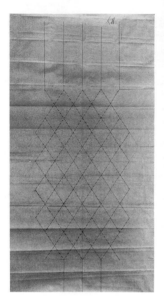

Fig. 7. Shop drawing for plotting tufting
pattern on the burlap of a Sleepy Hollow
chair, by Andrew Passeri, about 1975.
(Photo, Robert J. Bitondi.)

money, and we went along as best we could. That went along until
May or June of 1936. One day I was called at the house to come to
work, and I told them I couldn't come to work because I had injured
my hand. They said they would get back to me, and several days later
they called me and asked me if I could go back to work, and I said I
would.

When I got to the workshop, Mr. Archer began mumbling things
on the way up in the elevator, and I didn't know what he was getting
at. But when I opened the door, I saw a sofa partially done. Of course
I was irritated. I thought it was very unkind of Archer, after I had stayed
so many years at his beck and call, to go behind my back and hire
someone else just because I had an injured hand for a few days. The
person had botched the job and couldn't finish the job correctly, and it
had come to a halt in the middle of the sofa. Well, I told Mr. Archer
that I would finish that sofa, but I would never do another piece of
furniture for him. At that point, I finished the sofa and I took my tools
home.

Now, that's a tough time to take your tools home, because there
weren't many jobs. That weekend a friend asked me how things were
doing, and I told him the story, and he told me they were pouring

concrete at a post office site in Wakefield. The following day I went out to Wakefield, and I stayed there from that time until the dedication of the building, which was in December.

I'm talking now in my fifty-ninth year as an upholsterer, and that's the only part of my life that I was away from the art.

About the first week of January 1937, Sully Gangi called me and told me that there was a job opening at Fallona's at 1622 Beacon Street, Brookline. So I went there for an interview, and the man who was the working foreman was Dave Shea. Now, Dave Shea prior to this had been working with Sully Gangi and Johnny Murphy at John Riordan's and Sons in Boston. Riordan's was a highly respectable operation with a fine clientele. Sully had worked with Dave at Riordan's about two years or so, and Dave had wanted Sully to go to Brookline with him, but Sully wanted no part of him. Shea was a difficult man.

So I arrived at Fallona's to be interviewed, and Dave asked me, "What can you do?" And well, I says, "I can do all the straight work." And he says, "What about tufting?" I says, "I know nothing about tufting, only straight work." You will recall, the only person at Archer's who knew tufting was Fred Truman, and he never showed one person one iota of tufting. It's a mathematical formula with many subtle adjustments. So I told Dave Shea that I knew nothing about tufting, but I could do straight work, that is, untufted work, and I could cut and sew. That was one of the privileges of working at Archer's during the depression. I had had the opportunity to learn how to cut and to sew, because ordinarily, only the working foreman would have done that. He would do all the cutting and planning, and two women would do the machine sewing. So Dave says, "When do you want to start?" And I says, "Well, anytime." And he says, "You want to start today?" and I says, "Sure."

So I came back from Brookline by trolley and got my tools at my home in Revere and got back to the shop by twelve-thirty. I walked into the shop, and on a pair of horses which were designated as mine, there's a Victorian tufted chair. Lo and behold, I just told this man four hours before that I didn't know anything about tufting. So, I didn't know what to do with it. I started on the seat, which was a tight seat with no cushion, and I got the springs tied, and I got the horsehair stuffing picked, and I got it all stitched down.

And that night, I called Sully. And I said, "You won't believe it! I told Dave I know nothing about tufting, and this guy gives me a tufted job! The first job he gives me is a tufted job, and I know nothing about it!" Well of course, Sully had worked with him two or three years, and Sully knew nothing about tufting. And during the period that Sully worked with Dave Shea at Riordan's, Dave Shea showed nobody anything about tufting.

Now, Dave was the other man who had served his apprenticeship at Paine's and had then been asked to stay on as a journeyman. Dave Shea and Johnny Murphy were, to my understanding, the only two apprentices ever kept on at Paine's. So you can see, Dave knew what he was doing. He was a competent person.

I came back the next day after talking to Sully, and I worked on the tufting. I started to try to make some sense, and it was just guesswork. I plotted the tufts, and I allowed a quarter of an inch to the inch for the allowance on the tufts and hoped that it would work out. Anyway, when I got through, Dave said, "It's a reasonably good job. It's a good job." I says, "Well, look, I still don't know what I did, because I know nothing about tufting. Straight work, yeah, I can do it." He says, "It looks OK." I says, "OK, it may look OK, but I still don't know how I got to it." I made notes, you know, on what I did, but it was not the correct way of doing it.

So that was the first job. The second job he gave me was a Lawson sofa. The Lawson sofa was a new frame, and Dave was working on a new Lawson sofa at the same time. And I started going at it with the speed and desire that's normal with me, and I was going at it pretty good, and after I'm halfway through with it, he called me over to his bench (and to visualize Dave Shea, you have to picture [Gen. Douglas] MacArthur, the typical MacArthur attitude, corncob pipe and all), and he looked down at me, and he says to me, "What are you trying to do, show me up?" I thought I was trying to impress him because I needed a job, and I says, "No! You have so much more experience than I have, and the only thing I can hope for is that you'll be satisfied with my work." And apparently he believed me, because it was the gospel truth. I knew he was a difficult man. In the very near future, he took me under his wing and started teaching me the fundamentals of tufting, for which I'm grateful to this day.

Dave Shea stayed on at Fallona's about a year and three months. Then he was fired. He was a very capable man, but he would not put the effort into his work. And I've been thinking about why Dave showed me tufting, and I think I've arrived at the conclusion that *possibly*—Al

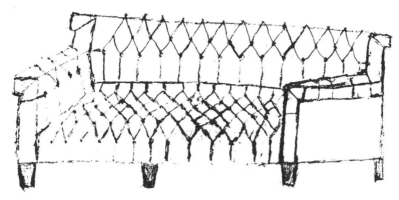

Fig. 8. Chesterfield sofa. (Sketch, Andrew Passeri, 1986.)

Mitchell at Fallona's could tuft, but Dave didn't want to give him any tufting to do, because there was no love lost between them whatsoever—did he teach me how to do it as a defense so he wouldn't have to rely on Al Mitchell, or did he simply not want to do it himself? But I never saw Al Mitchell do a tufted job. Any of the tufted jobs that came into Fallona's while Dave was still there, I got them, whether it was a Victorian lounge, or a big Chesterfield sofa [fig. 8]. He didn't teach me how to plot each of these different forms. He gave me the fundamental formulas. We were getting quite a few Chesterfields, big barges! They were a lot of work, and I don't think he wanted to put that much time into them. The term was, *if he had a bicycle pump, he'd fill it up with air.* On the first Chesterfield sofa, I didn't know what the hell to do with it. So he told me that on each tuft or biscuit, the diamond-shaped parts, make it two-and-a-quarter allowance back to front, and two-and-a-half side to side. And I'd find always that this use of two different allowances created a little crease along the biscuit. No matter how I regulated the hair in the thing, that strain, that little draw, was always there. And it bothered me. And it took me a long time to figure out that the allowances back to front and side to side should always be the same measure. He was setting me up a little. The only time you should use two different measures on the allowances for a biscuit is when your cover is a little stretchy, it'll pull along the fabric a little more than side to side. But these are things I reasoned out for myself.

Now, on the Victorian things I started to get, that's where I had to use my head. Now, if I came to a concave back, if I were allowing 2 inches, then I started learning, well, this is a big seat. On the small ones I started allowing 2 inches, then cut it to 1¾. You don't want something so puffy, so deep, so you cut on the allowance. So then I started figuring, well, wait a minute, this is concave, you don't need the same allowance as when it's flat. So I deducted what I thought was safe. Generally if there was any kind of concave back at all, I'd deduct half an inch.

From there I started reasoning, well, the sweeps, the curves, and the bends. Well, I started adding an inch, where you had to come up to a crest. Over here it sloped down, so I was minus half an inch. *That's not in any book.* It was trial and error, and sometimes they didn't come out right. One of the most difficult things were lounges or chaise lounges with curved backs. Now, you'd have individually tied springs, because you can't tie them all in one because you've got a concave, and they couldn't give if you did. And you'd have to plan that back out to button *in between* those springs. Well, sometimes you'd wind up on the spring itself, but then you had to make sure that the twine for the buttoning was not afloat, because it wouldn't hold. You've got to use your head. You can draw a picture of tufting in a book, but once you start getting into concave backs, you have to compensate for them all over.

So Dave Shea was fired. Another man was put on as the working foreman, and he stayed about a year and a half. And then he quit. The strain and the stress was a little too much for him. At that point, they asked me to take over the workshop. I was about thirty years old at that time.

As the working foreman, I always took the difficult pieces [fig. 9]. First, if anything went wrong, I was responsible, and second, it was a challenge. I wanted to learn, because Mr. Fallona had a wonderful clientele among the wealthy Brahmin families and wealthy Jewish families in Brookline. They brought the finest of period furniture to us. Remember, at Archer's I had only handled new frames, more or less on a production basis.

Mr. Fallona was an upholsterer of the old school. He started in Portland, Maine, and after World War I, he ran a government vocational school in Boston for veterans who were being discharged until it closed some years after the war. He then used the clientele he had

Fig. 9. Beacon chair designed by
Raymond Fallona and Andrew
Passeri about 1938. (Sketch,
Andrew Passeri, 1986.)

gathered among people who were sympathetic to the veterans to go into
business for himself. He was an excellent administrator.

In the workshop at 1622 Beacon Street, there were three floors.
Mr. Fallona had employed his brother, a contractor in Portland, to put
a new facade on the building with a big show window. On the ground
floor was the showroom and office. The showroom had five or six house
decorators, and there were three secretaries in the office, as well as Mrs.
Fallona herself, an extremely shrewd, tough, and difficult person to get
along with. I'm choosing my words very carefully here.

On the second floor was the upholstery shop, and on the third floor
were the drapery shop in front with about five or six women and a one-
man cabinet shop and a one-man finishing shop in the rear.

Now, Mr. Fallona liked the way I worked. And it was competition
from day one. If you didn't produce, you were the first one to go when
business slowed down. The policy was, no matter who came in the
door, you hired them, because he might be better than the next guy.
And that meant that my job was never secure. Fortunately, I was never
seriously challenged during my entire career, because I was a competi-
tor and still am. In my time at Fallona's, we developed a number of
techniques and practices. The first was the use of a cutting pad that Mr.
Fallona and I developed in 1938 [fig. 10]. Fallona wanted to make
money on fabric. All the jobs in his business were custom jobs, and the
show covers all had to be ordered specially for each job. And these show
covers and the matching trim were often exceptionally expensive silks.
Fallona figured that if he could calculate the absolute minimum amount

NAME

ORD. NO. PIECE

SEAT	
SEAT DECK	
SEAT BORDER	
BACK	
BACK BORDER-PANELS	
ARMS	
ARM PANELS	
WINGS	
OUT ARMS	
OUT BACK	
OUT WINGS	
SEAT CUSH.	
BOXING	
BACK CUSH.	
BOXING	
FLOUNCE	
PIPING	
	YDS.

WALTHAM SALESBOOK CO., WALTHAM, MASS.

Fig. 10. Sheet of the cutting pad developed by Raymond Fallona and Andrew Passeri about 1938.

of a given fabric needed to complete a job, he could overcharge for the supposed amount needed and make an additional profit. When you stop to consider that decorators always double the price of the fabric they obtain from the decorator houses like Scalamandré or Brunschwig and Fils, the amount of money involved could be enormous. And the technical aspects of laying out cuts were complex, especially if the fabric had a motif that had to be plotted on the object for balance and proportion. The only way to cut down drastically on yardage and not come up short was to calculate every last inch of fabric needed on a cutting pad, with each cut for each part of the object indicated. I've illustrated the pad in scholarly articles to teach curators how to figure their own yardage for museum projects, but its origin was strictly commercial.

And of course, Mr. Fallona wanted to keep his labor costs down to a bare minimum, as well. You will recall that at Archer's, they kept track of time with work tags. At Fallona's, they employed a more complex and efficient system. We kept our time in shop books in which you would record the name of the customer, the order number, and your hours. You had two such books that you rotated, one would be by your bench, and the other would be down in the office where the time spent on each job was logged on a cost sheet. This meant that Mrs. Fallona always had a perfect record of how long it took you to do something, and since she knew right to the minute how long you took, and since experience had taught the Fallonas how long a given type of job ought to take, they could tell if you were slacking off or if you had done the job too quickly to have done it correctly. They had you both ways. And your hours and wages translated directly into the final cost to the client.

The Fallonas' shop, like all custom shops, was small. It became like a family—you knew the owner intimately, and he knew you. At times, you were scandalized by the behavior of some workmen, who would go out on jobs in houses and make advances to the woman of the household or drink on the job. But the decorators who worked directly with the clients in the showroom were different. They didn't mingle with the upholsterers, they almost looked down on them. The owners discouraged conversation with anyone but employees, and there was little enough of that. There were no coffee breaks, no radios in the shop, no talking or hanging around. It was a harsh environment. The only time you saw the retail clients was when there was a complaint. And even then, usually it was the decorators who would come up in the shop from the showroom to register the complaint. This was an extremely touchy area, because often the clients were trying to get a break on the cost of the job, but Mr. Fallona maintained a strict policy that we would always strive to correct any flaws in the work but *never* lower the price. Only a very few times were the clients permitted to actually enter the shop, and not even salesmen were allowed in there. You didn't talk to people. Nobody knew who you were. I well recall that one of the few times I met a client at Fallona's was when I made a special chair for Dr. Serge Koussevitzky [1874–1951], the tyrannical conductor of the Boston Symphony Orchestra. This was his study chair, in which he would sit up to fourteen hours a day while studying and memorizing scores, and it had to be custom fitted to his contours. It took three fittings before he was satisfied.

Mrs. Fallona took an active part in policing the day-to-day operation of the shop, and as I say, she was a difficult person to work with. I'll tell you a little incident that happened one time. The workshop on the second floor was at that time in the rear of the building, and Mr. Fallona had rented two offices to dentists in the front part of the second floor. And they used to come in the workshop to dump their trash baskets every morning. And oftentimes there would be small talk, especially if you worked near the rubbish barrel, the first man over, you would hear, "Good morning, fine day," and so forth—some friendly small talk. And at one point, one of the dentists came to me and says, "You know, Mrs. Fallona doesn't want me to talk to you, she said that you're very nervous and I would be distracting you." Well, that was a pretty sad state of affairs, to go telling a stranger that I was nervous, as if I were mentally ill or something. The thing was that she didn't want the man to talk to me because that might distract me from my work for ten seconds. So that was the mentality. You had to concentrate on your work, and that's the way it was. So I repeat, the atmosphere was not nice. You tried to be friendly, you tried to be respectful, but it was just *produce*. And every second meant a major loss. Back in those days, the World Series was a major event, but no radio was permitted in the shop. A coffee break was unheard of. The only one who ever took a break was Dave Shea. He had the nerve to stand out on the back porch with his corncob pipe looking over a schoolyard for ten or fifteen minutes, doing nothing but smoking his pipe, because, of course, smoking was not allowed in the shop. That was probably one of the reasons he was fired.

After World War II, the government had a program to help veterans learn trades, and we had our share at Fallona's. And many of them wouldn't stay because civil service jobs were more secure. You had a steady week's pay, you had benefits, fringe benefits, and other options that didn't exist in the upholstery trade. Once one of these young men said to me, after my having put my heart and soul into all this stuff, "What's in it for you? Why are you putting in this much time training us?" Well, my philosophy was then and is now, that if I didn't help someone else's son, how could I expect the Good Lord to be kind to my sons? But a lot of the boys didn't stay, and you couldn't blame them. They would get jobs as policemen, firemen, or at the Registry of Motor Vehicles, and they were better off in a month than I was after a lifetime of working there.

And it was not as if I ever earned a word of praise from the Fallonas. Once Mrs. Fallona grudgingly admitted that I was the best upholsterer in the city of Boston, although she must have been terrified afterwards that I would ask for a raise. Mr. Fallona kept me working by promising me that one day, when he retired, he would divide the business between Malcolm Lord the decorator, Fallona's brother-in-law Dion who worked in the drapery shop, and myself. I rejected many other opportunities because of this promise, as the Fallonas knew I would. So about 1957, the Fallonas decided that they would retire and that they would let us run the business on their terms for a time. By this time, Malcolm Lord saw that this plan wouldn't work, and he resigned and went into business for himself. But then we were left to operate the business on the basis of Mr. and Mrs. Fallona's figures. We were told to operate the business at 10 percent above cost. We began to run the shop, and I took the paperwork home at night to figure the costs, and my wife, Mary, took over the payroll and the bills, and we were not being compensated for it. After two or three months, we started adding up the figures and were worse off than we ever were. We were working harder, and we were losing on everything we sent out. When you added up the cost that we were paying for the trucking alone, with the truck and the driver and the helper, we were losing every way. Finally, we took inventory, and we went to the Fallonas and explained that this was not working out. Of course, they talked us into keeping this arrangement for an entire year, because it was extremely advantageous for their taxes.

But after a year, we went back to the old system, and the Fallonas ran everything, Mrs. Fallona was always double-checking our accounts. In one instance, I did a favor for a neighbor of mine. His wife was running a small beauty parlor in their house, and I recovered some old chrome chairs for them. I went to the supply house and bought some fabric and paid for it. But then the salesman, Mr. Simmons, said, "Look, we'll put this on your bill and give you credit, that'll build up your standing." I said, "Well, if you have to, do it." But when Mrs. Fallona saw that item on the bill, she said, "What'd you do here?" I said, "Well, I bought some material that I used for a friend of mine, and I paid for it, and Mr. Simmons put it on the bill and gave me a credit." She said, "Oh, you should *never* do a thing like that. That is strictly wrong." I said, "How wrong is it? I paid for it, what's wrong about it?" She said, "Well! You shouldn't be doing those things at home, you shouldn't be doing it. " Of course, she was afraid that my private work and the work of the business would become confused, and heads of custom shops never wanted their upholsterers to do any outside work, for that reason and also because you would, in theory, become too tired working at night to perform well during the day. But Mrs. Fallona was, as I say, a difficult person. There's no gainsaying that. But I did like Mr. Fallona. About the fall of 1958, I was involved with building two houses and still had two sons in school, and on the first of December, Mr. Fallona informed me that he was going to retire at the end of the year. Well, that was it. That was a thirty-day notice, but as I looked around, it wasn't hard to get another job. I had half a dozen offers, and I accepted one from Kincaid and Kincaid in Brighton. That was in January of 1959. When I arrived in the shop, I brought my apprentice, Dick Wethers, with me, and there were already two other upholsterers in the shop, the working foreman and Kincaid's brother, Raymond Kincaid, who had been one of the upholsterers at Archer's when I was an apprentice there in the 1920s. A week after Dick and I arrived, the working foreman quit. He saw that the competition was a little stiff, and he saw no reason to postpone the inevitable.

Later on Kincaid found occasion to fire his own brother because of conflicts in the family. Melvin Kincaid was not a nice man. But I now had the opportunity to learn about drapery and upholstered walls. After a while, I lost my apprentice of nine years, Dick Wethers, because Kincaid wouldn't give him a raise, even though he now had a wife and five children to support. He went to the airport jockeying cars for the car rental places, and later he drove a cab. This was a very disheartening thing.

I might explain that in addition to the harsh environment in the shop, there was little in the way of fringe benefits. I got five days' vacation a year, eight paid holidays (but if the holiday fell on a Saturday, I didn't get paid for it), and no pension. Even as the working foreman, if I took an hour off, I was docked for it. Let me tell you my wages. When I was working as a common laborer prior to 1927, I was making $47.00 a week. When I began as an apprentice at Archer's, I made $14.00 a week, and that was a forty-four-hour week. When I went to Fallona's in 1937, I was making $.85 an hour. When I left Fallona's in 1959, the wage was $2.50 an hour. In 1973, I was making $3.85 an hour. Six weeks before I retired, Kincaid raised my salary to $4.00 an hour in a desperate attempt to keep me working, but I retired anyway.

So you see, the arts never did pay, and that's why we're suffering today. I certainly didn't want my sons to go through what I was going through, and I'm sure they never had the patience. They still don't have the patience and the dedication that I have today. Kincaid was bad news. I never had any respect for him, and he knew it up front, because of the way I spoke to him. He knew that I didn't tolerate that nonsense. He was a butcher. One time we were at Milton, working on a historical bed, and this man was destroying the thing, he was a destroyer. I was on the floor, putting on bases or dust ruffles under the rails, and Kincaid was up above, ripping off the original sacking bottom, and he yanked the bed so hard that the heavy corner post struck me in the temple. Well, you know, I was hurt pretty badly, and I yelled at him with a voice so loud—I think you could hear me four miles away—I said, "You son of a bitch, you're dangerous to work with!" And he knew I was angry, and I *was* angry, because he could have killed me that way. He didn't say a word, and it's a good thing he didn't, because I don't think I would have stayed still. That's another case where my hands wouldn't have been down at my side.

Anyway, I stayed with Kincaid until I retired in 1974. When I left the shop, he didn't even have the courtesy to shake my hand and wish me well.

Now I'm going to talk about my retirement. I'm going to talk about it. This has been the happiest time of my life. I feel younger now than I did when I was working in factories at fourteen. When I retired in January of 1974, after forty-seven years in the art, Michael Castaldi called me. Michael ran a workshop with Benny Arpino, who was the upholsterer. Michael is the drapery man. Both came out of the McLauren business in Boston. I had met Michael out in the field, hanging draperies in houses for Kincaid. After McLauren closed his business, Michael and Benny set up for themselves.

So Michael called me up about a week or two after I had retired and asked me what I was doing. I says, "Well, I retired a week ago, two weeks ago." He says, "Yeah, I know, I heard that, but what do you plan on doing?" I says, "Well, I want to keep busy, I enjoy it, I just want to supplement my income a little, because as you know, the only thing I get is Social Security, I have no other benefits." He says, "Well, fine, that's just what I wanted to hear. I have some work. Would you do it for me?" I says, "Well, of course."

So then Michael started giving me a few little projects. Benny was his upholsterer, but Benny didn't have the experience that I have. He had limitations. A fine human being, a wonderful man, but he had his limitations. That went along fine for six months or so. One day Michael called me and says, "Andrew, I have a chair at the Museum [of Fine Arts, Boston], and they won't send it out. You have to go there and help Benny." So the day came, and I met Benny in front of the museum, and he led me over to the staff entrance, and then Vincent Cerbone [furniture conservator] came to escort us to the cabinet shop on the third floor.

This was the first time I met Vincent Cerbone, although my second son knew of him because he was a friend of Vincent's nephew. I had lived around the corner from him in Revere for many years, but I didn't know him.

So we went up to the workshop, and there on the horses was an old English easy chair. It was quite fragile, and we were supposed to use the old fringe and galloon that was on it, and I could tell that Benny didn't want any part of it. He didn't say anything, but I knew it. I began working on the chair doing what I had to do. At certain stages, Vincent would call up Jonathan Fairbanks [curator of American decorative arts and sculpture] to approve of the work, and that's how I met him for the first time.

Now, it so happened that another upholsterer I knew from the trade, Lenny Pimentel, was in the museum doing work. He was never a good workman, because he only spent six or eight months in a professional shop and then he went into business for himself in a little corner shop. I didn't know what he'd learned in the time since I had known him in the trade, but it's competition that will make you a better workman. If a man leaves and goes into his own small business, he's not going to learn any more, because he hasn't got the competition, he hasn't got anyone that he can learn from. And that is not my idea of experience. That involves being in competition on a day-by-day basis and knowing that you have to account to someone.

Anyway, Lenny must have seen me and heard my voice as we passed in the hall on the way to and from Jonathan's office, and I guessed it must have scared him, because he knew who I was. A little while after, I heard that he had passed away, and I wound up doing some of his work that he had left behind.

So I started working with Jonathan, and the relationship was excellent. I could see his sincerity, something I've always respected. He appreciated my efforts, and when I was doing the [Samuel] McIntire furniture for the Oak Hill [period] rooms, he showed great interest in each object, something that no one had ever shown in forty-seven years. In the trade, it was strictly a question of how much money they were making, and the Fallonas lived well. It was thrilling to know that these people were sharing their expertise. I had always believed in it and practiced it, but others didn't.

Then Robert Trent [then a research associate at the museum] came into the picture. I found myself facing him in the shop quite often. He spent many hours with me, and we went over the Endicott leather chair [see Kirk, fig. 10] and restored the collapsed seat foundation together. And Jonathan Fairbanks was so pleased with it that he brought it to Jan Fontein, the museum's director, to show him the work. Hey, someone was appreciating what I was doing, you know?

And Trent wanted a seventeenth-century cushion to go on the chair. When I made the first pillow, I failed many times to cut the proper template, because it was something very unusual. I struggled with it. And I remember that finally I went into the museum with a template for it, and I went over it with Trent, and God, it looked terrible. Then we walked into Jonathan's office, and Jonathan very nicely said to me, "Andrew, what have you got there?" And I says, "I've got the pillow for the Endicott chair." He says, "Oh, let's look at it." I says, "Oh, no, no, no, it didn't come out right." He says, "Let's look at it." And someone who was helping to plan the upholstery conference was there, and they said to me, "Do you know Charlie Ianello, the upholsterer from the Metropolitan?" And I says, "No, I don't. I've heard of him, but I don't know him." They says, "Well, we'll let you and him fight it out." They said that to the wrong person, because I replied without thinking, "I'm not afraid of anyone." And that's the way it is, artistically or otherwise. I was sorry to have been so abrupt, but that's the way it is. Later on, I worked out that cushion template to everyone's satisfaction, including Peter Thornton's [then keeper of furniture and woodwork, Victoria and Albert Museum, London]. Those heavy-shouldered, rounded early cushions are tough.

Next Trent and I worked on the Franklin chair [fig. 11]. Robert Walker, the cabinetmaker at the museum, did a magnificent job of restoring a weak frame, riddled with tacks. Trent showed me the period

Fig. 11. Easy chair, Boston, 1705–20. Maple and pine; H. 48¾", W. 29⅛", D. 20½". (Museum of Fine Arts, Boston, gift of Robert L. Parker and Margaret S. Parker in memory of Winnifred Franklin Jones.)

sources, and we wrote to Thornton, and Trent stayed with me by the hours, and I was fascinated that someone would spend so much time working with me. He would tell me this particular thing should be finished at this point, and we experimented with the wing rolls and the depth of the cushion. And that was the beginning of our working relationship. He was teaching me, and I was teaching him.

And another tremendous experience was the upholstery seminar at the Museum of Fine Arts and at Sturbridge Village.[1] I was asked to

[1] Sponsored by the Museum of Fine Arts, Boston, Old Sturbridge Village, and the Decorative Arts Society, this conference was held in 1979. The proceedings were pub-

speak in front of educated people from all over America and from Europe.
The only nervousness I had was that when we arrived in Sturbridge
where I was to give my demonstration, the room where I was supposed
to work was still occupied, and we had only ten minutes to unload the
stuff out of the truck and into the anteroom and then into the room. It
was all jumbled, you know, horsehair and tools and horses and objects,
and I like to be organized. The first ten minutes, I wasn't at my best,
but we did get organized. And I demonstrated all the various techniques, and everybody seemed pleased. I was pleased when Peter
Thornton came over to me afterwards and said that he was taking my
techniques back to London with him. These were extreme honors.

As the years have passed, Trent and I have tackled many, many
objects, for museums and historic houses [fig. 12]. Trent has made me
the coauthor of articles about objects we have worked on, and now we
are planning a book on historical upholstery techniques, because we've
gained so much experience at restoring old foundations and replicating
old forms.[2] I want my work to be preserved in museums.

My life as a commercial upholsterer was entirely different from my
experience now. The conditions were bad, the wages were bad, and the
atmosphere was bad. On the other hand, I think you can understand
why I was surprised when Jonathan Fairbanks asked me what books I
had learned from. I have a ninth-grade education. All my experience
was in the workshop, and all the traditions were handed down from
master to apprentice, in a traditional manner. I improved upon what I

---

lished as *Upholstery in America and Europe from the Seventeenth Century to World War
I* (New York: W. W. Norton, 1987). Andrew Passeri and Edward S. Cooke, Jr., co-
authored two essays in this volume: "Evidence from the Frame of a Late Eighteenth-
Century Sofa," pp. 112–13, and "Spring Seats of the Nineteenth and Early Twentieth
Centuries," pp. 239–50.

[2] Andrew Passeri and Robert F. Trent have coauthored *The Regulator's Art: Early
American Upholstery, 1660–1830* (Hartford: Connecticut Historical Society, 1983); "The
Wheelwright and Maerklein Inventories and the History of the Upholstery Trade in America,
1750–1900," *Old-Time New England* 72, no. 259 (1987); as well as the following articles
in *Maine Antique Digest:* "The Franklin Easy Chair" (with Robert Walker), 7, no. 11
(December 1979): 26B–28B; "Two New England Queen Anne Easy Chairs with Original
Upholstery," 11, no. 4 (April 1983): 26A–28A; "Some Amazing Washington Chairs! or,
White-and-Gold Paint and the Square Stitched Edge," 11, no. 5 (May 1983): 1C–3C;
"Anglo-American Classics: A New Model Army of Cromwellians," 14, no. 9 (September
1986): 10C–16C; "American Classics: More on Easy Chairs," 15, no. 12 (December
1987): 1B–5B; "American Classics: More on Sofas" (forthcoming).

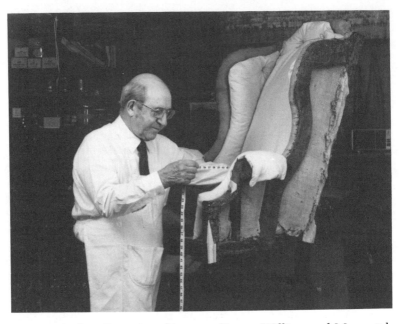

Fig. 12. Andrew Passeri working on a Boston William and Mary–style easy chair belonging to the Currier Gallery of Art in his shop in Revere, Mass., March 14, 1986. (Photo, Robert J. Bitondi.)

was taught, but even so, it was personal. This means that all it takes for all the techniques to be lost is for one generation to stop learning. And that, unfortunately, is what has happened since World War II. Foam rubber, zigzag springs, the staple gun, and other innovations have made traditional, hammer-driven tacks and hand-picked horsehair and hand-tied springs obsolete, insofar as the average furniture market is concerned. Now only museum curators can preserve the techniques, so that they can conserve objects in their collections. As with my career, they are faced with learning the historical techniques as they go, and only a painstaking process of recording and publishing the results of their work will educate other museum professionals.

I'm seventy-seven years old. I intend to keep on working as long as I can. I often joke with Trent that I'll only work with him another thirteen or fifteen years, and then he'll be on his own, but ultimately, it's no joke. My profession is almost gone, and now I hope that museum curators will help each other preserve the evidence and educate workmen. I will produce as many archival examples as I can. In the meantime, I hope that museum professionals can appreciate that most of my career was not spent in high-minded circumstances and that they are singularly privileged to be working in them.

GLOSSARY OF UPHOLSTERY TERMS

Bench
A pair of horses with attached well tops. Occasionally a flat work board will be laid on top of the horses to make a low table. When furniture is being placed on its side or back, padded inserts are set in the wells to protect the object. Upholsterers always have a separate high cutting table, about 6 feet wide and 12 feet long, on which to unroll and cut textiles.

Bias, cut on the
Diagonally across a fabric, at 45 degrees to both the warp and the weft. Welt cord is wrapped with material cut on the bias, and rounded structures like arms that are to be stitched are covered with material cut on the bias, because it models and yields under stitches better than material cut along the warp or the weft.

Buttoning
This refers to two kinds of structures. It can indicate a foundation where the stuffing is uniform but held down with twines and buttons, or it can indicate the mathematically planned buttoning found on tufted foundations.

Curved needles
All sewing on upholstered furniture is done with curved needles ranging from fine sizes about 2 inches in length on up to heavy needles 5 inches in length used to sew linen cord through bulky foundations. Upholsterers use double-ended straight needles for quilting foundations, some of which are 24 inches long.

Dead back or seat
Any upholstered back or seat made without springs, hence it is not intended to move and is "dead."

Edges
Several different structures are defined as edges. They can range from a simple sausage of hair stuffing sheathed in a burlap or linen tube to the most complex stitched square or Victorian edges. Generally speaking, the term *edges* means the perimeters where the transition from the frame to the foundation occurs.

Foundation
This refers to all components of the upholstery except for the show covers.

Gimp
A woven, flat braid or tape that is tacked or glued along the margins of a show cover. The seventeenth- and eighteenth-century term for *gimp* is *galloon*, from the French *galon*. The long, slender tacks with round heads used to attach gimp are called gimp tacks.

Hammer
A hammer about 11 inches long and 5¾ inches across the head, used exclusively for driving tacks and brass nails. The head, now made of drop-forged steel, was made of wrought iron before 1860. The two ends of the head are curved to conform to the radius of hammer blows swung from the wrist. Both ends are about equal in length, but one end is slightly narrower in diameter, in order to reach tight spaces. The narrow end is now an open loop and is magnetized so that the upholsterer can transfer tacks from his mouth to the work. This innovation was introduced about 1920. Before that, upholsterers transferred tacks to the work with their fingers.

Head coil
The top coil of a spring.

Horsehair stuffing
Long-staple hair from the manes and tails of horses, washed and dried to promote curling into a resilient mass. Short-staple hair mixed with hog bristles is also used for areas where the stuffing is stitched and compressed.

Lead twine
The first twine lashed to the springs, generally tacked to the top or the bottom of the seat rails.

Quilting
Stitches made with a straight needle through the sackcloth, stuffing, and undercover. Usually a row of quilting is made about 3 inches in from the perimeter of the seat, and then the center is filled with systematic rows of stitching as well.

Regulator
A stout, needlelike tool about 8¼ inches long, with one pointed end and one flattened, rounded end. Some have an oval eye in the rounded end. The regulator is used for numerous purposes. The pointed end traditionally is used for "regulating," or shifting and smoothing, curled horsehair stuffing. The rounded end is used principally for pushing covers through tuckaways or other tight places in the frame.

Ripping chisel
A dull chisel with a beveled edge and an offset blade, used for driving tacks out of frames being upholstered. Modern versions have plastic handles, while pre-1920 versions have wooden handles bound with iron.

Rolls
    In modern terminology, a "fox edge." This is a sausage made of stuffing
stitched in a burlap or linen tube. They are commonly used on seat rails and
on the edges of easy chair wings.

Sacking bottom
    A support system in beds employing flaps tacked on the rails and a center
panel that are laced together through grommets. This system went out of fashion with the introduction of box mattresses.

Shears
    A heavy pair of shears, about 10 inches long, with offset grips and flexed
steel blades, used exclusively for cutting fabrics. They are longer and heavier
than a draper's or a seamstress's shears. Upholsterers have at least three pairs,
which are rotated as they become dull with use.

Side-to-side stitch
    A form of stitch passed diagonally through the walls of a seat, a back, or
an arm to draw them up into a square shape.

Skewers
    Small pins with loop heads, about 2 inches long.

Stitched cake
    This is informal shop parlance and refers to any stitched seat or back held
together by quilting or edge stitching. *Cake* refers to the layers of sackcloth,
stuffing, and muslin or undercover.

Stitched seat
    Any seat where the layers or horsehair stuffing are held in place by through-
and-through quilting.

Straight work
    Any stuffing treatment that is not pleated or tufted.

Tight seat
    Any seat not intended to have a cushion.

Tuckaways
    Generally this refers to three locations on a chair frame: where the back
and arm or wing meet, where the back and seat meet, and where the seat and
arm meet. At these locations, the undercovers and the show covers must be
drawn through and tacked in place, hence "tucked away."

Tufting
    A decorative stuffing treatment where the horsehair is stuffed to accept a
series of diamond-shape pleats. The technique evolved in Paris about 1830 from
pleated foundations and was most popular from 1850 to 1900.

Upholstered walls
Walls that are covered in a textile stretched on battens.

Webbing
Woven strips that are tacked to the seat rails to support the foundation. Before 1830 they were made of linen; since then, of jute.

Webbing stretcher
A wooden tool with in-swept sides, six to eight sharpened teeth at one end, and a pad at the other end. Used to grip and stretch webbing as it is being tacked on the frames of furniture. Webbing stretchers came into use about 1830, when 3-inch-wide webbing became standard. Before that time, upholsterers may have used a webbing pincer with curved jaws, designed to rock against the frames and not mar the carving. Such pincers are illustrated in Denis Diderot's *Encyclopédie.*

Welt
A cord that is used to trim the seams of sewn covers, usually sheathed in the same material, in which case it is called a self-welt.

Zigzag spring
A patented type of long spring in a zigzag pattern that is tacked across the seat rails. It was mostly employed about 1945 to 1970, when other support systems were evolved.

Imagining the Parlor, 1830–1880

Katherine C. Grier

In 1853 New York daguerreotypist M. M. Lawrence opened his new heliographic establishment on the upper floor of 381 Broadway. Prospective clients first entered a 25-by-40-foot "reception room," described in *Humphrey's Journal of Photography* as "furnished with rich, heavy Brussels carpet . . . the walls handsomely papered, window shades, and appropriate lace curtains, gilt cornices and ornaments, rosewood furniture, upholstered and covered with green velvet." Gentlemen waiting for admission to the "operating room," site of the actual picturemaking, remained in this elegant interior. Women, however, were invited to prepare themselves for their portraits in a 25-foot-square "ladies parlor." This was "carpeted with rich tapestry," the walls were "covered with richest blue velvet and gold paper," and the furnishings included "rose wood furniture, covered with blue and gold brocatelle—reception, easy and rocking chairs, tete-a-tetes, &c.," and a "marble-top centre table" and "rose wood book-stand."[1]

Lawrence furnished his photography studio's reception room and ladies parlor as if they were drawing rooms in a well-to-do private household, and he was not alone in doing so. Between 1830 and 1880 a variety of quasi-public room settings appeared which, like Lawrence's heliographic rooms, were self-consciously designed as "parlors." Between 1830 and 1860, they included parlors in hotels, on steamboats, in the

[1] *Humphrey's Journal of Photography* 5, no. 1 (April 15, 1853): 10–11.

studios of daguerreotypists, and the meeting rooms of voluntary groups such as reading associations. By 1860 commercial parlors appeared on railroad cars and by 1880 in the form of ladies drawing rooms in big-city department stores. This essay focuses on publicly accessible "commercial parlors" in several businesses with which ordinary Americans had periodic contact—the hotel and the photographers' studio—and touches on parlors on steamboats and trains. It speculates on the reasons for their appearance and suggests that such public parlors served to focus new consumer demand on certain kinds of furnishing practices by allowing people to "imagine" parlors of their own.

The ordinary citizens who patronized these establishments received several messages from commercial parlors. They supplied not only an education in furnishing practices in three dimensions and glowing color but also the experience of simply being in a parlor. In so doing, they implied that parlor gentility was accessible through the great engine of American commerce and that the temporary inhabitants of the rooms were (or could become) "parlor people," comfortable with the parlor's social ceremony and its special middle-class milieu. Printed notice of and commentary on commercial parlors suggest that these elegant settings captured the imagination of at least those segments of the public that were middle class and urbane in their aspirations, if not yet in their actual means.

All forms of the commercial parlor predated the agencies to which most historians of consumer culture have given greatest credit for changing and educating public taste—the international exhibitions and the department store.[2] The "consumer revolution," however, had been under way for at least a century before the opening of the Crystal Palace in 1851, in both England and its American colonies. As British and American society became increasingly commercialized, citizens with new

---

[2] While a number of dissertations in progress are reported to be examining similar topics in American consumer culture, some of the oldest monographs on single businesses, such as John Hower's *History of Macy's of New York, 1858–1919* (Cambridge, Mass.: Harvard University Press, 1943), still stand as seminal works. Neil Harris's important essay "Museums, Merchandising, and Popular Taste: The Struggle for Influence," in *Material Culture and the Study of American Life*, ed. Ian M. G. Quimby (New York: W. W. Norton, 1977), pp. 140–74, linked department stores, expositions, and museums as nineteenth-century tastemakers, but no research since has expanded on his initial observations. One of the pioneering attempts at interpreting the first monographic studies of department stores, advertising, mass media, and other elements of American consumer culture is Daniel J. Boorstin, *The Americans: The Democratic Experience* (New York: Random House, 1973).

Fig. 1. Trade card, "Ray Hubbell's Patent Ornamental Metal Corners for Oil Cloths," 1880. (Margaret Woodbury Strong Museum.)

means to purchase what Neil McKendrick has labeled "decencies"—and, in time, luxury goods—were also eager seekers of information to guide their consumption.[3] These "green" consumers enthusiastically sought fashion intelligence through shopping and mass participation in forms of personal expression which relied on artifacts to convey social information. The first popularly available, personally expressive artifacts included articles of dress; eventually, as means allowed, articles of room decoration or objects that supported domestic social activities, such as formal calling or dining, became accessible to members of the growing middle classes and prosperous working-class families.

The popular practice of setting aside house space for a parlor, a room that could serve as the setting for the most formal social ceremonies of family life and that was furnished with the family's best things, is correctly associated with the development and maturation of Victorian culture (fig. 1). Even so, the reasons for public enthusiasm for parlors and their elaborate, difficult-to-maintain furnishings should not be considered self-evident. More than a mere expression of the culture,

[3] For discussion of the spread of habits of consumption beginning with the adoption of items of fashionable clothing by working people, see, for example, Neil McKendrick, John Brewer, and J. H. Plumb, *The Birth of a Consumer Society: The Commercialization of Eighteenth-Century England* (Bloomington: Indiana University Press, 1982).

parlormaking was a learned activity with complex motives, requiring that demand be created through the spread of information which both justified the parlor and taught proper furnishing practices. It was also an activity associated with cities, with urbane, if not urban, people. As late as 1850, *Godey's Lady's Book* felt obliged to chide rural readers who did not see the need for published intelligence on up-to-date furnishing fashions. Noting frequent requests by "those at a distance from cities, who wish to send orders" for "notice of new furniture," the editor anticipated complaints from the magazines' rural readership who still remained outside Victorian "parlor culture": "Now this may cause divers groans from 'honest country folk,' where chairs, a bureau, a looking-glass, and a table, are still considered the essentials of parlor furniture; and a sofa or centre-table luxuries, that call forth the remark from visitors, that 'Squire Smith, or Major Jones' people are living quite too stylish!' "[4]

Stating that commercial parlors in hotels, steamboats (fig. 2), photography studios, and railroad cars served as "model interiors," does not imply that all these rooms were copied exactly by aspiring parlormakers, although many of them could have been reproduced. Here "model interior" is used in the sense of being a setting which allows people to try on the idea of having a parlor; it is a setting in which one can picture oneself. Most of the rooms that served as models played a role in the creation of consumer demand by providing an experience—being in a carefully decorated room designed for social purposes similar to the domestic parlor. Commercial parlors introduced new consumers to the vocabulary of parlor furnishing, including wall-to-wall carpets, rich draperies and upholstered seating furniture in matching sets, large mirrors and chandeliers, decorative mantelpieces, and pianos. Some creators and observers of model interiors believed that contact with such spaces would make their clientele more refined (a form of popular deterministic thinking which I have labeled "domestic environmentalism").

How might this process of individual imagination have taken shape in the minds of thousands of individual consumers? Before demand for ownership of objects can be aroused in the minds of potential buyers, not only must they learn that the objects exist; the possibility of ownership must be perceived as *real*.

As McKendrick has argued in his study of the spread of fashion in

[4] *Godey's Lady's Book* 40, no. 2 (February 1850): 152.

Fig. 2. Main saloon, *City of Boston*, ca. 1865. From J. Hartand Gardner, "The Development of Steam Navigation on Long Island Sound,"
in *Historical Transactions, 1893–1943*, The Society of Naval Architects and Maine Engineers (New York: By the society, 1945), p. 107.
(Steamship Historical Society Collection, University of Baltimore Library.)

England between 1750 and 1780, the idea of a "consumer revolution"
depends on more than an increase in per capita income or productive
capacity, although these two factors are necessary components in this
kind of social change. There must also be a change in attitudes about
spending, including the belief that spending income on consumer goods
can make an actual difference in one's life, either in greater physical
comfort or in expressing one's social relationships. In other words, it
requires that some possibility of economic and social mobility exists—
that society be fluid, to some degree, without the restraints of ironclad
castes. Eighteenth-century England was such a place.[5]

[5] Neil McKendrick, "The Consumer Revolution," in McKendrick, Brewer, and Plumb,
Birth of a Consumer Society, pp. 20–21.

By the eighteenth century the aspiration to own furnishings became plausible for new groups of people, and this coincided with changing concepts of decor. Although it clearly had roots in the seventeenth century, the idea of creating self-consciously decorated rooms as personal settings for the display of *cultivation* (a highly refined form of social competition) and political power gained force in the eighteenth century, attaining its highest refinement in the French concept of "civilization," but also holding sway in England and her colonies.[6] It is possible to think of the tastefully decorated salons of men and women of cultivation as extensions of their dress, which also, within the dictates of fashion, became more personally expressive. Thus the habit of mind that perceived furnishing as a means of expressing social status (whether real or desired) was long-standing, but by the second half of the eighteenth century it was linked firmly to the developing notion of changing fashion and "taste," an association that remained strong through the nineteenth century.

Thus the motivation to furnish was in place as Victorian culture developed, but processes of consumer access to information about durable goods such as furniture were underdeveloped until the last decades of the nineteenth century. By the 1870s, furniture producers and various kinds of professional mediators (decorators, authors of domestic advice manuals, and retailers) stepped up their efforts to control the process of information dissemination and change. For example, furniture trade periodicals such as *The American Cabinetmaker, Upholsterer and Carpet Reporter* were new in the 1870s and 1880s. Their articles document the sometimes frenetic quality of trade efforts to keep ahead of consumer desires and to keep levels of interest and purchase high through the constant introduction of "novelties."[7]

The model room created by furniture manufacturers or interior decorators for commercial demonstration seems to have been a product of the 1876 Centennial Exhibition in Philadelphia. Before this time,

[6] For an analysis of this changing concept of unified decor and architecture, which included more complicated furnishings, see Peter Thornton, *Authentic Decor: The Domestic Interior, 1620–1920* (New York: Viking Press, 1984). For a discussion of "civilization," see Rosalind H. Williams, *Dream Worlds: Mass Consumption in Late Nineteenth-Century France* (Berkeley: University of California Press, 1983), pp. 8–9.

[7] An anonymous writer noted, "The demand for novelties in cabinet-work require a manufacturer to be constantly on the lookout for something fresh and new" ("Decorative Novelties," *American Cabinet Maker, Upholsterer, and Carpet Reporter* 14, no. 2 [November 25, 1876]: 4).

furniture warerooms were conglomerations of merchandise organized by price line or type. The model rooms at the exhibition seem to have suggested to furnishing manufacturers the efficacy of presenting what would now be termed "a total look" to potential buyers. Grand Rapids, Michigan, furniture companies, particularly Berkey and Gay, were the first to set up "rooms" offered for sale on the show floor, although the company's marketing strategy was aimed at sales to store owners during the semiannual furniture markets.[8]

Popular decorating advice books and articles were also largely a product of the 1870s and later, although domestic economy manuals often included a chapter on furnishing.[9] Specific decorating advice in mass magazines appeared sporadically until the 1870s, but much was unillustrated or included pictures of single objects out of context. Occasionally mass publications included images of exemplary parlors, as when *Frank Leslie's Illustrated Weekly Newspaper* published an engraving of Abraham Lincoln's parlor in 1860 (fig. 3). The costume prints in magazines such as *Godey's Lady's Book* also occasionally included enough detail of room furnishing to provide useful information to fashion-conscious readers. But extensive photomechanical illustrations of existing domestic interiors did not appear on the scene until the 1890s.

On the consumer's end, information on personal fashion—clothing styles, modes of hairdressing, and the like—seems to have been the easiest of all types of advice to obtain and the most widely disseminated. Information about new styles was readily transmitted through face-to-face contact between social classes, which in nineteenth-century America occurred in the mingling of street life. On her first visit to New York in 1832, British actress Fanny Kemble commented on the quality of clothing worn by lower-class people, including blacks, on Broadway: "After dinner, sat looking at the blacks parading up and down; most of them in the height of fashion, with every colour of the rainbow about them."[10]

Such casual mingling did not extend to socializing within the houses

[8] Richard Donald Jurzhals, "Initial Advantage and Technological Change in Industrial Location: The Furniture Industry of Grand Rapids, Michigan" (Ph.D. diss., Michigan State University, 1973), pp. 95–98; James Stanford Bradshaw, "Grand Rapids, 1870–1880: Furniture City Emerges," *Michigan History* 45, no. 4 (Winter 1971): 332.
[9] Martha Craybill McClaugherty, "Household Art: Creating the Artistic Home, 1868–1893," *Winterthur Portfolio* 18, no. 1 (Spring 1983): 1–26.
[10] Fanny Kemble, *The Journal of Frances Anne Butler, Better Known as Fanny Kemble*, vol. 1 (1835; reprint, New York: Benjamin Blom, 1970), p. 74.

Fig. 3. "Front Parlor in Abraham Lincoln's House, Springfield, Ill.," *Frank Leslie's Illustrated Weekly Newspaper* (1860). From Peter Thornton, *Authentic Decor: The Domestic Interior, 1620–1920* (New York: Viking Press, 1984), p. 300. (Margaret Woodbury Strong Museum.)

of the fashionable, however. New members of the middle classes in cities probably knew less about the style of living of their social betters, who received their fashion news through networks of contact with Europe, than even rural Americans who entered the houses of small-town leading citizens for special occasions such as funerals. In cities over the course of the nineteenth century, neighborhoods that once contained an economic cross section became increasingly stratified, as well as too large to encourage socializing among the upper and middle classes. The work of Richard Sennett on the Chicago neighborhood of Union Park and that of Sam Bass Warner on Philadelphia suggest that the upper and middle classes had little direct contact with one another, although the upper class and lower class were more likely to intermingle through domestic employment and charitable activities.[11]

[11] Richard Sennett, *Families against the City: Middle Class Homes of Industrial Chicago, 1872–1890* (Cambridge, Mass.: Harvard University Press, 1970), chaps. 1, 3; Sam Bass Warner, *Private City: Philadelphia in Three Periods of Its Growth* (Philadelphia: University of Pennsylvania Press, 1968).

There were ways for ordinary Americans with modest incomes and aspirations to gain admittance to the homes of the fashionable, however. One of the most important may have been the household auction, which provided not only furnishing information but also the possibility of ownership of furnishings which would otherwise have been beyond their means. Household auction catalogues confirm that public sales served as a means of contact with beautifully planned and furnished parlors, as well as elegantly appointed dining rooms and chambers.[12]

Preliminary evidence suggests that the first commercial parlors took their appearance from their domestic counterparts for several reasons. First, these rooms were new kinds of places, ones in which socializing was an element of the "product" being sold, whether accommodations, transportation, or likenesses. With the exception of the taverns, there existed no real precedent in America for spaces that commingled social and commercial functions in quite this fashion. At the same time, the function of the parlor in well-to-do private houses in the late eighteenth century and the first decades of the nineteenth was to serve as a social space which brought together sizable groups of the "best people," the select company rather than the more constricted domestic group of the middle-class parlor later in the nineteenth century. Some of the first commercial parlors may have served this function, as in the social gatherings that apparently characterized Tremont House.[13] Since the "best men" of communities such as New York and Boston were also the first to finance first-class hotels and steamboat companies, they appear to have chosen to furnish their commercial parlors along familiar lines, hiring firms that also provided furniture for their residences; George Henkels, the owner of Philadelphia's largest furniture emporium and manufactory at midcentury, supplied the interiors for the city's La Pierre House in 1853. Later commercial parlors probably took their decorating cues from public interest in these first rooms.

Commercial "parlors" could provide the first contact with consciously "designed" interiors—or even with as simple a novelty as spring-

[12] *Catalogue of Handsome Household Furniture, to be Sold by Bleeker and Van Dyke on Thursday, April 22, 1841, at No. 2 Albion Place* (New York, 1841); *Catalogue of Household Furniture, for Sale at Auction, by Henry H. Leeds and Co. on Friday, April 29, 1853, at Half-Past Ten O'clock, at No. 321 East 10th Street* (New York, 1853). Both catalogues are in the collection of Margaret Woodbury Strong Museum, Rochester, N.Y.

[13] For a "factual account" of social life in the hotel's setting, see Costard Sly (pseud.), *Sayings and Doings at the Tremont House in the Year 1832*, 2 vols. (Boston: Allen and Ticknor, 1833).

seat upholstery or lace curtains. In her popular novel of 1854, *High Life in New York*, Ann S. Stephens, speaking through the voice of the book's "author," Connecticut farmer Jonathan Slick, describes one such encounter in the parlor of the Howard Hotel. Upon Slick's being invited to take a seat on a "cushioned bench," the following incident occurs:

"Wal," sez I, a bowin, "I don't care if I du, just to oblige you"; so down I sot, but the cushion give so, that I sprung right up on eend agin, and when I see it rise up as shiney and smooth as ever, I looked at her, and sez I—"Did you ever!"
"It's elastic," sez she, a puckering up her mouth.
"I don't know the name on it," sez I, "but it gives like an old friend, so I'll try it agin."[14]

While we cannot know how many people developed a taste for parlor life through their contact with parlors in commercial buildings, articles and advertisements in newspapers and magazines suggest that the public was very interested in these rooms. The presence of a properly genteel parlor or a parlorlike setting became a selling point for photographers' studios, hotels, and steamboat and railroad lines. Parlors in commercial spaces were an integral thread in a web of ideas and images about the rapid advance of civilized living in America which resulted from commercial activity, a set of ideas that crystallized in the concept of "palaces of the people." If hotels and other commercial buildings, the kinds of steamboats commonly called "palace steamers," and railroad cars such as "Wagner's Palace Parlor Car" were all palaces of the people, commercial parlors in those spaces were publicly accessible rooms of state.

In a series of articles on new "first-class hotels" in America in the early 1850s, publisher Frederick J. Gleason associated the proliferation of hotels with "the advancements of civilization and refinement in our growing country" and claimed that by 1852 "nearly every city in this Union boasts of its first-class hotel, which, though devoted to the accommodation of the public, is yet equal to a European palace." Gleason's contemporary, New York journalist Reuben Vose, suggested that the appearance of such public palaces was the inevitable outcome of America's vigorous commercial life. New York had become a "city of

---

[14] Ann Sophia Stephens, *High Life in New York, by Jonathan Slick, Esq., of Weathersfield, Conn.* (New York: Bunce and Brother, 1854), p. 269.

palaces," he claimed, because "Commerce is the great civilizer of nations, and where merchants flourish, there all that adds charm to social existence will be found in the greatest abundance."[15]

The concept of the commercial "palace" and its related interior space, the commercial "parlor," were visible symbols which carried real power among commercially minded Americans. Winston Weisman has argued that the "dry goods palace" and "palace hotel" were examples of a specific American architectural type of the period 1845 to 1875 which carried on its exterior an iconography that contemporary observers recognized as "palatial" in character.[16] The prototype and most powerful example of the form was A. T. Stewart's Marble Palace, completed in 1846. "Commercial palaces" (the term was in use in the period) were multistory structures with elaborate symmetrical facades which quoted freely from past styles of architecture, including interpretations of the Italianate "palazzo" mode and the "Elizabethan" and "Gothic" styles. The popularity of the palace style may be attributed in part to reaction against the visual monotony of the neoclassical temple; its appearance coincided with the proliferation of historical-revival styles of furniture, for example. However, the "palace" mode's success also was encouraged by its flexibility in internal space arrangement for commercial purposes. Palaces also could be expanded easily by adding other symmetrically decorated units which often included cast-iron elements. The exterior of the St. Nicholas Hotel, for example, was faced with white marble and incorporated cast-iron elements painted to match.

By participating in the commercial, middle-class set of attitudes that supported the symbols of the "palace of the people" and the commercial parlor, middle-class Americans could become "parlor people," even if only for a short time, by occupying these rooms. They could imagine themselves possessing that space, one of the steps necessary to create demand for parlor furnishings. Vose, for example, described the pleasures of taking a seat in the "marble hall" of New York's Fifth Avenue Hotel in imaginary ownership: "If slightly fatigued a seat may be

[15]"Charleston Hotel," *Gleason's Pictorial Drawing-Room Companion* 2, no. 17 (April 24, 1852): 265; "The Girard House," *Gleason's Pictorial Drawing-Room Companion* 2, no. 8 (February 21, 1852): 113; Reuben Vose, *Reuben Vose's Wealth of the World Displayed* (New York: By the author, 1859), pp. 5, 40.

[16]Winston Weisman, "Commercial Palaces of New York, 1845–1875," *Art Bulletin* 34, no. 4 (December 1954): 285–302.

occupied in the hotel, and before him will pass more of the real beauty and wealth of the nation than in any other spot in the city. Here we recover from the toils that recur with every rising sun. Here as we gaze on the wealth of the world we feel at 'home.' *Yielding to the illusion of the place, and to a suggestive imagination, we often fancy that we are the happy owner of all that glides in beauty before us—except the ladies.*"[17]

Commercial "parlors" claimed their names by making use of a specific and recognizable vocabulary of Victorian parlor furnishing which developed during the first half of the nineteenth century. A particular kind of furnishings, placed in any kind of setting, denoted the presence of a "parlor," a space for social life in which the furnishings, in both their form and their quality, presented and represented the public face of a family. The artifactual vocabulary of the parlor included carpets, window draperies with lace curtains, a parlor suite, other fancy chairs, the center table, the piano, the decorated mantel, and myriad smaller objects. Additionally, certain forms for fabrics, carpets, and even wood types were so emblematic of ideal parlor decor that they provided a descriptive shorthand for authors or journalists describing rooms, as in the words *damask* or *satin*, and descriptions such as "richly carved" for furniture and "velvet" for carpets. Finally, in order to attain the parlor ideal fully, the room had to give the appearance of having been furnished all at once, in a coordinated—hence more expensive—manner; in Lawrence's elegant heliographic establishment, *Humphrey's Journal* noted, "every article . . . is selected with the greatest care to uniformity."[18] Within this set of parlor vocabulary terms there were also two "dialects," one that may be termed the "aristocratic" and the other the "middle-class" ideal of appropriate parlor furnishing. For our purposes, the image of Lincoln's front parlor may be taken as one visualization of the middle-class ideal of parlor furnishing, modest and appropriate for thrifty consumers with middling incomes. The view of a New York merchant's parlor from an 1854 issue of *Gleason's* serves here as a typical image of the "aristocratic" version of the parlor ideal, a mode that was decidedly French in inspiration (fig. 4).

Certainly the parlors in commercial spaces that received the most attention in print between 1830 and 1880 were those that expressed the "aristocratic" ideal of decoration. Although the scale of expenditure was

<hr/>

[17] Vose, *Reuben Vose's Wealth*, pp. 181–82.
[18] *Humphrey's Journal of Photography* 5, no. 1 (April 15, 1853): 11.

Fig. 4. "A Parlor View in a New York Dwelling House," *Gleason's Pictorial Drawing-Room Companion* 7, no. 19 (November 11, 1854): 300. (Margaret Woodbury Strong Museum.)

beyond the means of most consumers, the "vocabulary" and style of their furnishings was in keeping with the private households of well-to-do citizens. Take, for example, this description of the ladies drawing rooms of Philadelphia's Girard House in 1852: "The floors are covered with painted velvet carpets, that echo no footfall; the curtains, yellow damask, relieved by rich lace hangings, and the most costly trimmings; sofas, lounges, etageres, tables, rosewood, *inlaid*; the sofas, &c., seated and backed with yellow satin the chairs entire gilt, and yellow satin. The walls, from which gigantic mirrors blaze and multiply on every side, are decorated, and each parlor furnished with a massive chandelier of new style." Compare this account with the description provided by well-to-do Philadelphian Sidney George Fisher of the parlors at Mrs. Israel Pemberton Hutchinson's new house on Spruce Street some eleven years earlier: "The front room is in rosewood and some rich fawn colored stuff for draperies and sofas, with immense mirrors and splendid chandalier, candalabra, bronze ornaments etc; the back room, which is the dress room, is in blue and white damask & gold. The woodwork of the chairs, etc is massy gilt, the chandalier, candalabra etc ormolu of exquisite taste and execution."[19]

As decades passed, some kinds of commercial parlors grew even grander and less homelike. Beginning in the 1850s the public rooms of some first-class hotels and the most lavish steamboat interiors became so elaborate that their original relationship to domestic parlor furnishing became blurred. For example, with the remodeling of the *Isaac Newton* and the *New-World* in 1855, the grand saloons of Hudson River "palace steamers" took on a theatrical appearance, extending through several decks with gallery-level promenades. Russell Lynes correctly describes the interiors of the most elaborate hotels, as the Palace in San Francisco and the St. Nicholas in New York, as fantasy settings, but misses that for several decades after 1830 most first-class hotel parlors (and probably the more modest examples of respectable hotels) were essentially large-scale versions of the fashionable drawing rooms in private houses.[20]

The public rooms of city hotels, along with the parlors found in fashionable photographers' studios, were probably the most influential forms of commercial parlor between 1830 and 1860 because they existed in urban settings, where the power of fashion held greatest sway and where their information on roommaking could be most directly translated into purchases at nearby warerooms. The range and number of public rooms in good hotels varied; by 1837, Francis J. Grund considered a typical hotel in a larger American city to contain "besides the bar a ladies' and a gentlemen's drawing-room, a number of sitting and smoking rooms for the gratuitous use of boarders, a newsroom, and one or two large dining-rooms." With the exception of the bars and service areas such as barber shops, hotel public rooms were analogous to specific-use rooms in the homes of upper-middle-class and wealthy Amer-

[19] "The Girard House, Philadelphia," *Gleason's Pictorial Drawing-Room Companion* 2, no. 8 (February 21, 1852): 113; Nicholas B. Wainwright, ed., *A Philadelphia Perspective: The Diary of Sidney George Fisher Covering the Years 1834–1871* (Philadelphia: Historical Society of Pennsylvania, 1967), p. 116.

[20] David Lear Buckman, *Old Steamboat Days on the Hudson River* (New York: Grafton Press, 1907), p. 55; Russell Lynes, *The Tastemakers* (New York: Grosset and Dunlap, 1949), pp. 126, 84–87.

icans—for example, the reading room or newsroom corresponded to the private house library. Grund noted that the "elegantly fitted up" public rooms were intended to "supply, in a measure, the want of private parlours" which were few in number and expensive in hotels.[21]

As Vose's fantasy of "owning" the public room suggests, nineteenth-century hotels appear to have been even more open for the public's perusal, use, and informal instruction in "civility" than their descendants are today. Anthony Trollope was astonished at the number of local people, mostly men, who passed time in hotel public rooms in the West: "But the most striking peculiarity of the American hotels is their public rooms. . . . [There] is always gathered together a crowd, apparently belonging in no way to the hotel."[22] He considered such spontaneous but companionable crowding into public places a peculiarly American characteristic.

In this social meeting-place role, the hotels Trollope described were carrying on a function that inns had served in the eighteenth century, but with an important change in scale and appearance. While eighteenth-century inns were generally private houses converted to that use, between 1790 and 1830 a number of larger inns built specifically as inns appeared in East Coast cities, an effort to meet the needs of increasing numbers of transients. These larger inns, the first of which was New York's City Hotel (built 1794), continued the eighteenth-century inn's role as a social gathering place with "gaudy Long Rooms and Bar Parlors" (rooms that could be leased for social events such as balls).[23]

Not only did the appearance and size of hotels change, but the way people thought about them seems to have evolved as well. They too began to be described as "palaces." A "palace hotel" is here defined as a first-class hotel offering individual accommodations for guests, a variety of special services, and leasable space for public social gatherings. Jefferson Williamson, author of a 1930 history of American hotels, believed that the first published appearance of the term "palaces of the people" in reference to hotels occurred in a Washington, D.C., newspaper article regarding the opening of the National Hotel in that city in

[21] Francis J. Grund, *The Americans in Their Moral, Social and Political Relations,* vol. 2 (1837; reprint, New York: Augustus M. Kelley, 1971), p. 234.

[22] Anthony Trollope, *North America,* vol. 2 (1862; reprint, London: Dawson's of Pall Mall, 1968), p. 328.

[23] Jefferson Williamson, *The American Hotel: An Anecdotal History* (New York: Alfred A. Knopf, 1930), p. 12.

June 1827.[24] This new term suggests that the first-class hotel was a publicly accessible site which could still be associated with social ceremony and power and a kind of public civility; best of all, this social power and refinement was located in the acceptable world of commerce, a sphere of activity that seemed open to every man.

Foreign visitors observed the power of the hotel as a concrete symbol of American aspirations for a society that was both open and refined. In the 1860s Trollope wrote that Americans still were obsessed with hotels: "They are quite as much thought of in the nation as the legislature, or judicative, or literature of the country; and any falling off in them, or any improvement in the accommodation given, would strike the community as forcibly as a change in the constitution, or an alteration in the franchise."[25]

Tremont House of Boston, funded by a joint stock company of leading citizens and opened for business in 1829, is generally considered to have been the first "palace hotel." Its architectural plan and details, its provisions for privacy and security, its pioneering inclusion of systems for heating and rudimentary plumbing, as well as the size and grandeur of its public rooms, attracted so much interest that a book was published containing the plan and selected details, along with a brief history and description of the interior plan. Tremont's public room included two parlors for receiving new arrivals, two more "appropriated to the use of families," two sets of rooms for parties and clubs, six parlors attached to suites of rooms (promptly taken by permanent residents), and a large reading room with an attached "public Drawing-room for gentlemen." The reading and drawing rooms were free to hotel guests, but "a small annual subscription" allowed any male citizen to use them as a library and a club.[26]

No images of Tremont's first public parlors survive—if any were ever drawn or photographed. Their appearance can be suggested, however, by looking at known work and advertising by the twenty-one cabinetmakers, upholsterers, and importers of carpets, mirrors, and lighting devices who supplied Tremont's furnishings. Because the hotel was paid for by a stock company of the city's "better men," its furnishings prob-

[24] Lynes was the first social historian to call attention to the enthusiasm of the American public for these hotels and the power of their image as "palaces of the people" in *Tastemakers*, pp. 81–96. Williamson, *American Hotel*, p. 301.

[25] Trollope, *North America*, p. 314.

[26] *A Description of Tremont House* (Boston: Gray and Bowen, 1830), p. 12.

ably reflected their upper-class preferences, informed through contact with imported furnishings and publications. Sherlock Spooner, one supplier, advertised his firm in the 1829 Boston city directory as "constantly manufacturing every article in the CABINET, CHAIR, AND UPHOLSTERY hue." He offered "Spring-seat Rocking Chairs, Couches, Sofas, Mahogany Chairs, Music Stools," as well as a range of specialized tables, "in superior style." Another supplier, William Hancock, who seems to have been an upholsterer and furniture merchant, included a woodcut of a fancy Grecian couch in his advertisement that same year. Several examples of furniture made around 1830 with Hancock's paper label survive, including a reclining library chair and an elegant sofa with upholstered cylindrical arms in the collection of the Metropolitan Museum of Art.[27] The Tremont House parlors in 1830 may, in fact, have looked much like the large parlors of around 1824 depicted in Henry Sargent's *Tea Party* (fig. 5). Indeed, there was no American model for such an elegant hotel parlor except equivalent domestic spaces.

Between 1830 and 1860, large hotels were constructed in all sizable American cities as well as in communities with aspirations toward size and commercial greatness. In 1836, for example, the same year that John Jacob Astor opened New York City's first palace hotel, the Astor House, the metropolis of Buffalo, New York (population 16,000), welcomed the opening of the American Hotel, which was built in the "Grecian" style and had a center stained-glass dome. Preliminary evidence suggests the decor of these hotels' public rooms seems to have been supplied by warerooms and upholsterers who supplied domestic furnishings for middle-class and wealthier clients. The furniture of La Pierre House in Philadelphia, which featured a ladies parlor, a "reception parlor," and another for gentlemen, as well as an office, main dining room, and tearooms, was the product of George Henkels's manufactory. Henkels's sizable business provided furniture for middle- and upper-class households in the Philadelphia area between 1850 and 1876. His furniture fell well within the canons of middle-class taste as interpreted by *Godey's Lady's Book*, which promoted the firm's offerings in several articles in 1850.[28]

[27] *Boston Legal Advertiser* (1829), unpaged; E. Page Talbott, "The Furniture Industry in Boston, 1810–1835" (M.A. thesis, University of Delaware, 1974), p. 73.

[28] "La Pierre House," *Gleason's Pictorial Drawing-Room Companion* 5, no. 15 (October 8, 1853): 225, 239; "New Furniture," *Godey's Lady's Book* 40, no. 2 (February 1850): 152–53; "A Visit to Henkels' Wareroom," *Godey's Lady's Book* 41, no. 2 (August 1850): 123–24.

Fig. 5. Henry Sargent (1770–1845), *The Tea Party*. Boston, ca. 1821–25. Oil on canvas; H. 64¼″, W. 52¼″. (Museum of Fine Arts, Boston, gift of Mrs. Horatio A. Lamb in memory of Mr. and Mrs. Winthrop Sargent.)

A sixteen-page catalogue for Henkels's City Cabinet Warerooms, dating from about 1855, suggests the types of furnishings La Pierre's public rooms might have contained. With the exception of a group of comparatively inexpensive "Plain style" furniture (probably late neoclassical "pillar and scroll" style) and a passing mention of the "Elizabethan style" on the title page, the listed furniture was all based on fashionable French revival styles. The catalogue offered "Drawing-Room" furniture as a type distinct from "Parlor Furniture." While the range of forms offered in each of these lines was the same, the distinction between them was cost and degree of social pretension. Drawing-room furniture (which may have been imported) was offered in the "Antique" style, an interpretation of sixteenth-century furniture which was highly carved in the "grotesque" style with animal and plant imagery and which the French called "Renaissance." The drawing-room "Trio Tete-a-Tete" in the group ("elaborately carved, Satin covering") was offered at the breathtaking price of $350. Less expensive ($60 to $75) but still fashionable "Tetes" listed as parlor furniture were offered in a plainer version of the Antique style or in the popular Louis XIV taste. All three ranges offered customers tête-à-tête sofas, matching armchairs, ladies chairs, and side chairs—the grouping of forms that, sold together, comprised the typical seven-piece parlor suite of the 1860s through the 1880s. "Consol" and "Center" tables, étagères, and reception chairs rounded out the basic parlor line.[29]

More is known about the appearance of the draperies in La Pierre's public rooms, thanks to an illustrated article that appeared in the February 1854 issue of *Godey's*. The magazine touted the "celebrated depot" of W. H. Carryl, which supplied curtains, furniture coverings, window shades, and "all kinds of parlor trimmings" for La Pierre (fig. 6). The plates were one of a series of images of "parlor window drapery" furnished by Carryl that appeared in the magazine during the course of several years. The article marked no difference between the kinds of draperies used in houses and in commercial parlors, and the materials and forms listed corresponded to middle-class interior decoration. Among these were "heavy green lambrequins" (fabric window valances) in the parlor and the tearoom, whose "rich bullion fringe" was praised for being so close in appearance to real gold bullion that "it would take a practiced eye to detect it." Reading- and drawing-room curtains were made in brocatelle, an upholstery fabric which, at midcentury, was either all wool or had a linen warp and wool weft and was woven in

[29] Trade catalogue, George J. Henkels, Philadelphia, ca. 1855, Winterthur Library. For a discussion of Henkels's "Antique" furniture, an analysis of a group of surviving examples, and a brief business history, see Kenneth L. Ames, "George Henkels, Nineteenth-Century Philadelphia Cabinetmaker," *Antiques* 104, no. 4 (October 1973): 641–50.

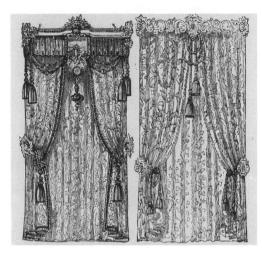

Fig. 6. "Fashion Plates for Decorating Parlor
Windows." From *Godey's Lady's Book* 48, no.
2 (February 1854): 97.

damask patterns with the figures formed by the warp in a satin weave.
It was a middle-class substitute for brocade fabrics and damask made
of silk.

The engraving represents curtains provided by Carryl for La Pierre.
The curtains designated "Fig. 1" were claimed to be "nearly identical"
in style to the window treatments found in the hotel's principal drawing
room. They were "draped with crimson, garnet, and gold brocatelle,
finished by heavy cornices and the richest corresponding decorations,"
along with "exquisite lace curtains, as in the plate, falling below." The
other draperies, labeled "Fig. 2," represented those found in the "elegant suite of parlors on the second floor," which were "curtains of brocatelle, crimson, yellow, and green and gold, equally rich and suited to
the style of the apartments, as in the drawing-room below." *Godey's*
congratulated Carryl for the part his curtains played in giving the hotel
"a cheerful welcome and homelike feeling."[30]

More modest hotels, in both the largest urban centers and the pro-

[30] "Fashion Plates for Decorating Parlor Windows: The Latest Styles," *Godey's Lady's
Book* 48, no. 2 (February 1854): 97, 166.

vincial cities, still tried to provide their clientele with elegant public rooms for socializing. Trollope noted that all the hotels he frequented during his 1861 visit, even in the West, contained the complete range of public rooms—"two and sometimes three" ladies parlors as well as "reading rooms, smoking rooms, shaving rooms, drinking rooms, parlors for gentlemen in which smoking is prohibited." In 1848, Waverly Hotel in Rochester, New York, contained "Reading, Receiving and Bar Rooms" on its first floor, "public Drawing Rooms," a number of private parlors and bedrooms, and the dining room on its second, and a leasable ballroom or lecture hall on its fifth floor. The local newspaper commented, "All are remarkable for their neatness, order and convenience, and are furnished in elegant style. . . . The whole arrangement of the house is such that all will feel at home."[31]

But it was possible for a middle-class American to be properly "at home" in the commercial parlors and sitting rooms of hotels, even though they were intended as paraphrases of the domestic parlor? Although only a small percentage of American families lived in hotels, their numbers were significant enough to inspire comment among European travelers and American commentators. These observers did not agree about the effects that attempts to experience gentility firsthand through hotel living had on the domestic sentiments of their residents, especially women. Grund thought that boarding was "commendable on the score of economy," both for single men and newly married couples, because it permitted marriages to take place "a little sooner than their means would otherwise allow them" and because it saved expenses on servants and rent. Thirty years later, the author of *Eighty Years' Progress in the United States* believed that hotels provided "an unrivaled combination of the applications of human ingenuity to the improvement of domestic life," with their "splendid furniture, elaborate food, economical yet liberal housekeeping, [and] labor-saving machinery."[32]

Public parlors in hotels seem to have served as sites for entertainments with a domestic flavor. The kinds of socializing that took place in the public parlors of Tremont House may have been much like the convivial gathering depicted in Sargent's *Tea Party. Sayings and Doings*

[31] Trollope, *North America*, pp. 328–29; "The Waverly Hotel," *Rochester Daily Advertiser*, May 6, 1848, p. 2.
[32] Grund, *Americans*, pp. 2, 236; *Eighty Years' Progress in the United States of America*, 2 vols. (Hartford, Conn.: L. Stebbins, 1867), p. 261.

at the Tremont House in the Year 1832, a two-volume miscellany of dialogues, sentimental and comic stories, and letters written pseudonymously by Costard Sly, describes several social gatherings in the hotel's public parlors in which the participants are both residents of the hotel and other Bostonians. These include formal calls and large parties, such as an after-theater gathering described as taking place in "a magnificent saloon, (the ladies' dining and drawing rooms in the TREMONT had been thrown into *one*,) brilliantly lighted, and so forth,—and already occupied by a large party of ladies and gentlemen,—their friends and acquaintances;—of course, the most approved fashionables of Boston. A band of music was in attendance." Another story, "A Second Scene in the Ladies' Drawing Room," brings all the characters in the book together for a party which has a decidedly domestic tone as the participants provide their own amusements: "The doings were simple—common-place enough. There was some dancing—some singing—and a good deal of eating and drinking between heats."[33]

An article on life along the Mississippi, published by the *Illustrated London News* in 1858, devoted considerable space to a description of social life at St. Charles Hotel. The anonymous author's comments suggested that such socializing was considered "domestic" enough to be suitable for the wives and daughters of planters, yet public and commercial in character.

The southern planters, and their wives and daughters, escaping from the monotony of their cotton or sugar plantations, come down to New Orleans in the early spring season, and, as private lodgings are not to be had, they throng to the St. Louis and St. Charles Hotels, but principalls to the St. Charles, where they lead a life of constant publicity and gaiety. . . . After dinner the drawing-rooms offer a scene to which no city in the world offers a parallel. It is the very court of Queen Mab, whose courtiers are some of the finest, wealthiest, and most beautiful of the daughters of the south, mingling in true Republican equality with the chance wayfarers, gentle or simple, well-dressed or ill-dressed, clean or dirty, who can pay for a nightly lodging or a day's board at this mighty caravanseri.[34]

Other observers of hotel life found this dual character of their parlors troubling, since they were neither exclusive nor domestic enough

[33] Sly, *Sayings and Doings*, pp. 220, 250.
[34] C.M., "Transatlantic Sketches—The Mississippi River," *Illustrated London News* 32, no. 912 (April 10, 1858): 378.

Fig. 7. "How We Sit in Our Hotel Homes." From William Brown, "American Homes in New York Hotels," *Harper's Weekly* 1, no. 52 (December 26, 1857): 825.

to be proper homes for middle-class living. However, at least one author acknowledged that access to parlor life was a common, if spurious, motive for choosing the hotel "mode of living" by young couples who could not afford to maintain a separate household (fig. 7).

Apart from the convenience of travel, the most common motive which persuades to the mode of living alluded to is economy. But it is quite clear that this idea of economy is founded upon a false standard of the necessities of life. . . . If gingerbread furniture, damask curtains, tapestry carpets and a French cook are essential to happiness, there is no doubt they can be secured in greater perfection and at a less price by the gregarious hotel system than by individual effort. Such luxuries, however, as well all know, are not essential to happiness, and however permissible as superfluous enjoyments, they certainly are too dearly paid for when at the expense of domestic virtue and happiness.[35]

The surviving interiors that probably bear the closest resemblance to public parlors in mid nineteenth-century hotels are to be found in what was, until the 1940s, a summer residence in Portland, Maine— one with a special connection to the hotel business. Known today as

[35] William Brown, "American Homes in New York Hotels," *Harper's Weekly* 1, no. 52 (December 26, 1857): 824–25; "Boarding Out," *Harper's Weekly* 1, no. 10 (March 7, 1857): 146.

the Morse-Libby House or "Victoria Mansion," the brownstone Italianate villa was constructed between 1858 and 1861 by Ruggles Sylvester Morse, a self-made man whose entire career was devoted to the hotel business. Morse was born in Leeds, Maine, in 1813, but family history (otherwise undocumented) states that he left the state in the early 1830s to work first at Boston's Tremont House and then at New York's Astor House. The Boydens, a father-and-son team who managed first the Tremont and then the Astor, may have brought an able young man, as was Morse, along as an assistant manager. After a brief sojourn to California to look for gold in 1849, Morse wound up in 1849 and 1850 as an employee of St. Charles Hotel, perhaps serving as manager. Between 1853 and 1870, Morse became proprietor of three New Orleans "caravanseries," the Arcade, the City, and the St. James hotels.[36]

Morse, who lived until 1893, became a wealthy man through the hotel business, so much so that he was able to own both a house in New Orleans and a "plantation" some miles outside of town, as well as the Portland villa, which served as a summer residence. As a self-made man, spending his entire working life in hotels, it seems safe to assume that Morse's tastes (and those of his wife, who was also a Maine native) were formed by his knowledge of hotel decor, especially in his adopted city.

Indeed, the floor plan of the house, with its grand central staircase and large drawing and reception rooms, the elaborate and brightly colored rococo-revival interior painting and architectural details, and the furnishings in the French taste, all recall the descriptions of first-class hotel parlors, especially the description of Philadelphia's Girard House. Two photographs of the drawing room from the end of the Morse era (ca. 1890) show wall-to-wall carpet of a large rococo pattern with a center medallion of roses, chair upholstery of satin with bullion fringe, and, on the seats of gilt reception chairs, what is probably French brocatelle. The windows are hung with satin valances and draperies, embellished with fringe and tiebacks in contrasting colors, with lace undercurtains (fig. 8). A slightly later photograph of the reception room during the ownership of the house by the Libby family (who left the interiors substantially unchanged), shows a button-tufted armchair which

[36] Nicholas Dean, "An Exquisite Victorian Puzzle," *Historic Preservation* 37, no. 5 (October 1985): 40–45; Arlene Palmer Schwind, Victoria Society of Maine, to Katherine C. Grier, February 6, 1986.

Fig. 8. Drawing room, Morse-Libby House, looking south, Portland, Maine, ca. 1890. (Victoria Society of Maine.)

would have been considered a *fauteuil confortable* (an easy armchair), as well as the presence of a *bourne*, the large, round, fabric-covered couch designed to occupy the center of rooms. The *bourne* was a French innovation, its design a reflection of the "Turkish taste" which was one aspect of French decor throughout the nineteenth century.

What is also striking about the Morse-Libby mansion public rooms, as they are depicted in turn-of-the-century photographs, is the absence of personal memorabilia and the restrained use of ceramics and other decorative accessories. When they appear, as in the mantel garniture of the reception room, it is because they are considered elements of the decorative scheme. This absence of knick-knacks and bibelots, along with the scale of the rooms and their exuberant decoration and French furnishings, suggests their fundamentally public character and origins in the hotel-trained tastes of Morse. At the same time, they still are furnished with what, to the mid nineteenth century, were recognizable terms of the parlor "vocabulary."

Assuming that the Morse-Libby Mansion represents the standard of hotel furnishing in the mid nineteenth century, before the decoration of these commercial parlors took off on an even larger scale and grander direction, we can speculate on the role these interiors also played in encouraging and sustaining the continuing American fascination with French taste in interior decoration. This preference for "Frenchified" rooms and their elaborate upholstery declined somewhat as the British-influenced aesthetic movement gained sway. The French taste never disappeared, however, and regained enormous popularity in the furnishings of the late 1880s through the 1910s—although the audience it gained was somewhat different in its socioeconomic status from the middle class of the mid nineteenth century.

Judging from *Humphrey's Journal* description of the two elaborate parlors in photographer M. M. Lawrence's New York City portrait studio, it is fair to conclude that their appointments were remarkable. Yet Lawrence's rooms were not unique. By the late 1840s many daguerreotype operators seem to have gone to great expense to create separate reception areas that incorporated virtually all the artifactual vocabulary of parlors—lavish draperies, suites of upholstered furniture, wall-to-wall carpeting, and large mirrors and center tables. Some, such as Ball's Great Daguerrian Gallery of the West in Cincinnati, furnished their reception rooms with pianos to encourage informal parlor musicales among waiting patrons (fig. 9). The gallery consisted of five rooms, the largest of which was the "Great Gallery" which displayed paintings, prints, allegorical figures representing the arts, and a handsome selection of Ball's half- and full-plate daguerreotypes (making the suggestion that they were both artistic and appropriate elements of parlor decor). The decor was described as "replete with elegance and beauty."[37]

Articles describing and praising such photographers' studios appeared in both middle-class periodicals and photographic journals, such as *Humphrey's* and the *Photographic Art-Journal*, throughout the 1850s. They tended to focus on the most elaborate and elegant studios as examples of what could be achieved by photographic practitioners of vision and ambition. However, parlormaking among photographers spread through all but the cheapest studios from the 1840s to the 1860s, in cities and larger towns across the United States.

[37] "Daguerrian Gallery of the West," *Gleason's Pictorial Drawing-Room Companion* 6, no. 13 (April 1, 1854): 208.

Fig. 9. "Ball's Great Daguerrian Gallery of the West." From *Gleason's Pictorial Drawing-Room Companion* 6, no. 13 (April 1, 1854): 208. (Margaret Woodbury Strong Museum.)

In the *Rochester Daily Advertiser* for March 3, 1848, daguerreotypist T. Mercer advertised the opening of a new set of "Branch Daguerrian Rooms" to accommodate the rapidly expanding city:

These Rooms are fitted up in a style of unusual splendor—are supplied with every thing the extravagant could desire, the luxurious sigh for. After naming *Sofas, Divans, Ottomans,* and *French Chairs,* comes one of ELDER's splendid *Golden Pier Tables,* with a Glass, (the first completed in Rochester) in which, 'tis said, the *Fair,* look more lovely still, and assume that pleasing expression so much coveted by Artists, and their friends. Carpets of downy softness are spread beneath the feet, and hush the noisy tread. Statuary from Italy, of *pure marble,* adorn the Rooms at various points; the walls are hung with some of the finest works of Art, both of pencil and engraver.[38]

Only after extolling the beauty of his receiving room did the advertisement mention *"premium* DAGUERREOTYPES," taken by Mercer him-

[38] *Rochester Daily Advertiser,* March 3, 1848, p. 1.

self, for a fee ranging from $1 to $12 apiece, depending on the size of the image and the case chosen for it.

By the 1860s, Rochester's photographers emphasized the range of photographic practices available in their studios—ambrotypes, photographs on papers, "Imperial" enlargements which could be painted over into "oil portraits"—as well as their prices. Attractive rooms were still important, but they were no longer a novelty worth numerous advertising lines. Powelson's "new and elaborate Photographic Rooms" in 1864 simply encouraged prospective patrons to "take a look at the new Gallery, which is acknowledged by everyone to be the best fitted up, finest carpets and most elegant furniture, the most commodious toilet room for the ladies to be found in the country." A recent article on photographers' studios in the West between 1850 and 1900 indicates that reception parlors fitted up with lambrequins, parlor suites, decorative chairs produced by the firm of George Hunzinger of New York City, and potted palms survived at least until the turn of the century, with style changes reflecting new taste in parlor decor.[39]

By the 1870s the efforts of ordinary studio photographers working in provincial cities to provide elegant parlors for waiting patrons had become so common that the activity was burlesqued in the photographic advice literature. H. J. Rodgers's *Twenty-three Years under a Sky-Light* (1872), was directed both to photographers and to prospective customers. Rather than presenting technical advice, Rodgers used anecdotes on good and bad clients encountered in his business to address etiquette questions related to behavior in the studio and to advise both photographers and patrons on obtaining the best possible portraits. He depicted the commercial portrait photographer as a long-suffering working man whose efforts at presenting a genteel public face were frequently tried by onslaughts of boors, rubes, and ignoramuses. In one such anecdote, Rodgers illustrated the trials of keeping up a refined reception room by describing the entry of a group of young men: "They step carefully over the door rug, and having approached the middle of the room, wipe their feet on the Brussels carpet. . . . When told that they must wait five or ten minutes, and after roughly handling specimens of art, especially selections framed in gold-leaf, they 'set down,' elevating their muddy *under-standings* (which are suitable for a Con-

[39]Advertisement for Powelson's photographic rooms, *Rochester City Directory* (1864); Peter E. Palmquist, "Behind the Scenes: A Potpourri of Western Photographic Studios and Darkrooms, 1850–1950," *Photographist* 66 (Summer 1985): 10–25.

necticut River fishing smack) into the best and most expensive upholstered chair."[40]

The sheer number of daguerreotypes made in the 1840s, which
Robert Taft estimated at 3 million annually, suggests that the experience of passing time in a photographers' studio was common and that
it grew even more ordinary in the next decade. Photographers encouraged their prospective patrons to visit newly redecorated studios for
inspection and to pass a pleasant hour or two in the reception rooms. A
properly decorated studio located in St. Louis in 1851 was praised as "a
most agreeable place to spend a leisure hour." An 1848 advertisement
for Rochester's Emporium Daguerreotype Gallery invited "ladies and
gentlemen" to visit its "Receiving Gallery," "whether they desire to sit
for portraits or not," and offered "a new and magnificent SERAPHINE, of
fine tone, for the amusement of visitors."[41]

Commercial parlors appeared on steamboats and trains (forms that
can only be touched on here), as well as in hotels and photographers'
studios. A complex set of motives attended and justified their proliferation. Partly it was due to the increase in the sheer numbers of Americans traveling for both business and pleasure during the first half of the
nineteenth century and, most particularly, to the increased presence of
women and children as travelers. An account by Thomas L. McKenney
of a barge trip up the Hudson in 1826 praised its "ladies cabin and
apartments," not only for their "splendid" furnishings but also because
"a lady has all the retirement and comfort which the delicacy and ten-
derness of her sex requires."[42]

Ladies parlors doubled as sleeping quarters, except on boats large
enough to have separate staterooms. In her short story "Mrs. Pell's Pilgrimage," Caroline M. Kirkland described the ladies cabin on a Hudson River steamer as containing rocking chairs and settees, which doubled
as sleeping couches. An illustration accompanying the story revealed an
elaborately draped doorway and wall-to-wall carpet (fig. 10).[43]

[40] H. J. Rodgers, *Twenty-three Years under a Sky-Light* (1872; reprint, New York:
Arno Press, 1973), p. 150.
[41] Robert Taft, *Photography and the American Scene* (1938; reprint, New York: Dover
Publications, 1964), p. 76; *Daguerreian Journal* 1, no. 4 (January 1, 1851): 58; advertisement for Emporium Daguerreotype Gallery, *Rochester Daily Advertiser*, March 23, 1848,
p. 1.
[42] Donald C. Ringwald, *Hudson River Day Line: The Story of a Great American
Steamboat Company* (Berkeley, Calif.: Howell-North Books, 1965), p. 96.
[43] Caroline M. Kirkland, "Mrs. Pell's Pilgrimage," in A *Book for the Home Circle*
(New York: Charles Scribner, 1853), pp. 144–61.

Fig. 10. Illustration from Caroline M. Kirkland, "Mrs. Pell's Pilgrimage," *A Book for the Home Circle* (New York: Charles Scribner, 1853), facing p. 144.

Another motive for creating separate women's parlors was considered so much a peculiar characteristic of American public life that many European visitors commented on it at length; this was the voluntary separation of the sexes, especially among the genteel classes. While separate women's parlors on steamboats (by the late 1820s) and railroad cars (from the 1840s) and separate family parlors and women's dining rooms in hotels allowed women to relax their public decorum temporarily, they also separated women from the coarse behavior of rough-natured traveling men, most particularly their drinking of spiritous liquors and their excessive and vulgar use of smoking and chewing tobacco. British actress Fanny Kemble complained: "It has happened to me after a few hours' travelling in a steam-boat to find the white dress, put on fresh in the morning, covered with yellow tobacco stains; nor is this offensive habit confined to the lower orders alone. I have seen *gentlemen* spit upon the carpet of the room where they were sitting, in the company of women, without the slightest remorse."[44]

Apart from the practical considerations associated with tending small

[44] Kemble, *Journal*, 2:172. See also Charles Dickens, *American Notes for General Circulation* (1842; reprint, Boston: Ticknor and Fields, 1867).

children or women's special sanitary needs in travel, the proliferation of commercial parlors—both ladies parlors and drawing rooms for mixed gatherings—may have gained momentum with the increasing power of the concept of separate masculine and feminine spheres in middle-class life—the cult of domesticity—reflected in voluntary separation of the sexes. This separation was not absolute; women could and did participate in mixed-sex social life in the saloons of steamboats, on railroad coaches, and in large parlors of hotels. Forms of internal public transportation of such an unprecedented physical scale as steamboats and railroads needed to be made suitably domestic. The ladies parlors were islands of domesticity in the realm of otherwise unregulated public life.

Most observers of commercial parlors in hotels also never doubted the appropriateness of the concept of a separate, feminine domestic sphere in the world. Their responses to hotel parlors depended on whether they found such spaces uncomfortably ambiguous or an ingenious solution to the problem of finding an actual, physical place for women in the world of commerce that was enough like their most proper place, the home. It seems clear, however, that the individuals who actually made use of public parlors were untroubled by the ambiguous status of the hotel parlor. They accepted it as a proper public place for middle-class women. And they seem to have used the hotel parlor as they might the comparable space in a private house—either the house they already owned or the one to which they aspired. The lessons of proper parlor decor gained by aspiring parlormakers were probably unintended consequences of many early commercial parlors.

The photographer's studio was a commercial setting that grew out of a combination of the pressures of competition: economic, professional, and artistic aspirations on the part of certain members of the community of photographers to join in the parlormaking and the willingness and interest on the part of the clientele (including middle-class women with leisure hours to spend) to patronize such "refined" commercial settings.

Thus a mixture of cultural attitudes, commercial pressures, and commercial or social aspirations led to the creation of quasi-public spaces that partook of the material vocabulary of gentility—the artifacts of the parlor—to attract and keep audiences. These pressures inspired photographers such as M. M. Lawrence to expend valuable rented space and scarce business dollars on parlormaking. Photography scholar Richard Rudisill has offered the hypothesis that such settings "allowed the photographer to control his clients more effectively" because the setting differed from their homes "only in degree."[45] Getting the best out of sitters was only one motive for photographers' parlormaking activity, however. Photographers sought to attract and hold patrons for repeat visits; some suggested that studio reception rooms offered an agreeable and socially acceptable site for spending leisure hours; the illustration of Ball's Great Daguerrian Gallery showed patrons socializing and enjoying an informal musicale. Additionally, displaying their own photographs alongside art in parlorlike settings suggested the proper place for photographic portraits and guided new habits of consumption by suggesting that they were genteel (as was the photographer who owned the parlor setting).

The domestic environmentalist assumption—that the appearance of the refined commercial parlor would discipline and civilize its clientele—also justified the expenditures to create parlors (fig. 11). The most articulate statement of this position appeared in an "interview" with George Pullman.

Putting carpets on the floors of cars, for instance, was considered a very useless piece of extravagance, and putting clean sheets on the beds was even more an absurdity in the minds of many. They said that men would get in between the sheets with their boots on. But they did not. So it was with the more elaborate and costly ornamentation and upholstery which has been steadily developed. It was criticised . . . as useless extravagance—a waste of money on things which passengers would only destroy. It was not proved to be the case. I have always held that people are very greatly influenced by their physical surroundings. Take the roughest man, a man whose lines have always brought him into coarsest and poorest surroundings, and the effect upon his bearing is immediate. The more artistic and refined the mere external surroundings, in other words, the better and more refined the man. This goes further than the mere fact that people will be more careful in a beautifully decorated, upholstered and carpeted sleeping car than they would were not such surroundings above them. It goes, when carried out under other conditions, to the more important matter of a man's productive powers and general usefulness to himself and society.[46]

[45] Richard Rudisill, *Mirror Image* (Albuquerque: University of New Mexico Press, 1971), p. 203; M. A. Root, *The Camera and the Pencil* (Philadelphia: By the author, 1864), p. 45; E. K. Hough, "Expressing Character in Photographic Pictures," *American Journal of Photography* 1, no. 14 (December 15, 1858): 211.
[46] This statement has been attributed to Pullman by Mrs. Duane Doty, as quoted in *The Town of Pullman Illustrated: Its Growth with Brief Accounts of Its Industries* (1893; reprint, Pullman, Ill.: Pullman Civic Organization, 1974), p. 23.

Fig. 11. "Pullman Parlor Car." From Thomas C. Clarke et al., *The American Railway* (New York: C. Scribner's Sons, 1889), p. 243.

Finally, an explanation of the development and proliferation of public parlors in commercial spaces between 1830 and 1880 is incomplete without reference to the way in which Victorian culture disseminated its symbols. "Victorianism" may best be thought of as the bourgeois culture of industrialization and commercialization in Anglo-America; further comparison of Anglo-America with the industrialized countries of northern Europe will probably indicate that Victorianism is in fact an Anglo-American subculture of Western industrial, commercial culture of the nineteenth and early twentieth centuries. As in the emergence of any new cultural form, Victorianism did not suddenly appear full blown, wielding a new, untried vocabulary of symbols. Instead, it worked as a culture first through the commercialization of existing symbols and then through the articulation of new symbolic forms which were peculiar to a modernizing, commercial world. The two powerful metaphors that permeate descriptions of the commercial spaces under investigation here are the "palace" and the "parlor." Palaces, symbols of the concentration of royal power, existed outside the world of commerce, in the realm of power divinely ordained and inaccessible to ordinary people. When Americans appropriated the symbol of the "palace" to describe the "palace hotel," "palace steamboat," or "dry goods palace," they were grafting an old symbol to a new situation, suggesting the simultaneously leveling ("every man a king") and uplifting effects of democratic society and commercially derived money.

The second symbol that was transplanted into the commercial sphere was the parlor, the site of formal social ceremony in the household and the room that most clearly bespoke the notion of gentility—of personal cultivation in appearance, etiquette, and education. The commercial parlor represented the commercialization of the concept of gentility, and its presence in commercial "palaces" may explain why the aristocratic version of parlor decor was preferred.

The significant commercialization of the artifacts associated with gentility began in the eighteenth century. More refined personal dress was the first element to become accessible across a broader social spectrum, but the tasteful furnishings and the rooms that constituted the stage set of the beau monde of cultivated people became the focus of middle-class attention in the first decades of the nineteenth century. Middle-class gentility also required appropriate settings in which to express itself, settings such as parlors. Evidence is beginning to emerge that suggests that the parlors in the best hotels were locations for entertainment and social ceremony, for guests, residents, and outsiders; they were a commercial version of the beau monde. At the same time, ladies parlors in particular provided a domestic haven which buffered their interactions with the broader public in commercial spaces, as well as providing an interim solution for a young society which was still looking for a "place" (in both the psychological and the spatial sense) for women in the public sphere. Finally, because anyone with the money and desire could create a commercial parlor, as photographers did, anyone could attempt to imply membership in the world of refinement and cultivation.

Americans experienced difficulties in controlling the uses of the public parlor, because it was open to such uncultivated individuals as tobacco chewers and ill-behaved photographers' clients. They also expressed ambivalence about the effects some commercial parlors had on domestic life, since new members of the middle classes seemed to relish parlor life, even in hotels, over a sparser yet more private domestic environment.

Still, commercial parlors served almost undoubtedly to stimulate demand for parlor furnishings in private households of the new members of the middle classes. In a world that provided few models for interior decor, commercial parlors introduced people to the "vocabulary"—the forms of furniture, carpets, draperies, and wall decoration for the parlor—as well as to the nuances of that vocabulary—matching color schemes and the use of certain woods, fabrics, and, as Jonathan Slick discovered, even the newest techniques of upholstery construction. Public parlors both expressed the aspirations of commercializing American society and provided models for the aspirations of new participants in Victorian culture, creating demand by priming the consumer imagination during the first decades of public-parlor making.

At Rest

Victorian Death Furniture

Ellen Marie Snyder

As urban centers grew in the nineteenth century, city dwellers lost touch with the intimacy of former small communities. Those whom they passed on the street were most often strangers. And in death, rituals of dying and mourning were no longer community events, but became private, family ones. In order to express beliefs publicly and tie into prevailing cultural norms, Victorians used an elaborate set of practices and objects that quickly became widely accepted and mass produced. This paper is a study of a body of such diverse goods. What I identify as Victorian death furniture—coffins, grave beds, graveside seats, and vacant chairs— was linked by common beliefs about death and the role of the deceased. Involving changing concepts about religion, the need to express properly true Christian gentility, domesticity, and the role of memory, death furniture was the creation of a largely Protestant, urban, northern, middle-class, white audience.[1] It offers a graphic illustration of prevailing Victorian attitudes about life, death, and the afterlife.

[1] Kenneth L. Ames, "Ideologies in Stone: Meanings in Victorian Gravestones," *Journal of Popular Culture* 14, no. 4 (Spring 1981): 641–56. Karen Halttunen, *Confidence Men and Painted Women: A Study of Middle-Class Culture in America, 1830–1870* (New Haven and London: Yale University Press, 1982), p. 124. I use the term *Victorian* as Daniel Walker Howe describes it in *Victorian America* (Philadelphia: University of Pennsylvania Press, 1976), pp. 8–13. Not all of those living in America during the nineteenth century were Victorians. In general, *Victorian* encompasses Protestants, but also extends to Catholics and Jews; it largely characterizes a new urban middle class, but can also be applied to other classes; and most of its spokesmen were northerners. For several good essays on the role of mourning in Victorian America, see Martha V. Pike and Janice Gray Armstrong, *A Time to Mourn: Expressions of Grief in Nineteenth-Century America* (New York: Museums at Stony Brook, 1980).

Victorian death furniture was the direct product of a Victorian ideology which held that the dead did not die but rested and slept. "It is not death to die / To leave this weary road, / And 'mid the brotherhood on high / To be at home with God," wrote the popular late nineteenth-century minister Theodore L. Cuyler in *Beulah-Land; or, Words of Cheer for Christian Pilgrims,* quoting George W. Bethune. Cuyler believed that Bethune's bit of poetry put forth "the right way for a redeemed child of Christ to think and to speak about dying." During the second half of the nineteenth century, mainstream Protestantism moved away from the Puritan concept of predestination and salvation for a few lucky elect, as its concern with numbers and popularity overtook its former emphasis on doctrine and issues. Hoping to retain its power through increased attendance, the clergy relaxed old standards of entry into the church. The creed of American Protestants—liberal, sentimental, and softened—meant that grace had fewer strings and heaven more openings. Those who died in Christ did not die, but slept eternally, assured of an afterlife with Jesus. This religious atmosphere was complemented by more secular beliefs as well, leading to what Charles O. Jackson calls a change in vision. "Increasingly, death was perceived within a context of attachment to life as well as some disquieting uncertainty about the future of the dead." As the living became "less willing to conclude their relationship with the deceased," writes Jackson, they "would seek comfort through a substantial reduction in social distance between the living world and the dead world."[2] This reduction was achieved in part by language, as the words *sleep* and *rest* were used again and again as Victorian metaphors for death.

Sleep itself was seen as a state midway between life and death. In Julian Cramer's 1850 poem "On a Sleeping Wife," the poet watches his slumbering spouse and notes, "the features of that state / Dividing death from life." Sleep was perceived as an escape. And in a Victorian

---

[2] Theodore Cuyler, *Beulah-Land; or, Words of Cheer for Christian Pilgrims* (New York: American Tract Society, 1896), p. 191; Ann Douglas, *The Feminization of American Culture* (New York: Avon Books, 1977), pp. 6, 17–19, 162–67; Charles O. Jackson, "'Reaching for the Choir Invisible': The Nineteenth Century," in *Passing: The Vision of Death in America,* ed. Charles O. Jackson (Westport, Conn.: Greenwood Press, 1977), pp. 61–64. It is significant that another example of reducing the distance between this world and the next, spiritualism, became somewhat popular in the United States during the 1850s and 1860s, peaking around 1870 "when the movement claimed eleven million adherents." Spiritualists believed that living mediums could "make contact with the spirit world" (Sydney E. Ahlstrom, *A Religious History of the American People* [New Haven: Yale University Press, 1972], pp. 488–90).

consumer society that embodied the worldliness that Puritan ministers had condemned years before, the escape was a road away from worldliness to a pure haven. "How sweet her slumber!" wrote Cramer of his wife. "None but those / Whom heaven hath numbered for its bliss / Have promise of such calm response—/ Such perfect rest—as this. / Unconscious of the woes and cares / That weigh us down in waking hours." In "The Land of Dreams" by William C. Bryant, living dreamers and the deceased meet and mingle in a shadowy halfway world. "A mighty realm is the land of dreams," writes the poet; there "The souls of the happy dead repair / From their bowers of light to that bordering land, / And walk in the fainter glory there, / With the souls of the living, hand in hand."[3]

Gravestone epitaphs resonate this nineteenth-century belief in death as sleep. Such stock phrases as "At Rest," "Not Dead but Gone Before," and "Farewell my wife and children dear / I am not dead but sleeping here" appear frequently on Victorian stones. Cuyler, author of various late nineteenth-century mourning manuals, noted in *God's Light on Dark Clouds* that the most popular tombstone inscription was "Asleep in Jesus," and "No scriptural description of death is so suggestive as that which is conveyed by the familiar word *sleep*."[4]

According to Victorian literature and graphics, the commonest stage for the Victorian death was the bed (probably seconded only by the battlefield). The deathbed could be any bed, plain or ornate, but above all it was sacrosanct space. It assumed its ritual significance as a person passed from life to afterlife upon its sheets. Frequently hopefully it was a scene of revelation and instruction as well as farewell, drawing survivors together to learn from a moving death. Like other illustrations of the genre, a view of Charles Sumner's deathbed shows his colleagues clustered around him, leaning toward his face as if to hear him utter any stirring last words (fig. 1). Lyman Beecher described the death of a cholera-stricken seminary student as related to him by a Mr. Weld of that school. He portrays the bed as a doorway to eternal life, not as an entranceway to death. Wrote Weld to Beecher: "His last words were, addressing me as I was bending over him, 'Brother, I feel as if I was

[3]Julian Cramer, "On a Sleeping Wife," *Godey's Lady's Book* 40, no. 3 (March 1850): 220; William C. Bryant, "The Land of Dreams," *Brooklyn Daily Eagle and Kings County Democrat*, December 18, 1847, p. 2.
[4]Theodore L. Cuyler, *God's Light on Dark Clouds* (New York: Baker and Taylor Co., 1882), pp. 164, 163.

Fig. 1. Theo. R. Davis, "The Death of Charles Sumner." From *Harper's Weekly* 18, no. 901 (April 4, 1874): 292. (Winterthur Library.)

beginning to die. Don't you think I am?' 'Yes, my dear brother. Your Father calls you.' 'Yes, he calls me—yes, I am beginning to die. Oh, blessed be God through Jesus Christ, I am beginning to live!' " The Reverend Cuyler wrote that the suitable deathbed—such as the one witnessed by Weld—was a tranquil one. According to Cuyler, the bed— a "transformed" piece of furniture—was an instrument of passage to a Christian afterworld. "To a genuine Christian few things in life are less painful than life's close," he wrote. "Death is very often a slow fading out of the faculties, like the coming of a tranquil twilight."[5]

Thus Victorians who died passed from sleep to death in a kind of sanctified suspended animation. Theoretically, nothing changed for the deceased, and it was important to arrange for them an appearance that best resembled the peace and calm of sleep. "After being properly laid out," commented one journalist in "The Remains of John Brown" (1859), "the deceased looks as though he had sunk into a quiet sleep." In order to preserve the body and, in the process, the look of sleep, ice, corpse preservers, and embalming fluids were often used. Sold under such names as "Oriental" and "Crane's Electro Dynamic Mummifier," embalming fluids were originally developed primarily for medical reasons (fig. 2). However, they were repeatedly celebrated by morticians for their ability to return the lifelike look of the deceased. Not widely popular until the 1880s and 1890s, by the 1920s almost all bodies were embalmed. Revealing an Egyptianlike desire to preserve the corpse and an emphasis on appearances, embalming preserved the visual memory of the deceased. It was essential, reasoned one nineteenth-century writer, because "the memory of our dear departed being always associated with our last look upon them, it is preferable to have their last appearance free from the pallor of death."[6]

---

[5] Lewis O. Saum, "Death in the Popular Mind of Pre–Civil War America," in *Death in America*, ed. David Stannard (Philadelphia: University of Pennsylvania Press, 1975), pp. 30–48; Douglas, *Feminization of Culture*, p. 240; Charles Beecher, ed., *Autobiography, Correspondence, etc. of Lyman Beecher, D. D.* (New York: Harper and Brothers, 1865), p. 315; Cuyler, *Beulah-Land*, pp. 191–92.

[6] "The Remains of John Brown in New York—Interesting Particulars," *Brooklyn Evening Star*, December 5, 1859, p. 2; Robert W. Habenstein and William M. Lamers, *The History of American Funeral Directing* (rev. ed.; Milwaukee: Bulfin Printers, 1962), pp. 340–48; James J. Farrell, *Inventing the American Way of Death, 1830–1920* (Philadelphia: Temple University Press, 1980), p. 159; "The Spread of Embalming. The Public Waking Up to Its Importance," *Sunnyside* 4, no. 30 (January 1, 1888): 1.

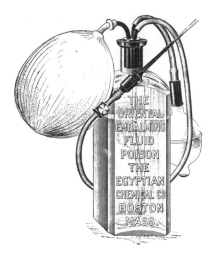

Fig. 2. The New Wagner Injector. From *Sunnyside* 4, no. 35 (June 1, 1888): n.p. (Winterthur Library.)

The sleeping body found final repose in a bedlike container: the coffin. Before the undertaking business became totally specialized in the late nineteenth century, cabinetmakers frequently crafted, or had on order from manufacturers, caskets in addition to their regular furniture line (fig. 3). Available in a wide variety of styles by midcentury, caskets often resembled elaborate parlor furniture—wooden on the outside and generously tufted on the inside. For instance, the Crane casket, pictured in an 1867 catalogue, was available "Lined, Full Satin," or "Lined, Full Merino," in sixteen sizes ranging from 29 inches long by 9½ inches wide to 80½ inches long by 23 inches wide (fig. 4). In an 1860 *Atlantic Monthly* article titled "A Day with the Dead," the unnamed author addresses this phenomenon. "Nothing in New York astonishes visitors from the country so much as the magnificent coffin-shops, rivalling, in the ostentatious and tempting display of their wares, the most elegant stores on Broadway. Model coffins, of the latest style and pattern, are set up on end in long rows and protected by splendid showcases, with the lids removed to exhibit their rich satin lining. Fancy coffins, decorated with glittering ornaments, are placed seductively in bright plate-glass windows, and put out for baiting advertisements upon the side-walks." With dry humor, he speculates on the future of the trend. "Why, I expect in a year or two to see coffins introduced into the parlors of the Fifth Avenue," he wrote, "and to find them, when their

A. C. CHAMBERLIN,
CABINET MANUFACTURER
AND
UNDERTAKER.

Bureaus, Tables, Sofas, Sofa Beds, Chairs, Bedsteads, and Mattresses
Of all kinds.

FEATHERS, of the first quality.

As I have now made complete arrangements for the prosecution of the Undertaking business in all its branches, I intend to make it a prominent part of my business, and therefore hold myself ready at all times, by day or night, to do any thing which the friends of the dead shall require.

A COFFIN WAREROOM,
In which are full sets of Mahogany, Black Walnut, Cherry, and Whitewood Coffins. Also,

METALLIC AIR-TIGHT BURIAL CASES,

At prices for full sizes from $22 to $30. Those of silver trimmings, cloth covered, &c., at a higher price.

SHROUDS, of various styles, constantly on hand.

The subscriber having had much experience in the Undertaking business, would most respectfully solicit a share in this branch of business, by those who are called to give patronage to the Undertaker.

Warerooms, No. 68 Orange Street. Dwelling House, Park Place, east side, first house south of George Street.

A. C. CHAMBERLIN.

Fig. 3. Advertisement for A. C. Chamberlin, cabinet manufacturer and undertaker. From J. H. Benham, *Benham's New Haven Directory and Annual Advertiser, 1853–1854* (New Haven, 1853), p. 270. (Winterthur Library.)

owners fail . . . advertised for sale at auction, with the rest of the household furniture, at a great sacrifice on the original cost. 'ONE SUPERB COFFIN OF ELEGANT PATTERN AND SUPERIOR WORKMANSHIP, AS GOOD AS NEW. TWO DITTO, SLIGHTLY DAMAGED.' " He prophesied that the fashion would eventually "trickle down" to the masses and that elegant coffins would become "popular with the less aristocratic portion of the community." He imagined that one would see "crowds of servant girls

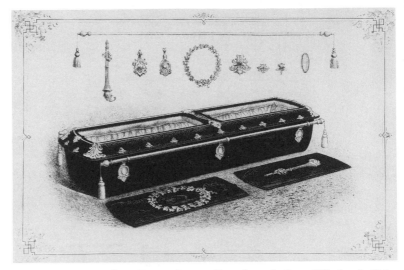

Fig. 4. Crane casket. From Crane, Breed, and Co., *Wholesale Price List of Patent Metallic Burial Cases and Caskets, Hearses, Name Plates and Handles, Plumes & Sockets, Etc.* (Cincinnati and New York, 1867), p. [25]. (Winterthur Library.)

and street-loungers around the windows of our magnificent coffin-bazaars, and hear from them such exchanges as these: 'Oh! Do look here, Matilda! Wouldn't you like to have such a nice coffin as that!' or, 'What a dear sweet sarcophagus that one is there!' or 'Faith, I should like to own that air-tight!' "[7]

The author was not totally off the mark. Manufacturers, furniture dealers, and undertakers—what one newspaper called "dealer[s] in death's furnishings"—marketed coffins that not only looked good, or promised to preserve and protect well, but also were extraordinarily bedlike and reflected the size, status, sex, and age of the occupant. Children's caskets were small and white, for purity (fig. 5); those for adults were larger and generally came in different hues. In one of their advertisements,

[7] Crane, Breed, & Co., *Wholesale Price List of Patent Metallic Burial Cases and Caskets, Hearses, Name Plates and Handles, Plumes & Sockets, Etc.* (Cincinnati and New York, 1867), p. 6; "A Day with the Dead," *Atlantic Monthly* 6, no. 35 (September 1860): 326–42, quotations pp. 338–39.

Fig. 5. Children's elliptic-end, covered caskets. From National Casket Co., *Catalogue A* (Buffalo, N.Y., 1891), p. 101. (Winterthur Library.)

New York and Brooklyn Casket Company noted the trend of "delicate colors used for Children, and snowy satins for Brides." And they reminded buyers, "the stately 'SENATOR' and the magnificent 'GOVERNOR' . . . are intended only *for Men*—from the MASSIVE GRANDEUR OF THEIR PRO-PORTIONS." Their "Governor casket," illustrated in the June 1888 issue of the undertakers' journal, *Sunnyside*, is lauded by the company as the only suitable receptacle for "great men" (fig. 6). "Very grand and truly beautiful caskets have been provided for OUR GREAT MEN, as one by one they have 'wrapped the drapery of their couch about them and lain them down to pleasant dreams,' " they wrote, "but it has been given to THE NEW YORK AND BROOKLYN COFFIN COMPANY to place upon the market the noblest conception of such a couch, and to embody in richest material the ideas which such a last resting place should convey." Stein Manufacturing Company of Rochester, New York, and Boston adver-tised, "[We] Are the Only Firm in the World who manufacture a com-plete line of Caskets adapted to every age and condition of life." Indeed, their April 1, 1888, advertisement in *Sunnyside* listed casket trade names under headings that corresponded to stages of life: "Caskets for the Infants," "For the Schoolboys," "For the Lovers," "For the Soldiers," "For the Justice," and "For the Aged." The "Duchess," no doubt intended for a

Fig. 6. Governor casket, New York and Brooklyn Coffin Co. From *Sunnyside* 4, no. 35 (June 1, 1888): n.p. (Winterthur Library.)

lady, came with the "Finest White Silk Brocade Body and Drapery" and a satin pillow (fig. 7).[8]

Fabrics, tufting, and pillows, like bed furnishings, lined coffins constructed of wood and metal. In an 1859 article on the particulars of abolitionist John Brown's death, the author makes a point of mentioning the absence of such features. "The body was dressed in the clothes Brown wore when executed—there was no pillow under the head, nor any sort of trimmings usually placed in coffins." Such seemingly requisite embellishments ranged from simple to elaborate. On a page entitled "Coffin and Casket Linings," Columbus Coffin Company illustrates options ranging from "11-inch Corded Mohair, Looped Apron, Velvet Bows, White Silk Trimming" to "8-inch Fancy Piqueteen, Embossed

[8] *Brooklyn Evening Star*, September 23, 1859, p. 2; *Sunnyside* 20, no. 2 (February 1, 1890): n.p.; *Sunnyside* 4, no. 35 (June 1, 1888): n.p.; *Sunnyside* 4, no. 33 (April 1, 1888): n.p.; National Casket Co., *Catalogue* A (Buffalo, N.Y., 1891), p. 81. The five major themes necessary to understanding the "historical development of coffin styling and composition," particularly in the nineteenth century, were "utility, status indication, preservation of the body, protection, and aesthetic representation" (Habenstein and Lamers, *History of Funeral Directing*, p. 262).

Fig. 7. Duchess full-circle-end, silk-brocade, draped casket. From National Casket Co., *Catalogue* A (Buffalo, N.Y., 1891), p. 81. (Winterthur Library.)

Spanish Satin Apron with Blue Silk Needle-work, Silk Trimming" (fig. 8). In their 1887 trade catalogue, Chappell, Chase, Maxwell, and Company offered "a very large line of the Richest Broadcloths, Silk Velvets, Silk Plushes, Plain and Brocaded Satins, in all shades, with Fringes, Tassels, &c., to match. Any casket in our list covered with these goods, to order, on short notice." The fabrics were available in such colors as "Baby Blue," "Peach Pink," "Lavender," "Steel Gray," "Cream," and "Purple."[9]

Interchangeable and highly ornamental hardware could be bought and added to caskets to individualize them further. Handles and bars for the sides of caskets came in a variety of styles and finishes (fig. 9). These could be matched with screws, moldings, tacks, and other hardware bearing the same or different design motif. Shields, or plates, derived from the silver, wooden, and glass coffin plates of the eighteenth and

[9]"Remains of John Brown," p. 2; "Price List of Burial Caskets, Pedestals, Robes, Wrappers, Linings, Hardware, &c.," as shown in the *Eighth Illustrated Catalogue and Supplement Issues by Chappell, Chase, Maxwell, & Company* (Oneida, N.Y., 1887), pp. 4, 14.

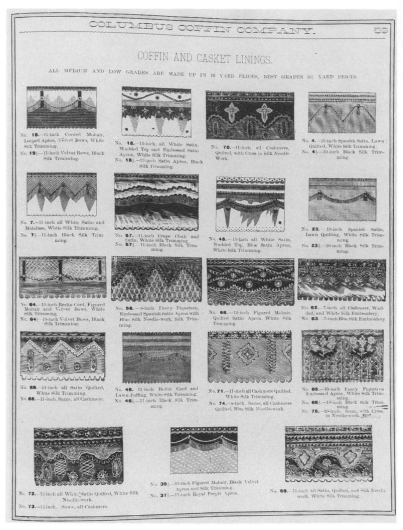

Fig. 8. Coffin and casket linings. From Columbus Coffin Co., *Illustrated Catalogue of Wood and Cloth Covered Coffins and Caskets, Undertakers' Hardware and Sundries, Robes, Linings, and General Supplies* (Columbus, Ohio, 1882), p. 59. (Winterthur Library.)

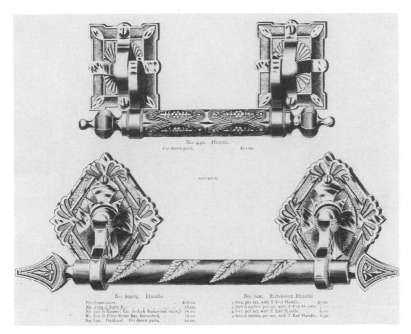

No. 440. Handle.
Per dozen pairs, $11.00.

PATENTED.

No. 600½. Handle.
Per dozen pairs, $18.00.
No. 1199 is Satin Bar,   18.00.
No. 500 is Enamel Bar, (a dark Rosewood color,) 18.00.
No. 600 is Plain Silver Bar, Burnished,   15.00.
No. 600. Oxidized. Per dozen pairs,   22.00.

No. 600. Extension Handle.
3 feet, per set, with T End Handle. $5.00.
3 feet 6 inches per set with T End Handle,   5.00.
4 feet, per set, with T End Handle,   6.00.
4 feet 6 inches, per set, with T End Handle,   6.50.

Fig. 9. "Fine electro silver plated" casket handles. From Meriden Britannia Co., *Illustrated Catalogue and Descriptive Price List of Wm. M. Smith's Fine Silver, Bronze, Gold Plated and Oxidized Silver Casket Trimmings* (West Meriden, Conn., 1880), p. 13. (Winterthur Library.)

early nineteenth centuries were also available. These mass-produced plates adapted an old form to a generic format, allowing consumers to choose from an assortment of types and inscriptions (fig. 10).

Instead of a traditional, loose, ill-fitting shroud, the well-dressed Victorian deceased could wear clothing specifically designed for death. Manufacturers described such wear in bedchamber terms. "The manufacture of proper Habiliments for the dead is a special feature of our business," proclaimed H. E. Taylor and Company in its 1879 trade catalogue. "Our Robes are well and liberally made, and are of good value."[10] The garments shown here are fairly elaborate examples of

[10] H. E. Taylor and Co., *Robes and Linings* (Hadlyme, Conn., 1884), p. 189.

Fig. 10. "Fine electro silver plated" casket shields. From Meriden Britannia Co., *Illustrated Catalogue and Descriptive Price List of Wm. M. Smith's Fine Silver, Bronze, Gold Plated and Oxidized Silver Casket Trimmings* (West Meriden, Conn., 1880), p. 43. (Winterthur Library.)

women's dress (fig. 11). Corresponding menswear closely resembles formal tuxedos.

All these trappings helped to make the casket a more familiar object and made the deceased within seem more a part of the living world than the dead. Fancy casings and dressings also showed others that proper sentiment had been used in caring for the deceased. Expounded one

Fig. 11. Ladies' burial robes. From H. E. Taylor and Co., *Robes and Linings* (Hadlyme, Conn., 1884), p. 14. (Winterthur Library.)

casket dealer, "Why, the Burial Art to-day EXISTS on Sentiment! The very word ART implies it. For if there were not The Sentiment of Love! The Sentiment of Religion! The Sentiment of Grief! we should thrust the bodies of our friends into rough boxes, and the Manufacturers of Caskets would be an *unknown quantity in modern civilization!*" Elaborately dressed caskets that looked like overstuffed parlor furniture and were in the form of beds helped the bereaved to become more comfortable with their beloved's transition to the next world. But the practices themselves caused at least one writer to ask in 1860, "Are we not, in this class of our tastes and feelings, becoming rapidly Egyptianized?"[11]

Ultimately the dead found their "final rest" in the cemetery. The Victorian rural cemetery offered the dead an abode intended as a place of "leisure and gentle assurance for the living," far different than many earlier church graveyards of the eighteenth century, which by the nineteenth century were often crowded and unkempt. The new rural cemetery, located at a distance from the city center, was designed as a healthy alternative to the graveyard and a refuge from the world of business. It was a place where one kind of bed and one kind of home were exchanged for another. For while far from the home itself, the Victorian rural cemetery nonetheless bore a layout that reflected "the ideology of domesticity and an emphasis on family," particularly in its use of enclosures around family plots and the layout of plots with graves surround-

[11] *Sunnyside* 20, no. 2 (February 1, 1890): n.p.; "Day with the Dead," p. 338.

ing family monuments.[12] But perhaps the clearest effort to establish a home in the cemetery was the use of stone beds and iron, wooden, and stone seats.

Single grave enclosures, or "beds"—some no more than simple low surrounds—furthered the thought that the deceased was sleeping. Stone, and sometimes wooden, surrounds delineated the shape of the coffin which lay in the ground beneath.[13] Most elaborate were the grave beds with low sides, low footstones, and raised headstones. The name used to describe them in period literature—"French Beds"—is derived from wooden furniture of the same name (fig. 12). The stone model shown here is called a French scrolled bed in Richard Wathan's 1875 catalogue, *Monumental and Headstone Designs* (fig. 13). The centers of these enclosures were planted with flowers or greenery. What appears to be an example from Wathan's catalogue still bears traces of greenery within its slightly sunken sides (fig. 14). With their raised headboard- and footboard-type ends and low sides, such objects clearly replicated the massive beds frequently used in the bedroom at home.

The belief that the dead slept in beds is most graphically expressed by children's grave furniture. Occasionally the French beds used by adults appear in miniature for children. But more often those stones that use furniture motifs employ startlingly realistic beds replete with slumbering infants. Some of these beds contain one or two children who sleep on top of the gravestone; the Groots, brother and sister, clasp

[12] Jackson, *Passing*, p. 62; Ames, "Ideologies in Stone," p. 653. One author wrote: "The advantages of rural cemeteries are so obvious, that a large city which did not have several of them within easy access, would be deemed uncivilized. Indeed we may go farther and say that it is now considered quite as essential in the arrangement of our social life (certainly in this land), to own a burial plot in the country, as to own any kind of property in the city" *(The Loved and the Lost* [New York, 1856], p. 49).

[13] It is difficult to determine just how many cemetery "beds" and furniture were used in the nineteenth century, since many cemetery owners have removed them in recent times to facilitate mowing. Additionally, chairs and settees have fallen prey to age and vandals. However, the survival of many examples to this day, along with their mention in period literature, trade catalogues, and appearance in old photographs, clearly shows their use by middle-class Victorians. Terry Jordan is one of the few historians to look at the phenomenon of grave surrounds. He studied the use of grave curbings by Texas Hispanics and Germans in the early twentieth century and concluded that Germans used curbings to indicate visually that "each burial is an entity unto itself" and as outlets for "craftsmen to display their skills at working wood and stone" (Terry G. Jordan, *Texas Graveyards: A Cultural Legacy* [Austin: University of Texas Press, 1982], p. 96). While it is true that curbings and surrounds do appear frequently in Hispanic and German plots, even in the North, their use by others, even earlier, clearly commands deeper explanations for their use.

Fig. 12. French bedstead. From Blackie and Son's, *The Victorian Cabinetmaker's Assistant* (London, 1853; reprint, New York: Dover Publications, 1970), pl. 77. (Winterthur Library.)

Fig. 13. French scroll bed gravestone. From Richard Wathan, *Monumental and Head Stone Designs* (New York: by the author, 1875), t.p. (Winterthur Library.)

Fig. 14. French-bed-type gravestone of George Fernald (d. 1855) and Mary A. Fernald (d. 1863), Green-Wood Cemetery, Brooklyn, N.Y., ca. 1855–63. Marble; H. 54″, W. 30½″, D. 87½″. (Photo, Ellen Marie Snyder.)

each other upon a bed complete with sheets, a pillow, and a fringed spread (fig. 15). Other beds are part of the interior of the stone, while still others are vacant. Three such examples poignantly evoke the presence of the dead babe. On a tiny bed unmarked except for the word GRACE and a symbolic broken flower, sheets of stone are drawn back as if waiting for the child's entry (fig. 16). In a similar format, sheets are drawn back, and pillows are full and fluffy (fig. 17). A baby, partly shrouded in clouds and reaching toward heaven, indicates the fate of the child who has died. Next to the marker is another bed, occupied by mother and child (whose sculptured marble head is missing after years of erosion). In Mount Auburn Cemetery, an uncannily realistic stone bassinet bears the name of the dead infant on its ruffled pillow (fig. 18).

This clearly domestic furniture expresses the children's own strong domestic ties. Dying before they had the chance to grow up, leave the home, and venture into the world of business, they were, in nineteenth-century liberal ideological terms, untainted beings in an impure world. In "Heaven Our Home," Ann Douglas identifies the dying children in mid nineteenth-century consolation literature as "guides to their adult

Fig. 15. Reclining children on bed gravestone of William P. Groot (d. 1849) and Lydia Groot (d. 1846), New York cemetery, ca. 1849. Marble; H. 20½″, W. 14″, D. 20¼″. (Photo, Ellen Marie Snyder.)

Fig. 16. Bed gravestone, New York cemetery, ca. 1849. Marble; H. 10″, W. 11¼″, D. 18″. (Photo, Ellen Marie Snyder.)

Fig. 17. Mother and child in bed and empty bed gravestones of Mary Louisa Hawley Whitlock (d. 1840) and Sarah Louisa Hawley Whitlock (d. 1831?), Green-Wood Cemetery, Brooklyn, N.Y., ca. 1831–40. Marble; mother and child: H.70½", W. 29", D. 60"; empty bed: H. 34", W. 22", D. 42". (Photo, Ellen Marie Snyder.)

supervisors." The stock, lifelike markers with children which manufacturers produced often functioned first as information bearers, looking much like ordinary inscribed stones. But the sleeping babes atop these monuments obliquely set them apart from their adult counterparts (fig. 19). The small beds were dramatic visual statements; visitors who passed by had much to learn from their small forms.[14]

    Children's deaths served to remind worldly people of purity. "Sanctified by death," wrote the Reverend John H. Morison in 1842, they were "angel teachers, calling us away from our worldly thoughts to the purity, humility, and submissive, affectionate trust, through which they have entered, and through which alone, by the mercy of God, we can enter, into the Kingdom of heaven." To Morison, as to many others of his time, they were the only pure beings who could truly touch hearts and evoke sincere emotions. "Blessed ministers of God's love . . .

[14] Ann Douglas, "Heaven Our Home: Consolation Literature in the Northern United States, 1830–1880," in Stannard, *Death in America*, p. 57.

Fig. 18. Bassinet gravestone of Mary Wigglesworth (d. 1884), Mount Auburn Cemetery, Cambridge, Mass., ca. 1884. Marble; H. 32″, W. 20″, D. 37″. (Photo, Ellen Marie Snyder.)

Fig. 19. Child's gravestone. From Robert Wood and Co., *Portfolio of Original Designs of Ornamental Iron Work of Every Description* (Philadelphia, [1870]), p. 163. (Winterthur Library.)

lent just long enough to touch our dearest feelings, and then with-
drawn;—shall they not lift up our desires and affections to that pure
world, of which while here they were the purest emblems, and to which
they are now gone?" Children looked forever young and pure in the
cemetery, as they did in the minds of their loved ones. "They who have
lost a child in infancy, have a child which shall not grow old," assured
Morison. "No change is there. Its countenance is not hardened into the
rigid features of the man, but remains always the countenance of a
child; Eternity has there fixed its seal."[15]

"Deriving from longstanding Protestant anxieties about commercial prosperity," what T. J. Jackson Lears identifies as a Victorian "nostalgia for childish innocence," was thus translated into literal, physical
representations: furniture filled by sleeping babes.[16] Asleep in beds like
those in their parents' homes, children were best suited to evoke the
goodness of the domestic world and heaven beyond. In a nineteenth-
century Protestant culture which interpreted the religious fight as a struggle
to attain purity, they represented a battle fought and won.

Grave beds visually conveyed the Victorian belief that the tomb
was more than a repository for physical remains. A new emphasis on
memory and a belief in an immortal soul transformed the gravesite into
a place to go to remember, pray, and mourn: a scene of powerful emo-
tions where the dead could be mentally revived. "Where is it, indeed,
that the heart is likely to be so feelingly moved, or the memory to be so
powerfully roused, as at a parent's grave or at a sister's tomb?" rhetori-
cally asked the author of *Necropolis Glasguensis* in J. Jay Smith's 1846
Designs for Monuments. And Cuyler wrote of the plot as a familial
home away from home: "When I am visiting my beautiful plot in peer-
less 'Greenwood' I often forecast the inevitable hour when my earthly
vesture shall be laid down beside those of my beloved children in our
family bed-room—'asleep in Jesus.' "[17]

[15] John H. Morison, *A Sermon . . . Preached before the First Congregational Society
in New Bedford, Sunday Morning, November 27, 1842* (New Bedford, Mass.: Press of
Benjamin Lindsey, 1842), pp. 16, 11.

[16] T. J. Jackson Lears, *No Place of Grace: Antimodernism and the Transformation of
American Culture, 1880–1920* (New York: Pantheon Books, 1981), p. 146.

[17] Philippe Ariès, *The Hour of Our Death* (New York: Vintage Books, 1982), p. 526;
J. Jay Smith, *Designs for Monuments and Mural Tablets. Adapted to Rural Cemeteries,
Church Yards, Churches, and Chapels. With a Preliminary Essay on the Laying Out,
Planting and Managing of Cemeteries and on the Improvement of Church Yards, on the
Basis of Loudon's Work* (New York: Bartlett and Welford, 1846), p. 6; Cuyler, *Beulah-
Land*, p. 190.

Fig. 20. Trade card of J. C. Chandler, proprietor of Newton Marble Works, ca. 1890. (Winterthur Library.)

Places in which the grieving could mourn properly, in appropriate surroundings, were considered mandatory for true, sincere Victorians. Proper mourning, like dress and polite social conduct, was equated with good character. Unkempt cemeteries indicated a lack of gentility and, even worse, the presence of the hypocrisy so strongly condemned by Victorians. In a stock illustration, used here on a trade card (fig. 20), the "REMEMBERED," and hence "good" plot is one that is in the form of a family plot—enclosed, well manicured, and replete with prominent marble grave markers. One of the markers is a French-bed type, strategically placed near the steps and central path, much as a bedroom might be placed in a house, to the rear of the threshold and off a central hallway. One mid nineteenth-century book condemned any graveyard that did not have space for "benches where the mourner may sit and meditate upon the 'loved and the lost.' "[18]

Cemetery chairs and settees helped mourners to grieve, becoming visible signs that the dead were indeed remembered. An illustration of a woman seated in a small iron chair, next to a tomb, appears in a variety of nineteenth-century sources, including cards of memorial verse and a tomb catalogue (fig. 21). The chair she sits in adds visual importance to the small image: it implies that her visit is not short and perfunctory, but deliberate and, perhaps, lengthy, since she must sit. Set

[18] Halttunen, *Confidence Men and Painted Women*, pp. 134–35; *Loved and Lost*, p. 48.

Fig. 21. Seated woman and child at graveside. From Crane, Breed, and Co., *Wholesale Price List of Patent Metallic Burial Cases and Caskets, Hearses, Name Plates and Handles, Plumes & Sockets, Etc.* (Cincinnati and New York, 1867), facing p. 26. (Winterthur Library.)

by the sides of graves and within family plots, they transferred a familiar domestic quality to the cemetery. When mourners placed seats near the "sleeping deceased," it became possible for them to reenact repeatedly the deathbed scene. In an 1856 guidebook to Brooklyn's Cypress Hill Cemetery, the author wrote that most of the enclosures in the cemetery "are surrounded by costly fences with iron or stone posts. Within are iron seats wrought in a graceful pattern, upon which mourners may sit and weep over the grave."[19]

The cast-iron Gothic settee depicted in figure 22 is probably similar to the one described by the Cypress Hill commentator. Iron furniture was particularly well suited to the cemetery because it could withstand the elements if cared for properly. Also used in gardens and on porches, it could be purchased in styles that resembled parlor furniture used in

[19] *Loved and Lost*, p. 63.

Fig. 22. Cemetery plot with Gothic cast-iron settee. From Stewart Iron Works Co., *Iron Reservoir Vases Catalogue No. S* (Cincinnati, Ohio, [1910]), back cover. (Winterthur Library.)

the home. Or it could look quite naturalistic, drawing on organic motifs.[20] But iron was only one of many kinds of seats that graced graves and plots. Stone seats, fairly durable as well, also drew on the natural world. Branchlike legs support the serpents and leaves adorning one example (fig. 23). A wooden rustic chair, such as one from an unidentified cemetery (probably in New York) (fig. 24), was hardly as durable and seems to have been less popular than more lasting seats.

All these seats, large and small, iron and wood, ultimately served as symbols. They represented not only the home but also the presence of mourners, even when no mourners were present. In a culture that exalted sentiment and stressed appearances, these chairs visually told others that mourners did indeed come to visit the grave.

Thus grave beds and cemetery furniture helped to make the cemetery less mysterious, more understandable, more comfortable, and more

[20] For a discussion of cast-iron furniture in cemeteries, see Ellen Marie Snyder, "Victory over Nature: Victorian Cast-Iron Seating Furniture," *Winterthur Portfolio* 20, no. 4 (Winter 1985): 238–41.

Fig. 23. Stone sofa, Green-Wood Cemetery, Brooklyn, N.Y., ca. 1865–85. Marble; H. 25″, W. 59″, D. 15″. (Photo, Ellen Marie Snyder.)

Fig. 24. Cemetery plot, with rustic chair (left), probably New York. Photo, ca. 1862. (Brooklyn Historical Society.)

Fig. 25. Child's chair gravestone, Green-Wood Cemetery, Brooklyn, N.Y., ca. 1850–65. Marble; H. 23″, W. 13½″, D. 14½″. (Photo, Ellen Marie Snyder.)

like the middle-class American world of the living. Their domestic con-notations created direct links to the Victorian heaven, which was per-ceived as a domesticated sphere, a pure home better than the earthly one. "Oh we are happy now dear mother," sing small deceased children in Isaac Baker Woodbury's 1853 parlor song. "Would we come back, dear mother, and leave our glorious home? No! No! No!" they sing, "For though we love you dearly, from heav'n we would not roam."[21]

The use of death furniture came full circle in the "empty" or "vacant" furniture used to represent someone who had died. This genre of fur-niture served much the same function as the recreated domestic furni-ture of the cemetery. An unusual and disarmingly realistic child's chair in Green-Wood Cemetery is a Victorian tearjerker. Draped by a tiny coat and shoe, it evokes the lost babe who was the right size for it (fig. 25). But unlike this chair, the "empty chair" of nineteenth-century lit-erature was reserved for the homes of the living. Seats, beds, and cradles

[21] Isaac Baker Woodbury, "We Are Happy Now, Dear Mother; or, Heavenly Voices," from *Angels' Visits and Other Vocal Gems of Victorian America*, ed. Richard Jackson, New World Records 220, 1977, p. 3 of notes.

Fig. 26. Theo. R. Davis, "The Vacant Chair." From *Harper's Weekly* 18, no. 901 (April 4, 1874): 289. (Winterthur Library.)

were used as visual records of the dead. A draped armchair represents its deceased former occupant, Charles Sumner (fig. 26). Acting as magnets for their spirits, empty furniture brought the dead near, closing the gaps between the worlds of life and death and between heaven and home. Hovering spirits, especially those of children, thus extended the maternal sphere. In "Cradles Empty, Babys Gone," an empty cradle becomes a kind of memory transmitter for a baby now dead (fig. 27). Sings the mother: "Little empty cradle, treasured now with care, though thy precious burden it has fled. / Now we miss the locks of curly golden hair, Peeping from thy tiny snow-white bed; when the dimpled cheeks and little laughing eyes from the rumpled pillow shone; / Then I gazed with gladness, now I look and sigh; Empty is the cradle, Baby's gone."[22]

Similar sentiment is expressed in "The Vacant Chair," a poem published in 1850. The subject of the poem, Little Mary, has died. But

[22] Douglas, "Heaven Our Home," p. 62; *Cradles Empty, Babys Gone Songster, No. 112* (New York: Popular Publishing Co., 1883–90).

Fig. 27. *Cradles Empty, Babys Gone Songster*, No. *112* (New York: Popular Publishing Co., 1883–90), cover. (Shirley Sue Swaab: Photo, Helga Photo Studio.)

through her chair, she lives. "Oft we see her in our dreams," cry the bereaved family. "Then an angel one she seems! / But we oftener see her, where / Stands, unfilled, the vacant chair." In a poignant plea, they ask her spirit to return to the chair, which, in typical fashion, acts as an inanimate medium to the world beyond: "Little Mary! angel blest! / From thy blissful place of rest, / Look upon us, angel child, / Fill us with thy spirit mild. / Keep o'er us thy watchful care; / Often fill the vacant chair."[23]

[23] Richard Coe, Jr., "The Vacant Chair," *Godey's Lady's Book* 40, no. 1 (January 1850): 69.

Through memory, the empty chair could be filled. "THERE *is* no vacant chair," wrote Elizabeth Stuart Phelps. "To love is still / To have. Nearer to memory than to eye / . . . will / We hold him by our love, that shall not / die."[24]

The use of Victorian death furniture reflects a nineteenth-century American Protestant ideology in which judgment was suspended at death. Theoretically, when urban, northern Victorians died, they entered a world of sleep. The thin line between life and death became blurred. With this blurring came new sensibilities about the ways mourners could assist the deceased in their journey from the deathbed to the coffin, to the grave, and ultimately to heaven. In an effort to preserve the look of this world for a receptive next world, embalming fluids, clothing, and decorative, bedlike caskets were employed. Bedlike gravestones were produced. Often resembling the beds people died on, they assumed some of the deathbed's charged function. Like deathbeds, cemetery beds became places where people gathered to observe and mourn the passage of the dead, for beds—filled and empty—symbolized a physical presence. Mourners' chairs found a home in a domesticated cemetery because a religious ideology said there was still someone there to mourn, and the need to express Christian gentility was satisfied by this proper care of the grave. Furniture made the cemetery familiar and homelike in a changing world. In the home, where the vacant chair conjured up the presence of a long-gone loved one, it made memory tangible. Finally escaping to a world of purity from a world of worldliness, the Victorian dead found rest in heaven, and the furniture used by those left behind insured that they were dead—but not forgotten.

How a culture treats its dead reveals much about the role of its living. In Victorian America, an emphasis on religion, home, and appearances was reflected in a desire to project the trappings of home and life ever farther into the next world, slowly domesticating not only the cemetery but heaven as well and then bringing the dead back into the home through the power of the vacant chair. Ultimately the world of the dead became the mirror world of the living. As caskets became more elaborate and bedlike (fig. 28), as seats took on new styles (fig. 29), and as the metaphorical language of sleep and rest pervaded a cul-

[24] Elizabeth Stuart Phelps, *Songs of the Silent World* (Boston: Houghton Mifflin Co., 1885), pp. 11–13.

Fig. 28. Lucretia casket. From National Casket Co., *Catalogue M* (Buffalo, N.Y., 1911), n.p. (Winterthur Library.)

Fig. 29. Stone chair, West Laurel Hill Cemetery, Bala Cynwyd, Pa., ca. 1908. Granite; H. 36″, W. 31½″, D. 24½″. (Photo, Ellen Marie Snyder.)

ture, the Victorian legacy became so strong that in some ways it has persisted to the present. Today, the deathbed, vacant chair, and bedlike gravestone have lost both popularity and cultural significance, but the use of elaborate caskets and a general desire to preserve the look of sleep continues, cutting across economic, cultural, and religious backgrounds. What began as a Victorian practice has become, for many, an accepted way of life. [25]

[25] See, for example, Jessica Mitford, *The American Way of Death* (New York: Crest Books, 1964).

Furniture as Machinery
Nineteenth-Century Patent Rocking Chairs

David B. Driscoll

Even objects will become speech, if they mean something.
—Roland Barthes, *Mythologies* (1972)

Historically and symbolically, the rocking chair is a characteristically American artifact. Ellen and Bert Denker conclude their 1979 study, *The Rocking Chair Book,* with a discussion of the rocking chair as an icon of an idealized American past, symbolic of the stability and tranquility of a preindustrial, or perhaps extraindustrial, era. Nineteenth-century patent records, however, reveal an alternative tradition of rocking-chair design which viewed the rocker not as furniture, but as a machine. "Machine rocking chairs" were rockers arranged to operate some type of mechanical device, usually but not always a fan. Rocker-powered cradles, washing machines, butter churns, and other household equipment were also patented. No less "American" than ordinary rocking chairs, machine rockers embodied some of the fundamental contradictions and ambiguities of nineteenth-century America's notions of work, leisure, progress, and technology. [1]

The author thanks Kenneth L. Ames for his guidance in the early formulation of this paper and Eugene S. Ferguson for his perceptive critical reading of an earlier draft. The paper is stronger for each of their contributions.

[1] Ellen Denker and Bert Denker, *The Rocking Chair Book* (New York: Mayflower Books, 1979). For an invaluable history of the changing cultural definitions of such important words as *class* and *history,* as well as *work, progress,* and *technology,* see Raymond Williams, *Keywords: A Vocabulary of Culture and Society* (rev. ed.; New York: Oxford University Press, 1983).

When machine rockers have been noticed in print at all, they have been presented as amusing relics of a quaintly primitive age. This treatment may be partially explained by their lack of commercial success. Although evidence indicates that at least two of the dozens of machine rockers patented in the nineteenth century were actually offered for sale (fig. 1), the great majority were not.[2] Machine rockers have existed, primarily in the form of patent descriptions, drawings, and models, as the unrealized dreams of unknown inventors. Compared to such dramatically influential inventions as the telegraph or Bessemer steel, machine rockers have been understandably overlooked. The openly condescending attitude adopted in the literature on machine rockers, however, reveals a failure to understand the ways in which artifacts can inform us about the past.

Objects can be meaningful in two separate, although often overlapping, ways: in use and in thought. Telegraphs, uniforms, waiting rooms, theater tickets, and handcuffs actively define and facilitate social relationships; their importance is in their function as mediators. Others, like flags, gravestones, and crowns, are meaningful on a more abstract plane as well, as expressions of ideas, symbols of aspiration, or signifiers of rank. In both cases, the objects serve as a means of human communication.

Because machine rockers were never widely manufactured or used by large numbers of people, the specific influence they may have exerted in mediating relationships is beyond our speculation. In their existence as patent records, therefore, machine rockers must be considered primarily intellectual artifacts, whose significance lies in the attitudes they expressed rather than in the behavior they modified. Nevertheless,

---

[2] For examples of the treatment usually given unsuccessful patents, see Leonard de Vries, *Victorian Inventions* (New York: American Heritage Press, 1972); and A. E. Brown and H. A. Jeffcott, Jr., *Absolutely Mad Inventions* (1932; reprint, New York: Dover Publications, 1970). Both contain examples of machine rockers. An 1873 description of a rocker-powered household "motor" referred interested readers to the New York Exposition and Manufacturing Co. of New York City for further information ("A New Domestic Motor," *Scientific American*, n.s., 29, no. 8 [August 23, 1873]: 118), and nineteen years later Thomas Madden, Son, and Co. advertised "the Wonderful Pneumatic Chair, . . . a Chair that Fans You with Perfumed Breeze as You Rock." Neither of these chairs was notably successful; indeed, it is characteristic of the machine rocker's commercial failure that, although they had been patented repeatedly since 1827, Madden, Son, and Co. still refer to its chair as a "novelty." The author is indebted to Michael H. Knight for bringing this advertisement to his attention.

Fig. 1. The Wonderful Pneumatic Chair. Manufactured by Thomas Madden, Son, and Co., Indianapolis, Ind., 1892. From *Michigan Artisan* 12, no. 10 (April 1892): 67. (Winterthur Library.)

machine rockers were mechanical inventions, and the search for their meaning must begin with a mechanical analysis.

Considerable technical information exists on machine rockers. By law, patents have always required both drawings and a detailed written description of how the invention was supposed to work. Between 1836 and 1880 a working model was also required.[3] While patent records occasionally fail to provide all the information pertinent to an invention, the great majority convey both the mechanical principles used and the specific features claimed as novel. In the terms in which they are described and presented, little distinguishes machine rockers from contemporary types of patented machinery.

Franz Reuleaux, a leading nineteenth-century theoretician of machinery and founder of the science of kinematics, defined a machine as "a combination of resistant bodies so arranged that by their means the mechanical forces of nature can be compelled to do work accom-

---

[3] The patent model requirement was statutory until 1870 and continued within the Patent Office until 1880. For more information on the Patent Office, see P. J. Frederico, ed., "Outline of the History of the United States Patent Office," *Journal of the Patent Office Society* 18, no. 7 (July 1936): 3–234.

panied by certain determinate motions." Many concepts first formulated by Reuleaux, particularly those of the "kinematic pair" and the "fixed link," have become standard kinematic definitions, and his description of the machine the accepted one. According to Reuleaux's conception, a machine has four characteristics: it is an assemblage of parts, the parts resist each other, motion is constrained to a fixed path, and energy is transmitted to perform work.[4] The machine rocker fulfills all these criteria.

Machine rockers are composed of a number of moving parts that resist each other in operation (otherwise motion would not be transmitted from one part to the next). The machine rocker epitomizes Siegfried Giedion's observation: "The basic problem of patent furniture was above all a problem of motion. The Americans . . . drew upon an almost inexhaustible fantasy to solve the motion problem for furniture."[5] Machine rockers were indeed concerned with the problem of motion, and the variety of mechanisms they employed to operate fans and other paraphernalia is extensive. These devices can be separated into those that are mechanical in nature and those that are pneumatic.

Patented rockers used numerous mechanical methods to operate fans, including pulleys and a continuous rope (fig. 2), weighted levers (fig. 3), mechanical linkages (fig. 4), a variety of bows and looped cords (figs. 5, 6), racks and pinions (fig. 7), and pendulums (fig. 8). Pneumatic machine rockers were somewhat simpler, consisting essentially of a bellows mounted beneath the seat of the chair (fig. 9). What they lacked in technical sophistication, however, pneumatic rockers made up in imagination. One patented rocker cooled the air in a scented-ice box before directing it back at the occupant (fig. 10); a "musical rocking chair" had an accordionlike instrument fixed beneath its seat (fig. 11); and, although no one seems to have taken him up on it, a writer in *Scientific American* proposed building a rocker with harp strings in its air tubes, to serenade its rocking occupant.[6]

    [4] Franz Reuleaux, *The Kinematics of Machinery: Outlines of a Theory of Machines,* trans. Alexander B. W. Kennedy (1876; reprint, New York: Dover Publications, 1963), p. 35. For additional technical descriptions of machines, see T. M. Goodeve, *The Elements of Mechanism* (London: Longmans, Green, 1905); and John H. Barr, *Kinematics of Machinery: A Brief Treatise on Constrained Motions of Machine Elements* (New York: John Wiley and Sons, 1899).
    [5] Siegfried Giedion, *Mechanization Takes Command: A Contribution to Anonymous History* (1948; reprint, New York: W. W. Norton, 1969), p. 390.
    [6] *Scientific American* 3, no. 7 (November 6, 1847): 52.

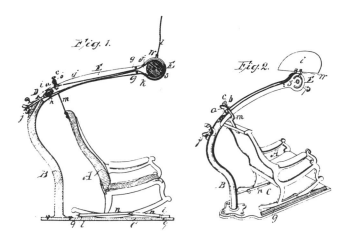

Fig. 2. Rocking Chair and Fan, U.S. Patent 5,231 to Charles
Horst, August 7, 1847. (U.S. Patent and Trademark Office.)

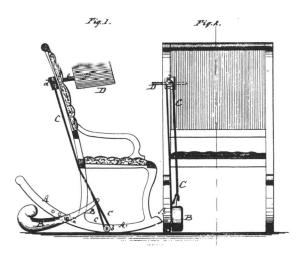

Fig. 3. Rocking-Chair Fans, U.S. Patent 135,282
to A. Nissle and J. Schoberl, January 28, 1873.
(U.S. Patent and Trademark Office.)

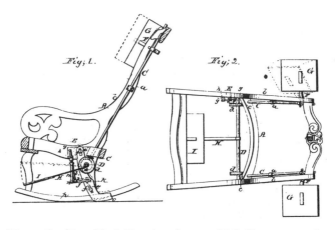

Fig. 4. Rocking-Chair Fan Attachment, U.S. Patent 14,506 to Konrad Kiefer, March 25, 1856. (U.S. Patent and Trademark Office.)

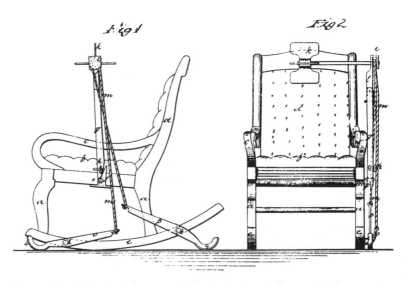

Fig. 5. Combined Rocking Chair and Fan, U.S. Patent 89,897 to Martin Stiefenhofer, May 11, 1869. (U.S. Patent and Trademark Office.)

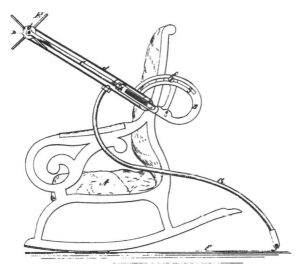

Fig. 6. Improvement in Fan Attachments for Rocking Chairs, U.S. Patent 123,626 to William H. Fletcher, Jr., February 13, 1872. (U.S. Patent and Trademark Office.)

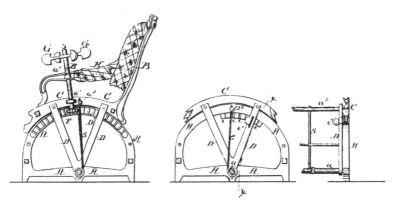

Fig. 7. Rocking-Chair Fan-Attachment, U.S. Patent 76,452 to Augustus R. Hobbs and Nathaniel F. Wright, April 7, 1868. (U.S. Patent and Trademark Office.)

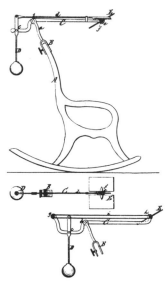

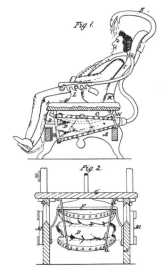

Fig. 8. Rocking-Chair Fan, U.S. Patent 139, 112 to Otto Brueck, May 20, 1873. (U.S. Patent and Trademark Office.)

Fig. 9. Rocking Chair, U.S. Patent 92,379 to C. Singer, July 6, 1869. (U.S. Patent and Trademark Office.)

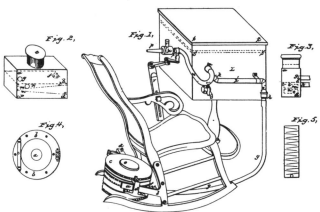

Fig. 10. Ventilating Rocking Chair, U.S. Patent 18,696 to David Kahnweiler, November 24, 1857. (U.S. Patent and Trademark Office.)

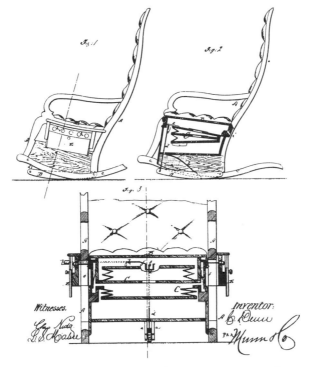

Fig. 11. Musical Rocking Chair, U.S. Patent 106,790
to Clayton Denn, August 30, 1870. (U.S. Patent and
Trademark Office.)

In each of these devices, the moving parts repeatedly traversed a single, fixed path, thereby fulfilling the third of Reuleaux's criteria. Reuleaux identified the importance of the "fixed link," or nonmoving element, in a mechanical chain. Fixed links act as stops or pivots for the movable links in any mechanism and are indispensable to the whole. It is significant, in light of this description, that many of these rockers were fixed in position, attached to stationary frames, platforms, and iceboxes. In kinematic terms, fixing them within a rigid framework reduced certain machine rockers to components of a larger mechanism, thereby making them conform even more closely to the classic conception of a machine.

Another integral part of that conception is the notion of work.

These chairs could be called machine rockers simply because of the complexity of their mechanical components, but they are mechanical in a more fundamental way. Each of these chairs is a machine for channeling the energy of rocking into a desired effect—that is, for converting motion into work. Although the mechanisms are not identical, there are certain visual similarities in the shapes and motions of beam engines and rocking chairs. In both chair and engine, power is transmitted through a central rocking member and a series of linkages to the point of application. And in most of the mechanical machine rockers, the kinematic problem is exactly that of the early steam engine (the solution of which assured its widespread application); namely, how to convert reciprocal motion into circular motion. In fact, all the mechanisms used by nineteenth-century machine rockers—pulleys, linkages, racks and pinions, pendulums, and bellows—had had prior technical applications in transforming unproductive motions into productive ones. Machine rockers sought to harness the previously "wasted" motion of the rocking chair and apply it to a variety of uses. Some of these uses were decidedly productive, such as Daniel Sheldon's 1827 patent for a rocker-powered butter churn (fig. 12). Most machine rockers, however, were intended to keep their occupants comfortable, a point to which we will return.

It is not merely in retrospect that rocking chairs have been described as machines: in his 1831 patent for an "invalid rocker," Daniel Harrington referred to his invention as an "engine." If a rocking chair is considered a machine—that is, a means of applying power constructively—then its user, as motive force, must also be considered part of the machine. In the world of the mid nineteenth century, so much of which was being built by unassisted human labor, such a mechanistic view of human beings was not uncommon. Thomas Ewbank, commissioner of patents from 1849 to 1852, saw the human race in exactly these terms. In 1855 he remarked, "Like artificial motors—we are created for the work we can do—for the useful and productive ideas we can stamp upon matter."[7] In construction and conception, machine rockers expressed the nineteenth-century understanding of the machine and began to apply it to humankind as well.

[7] Harrington's patent description is quoted in Denker and Denker, *Rocking Chair Book*, p. 78. Ewbank quoted in John F. Kasson, *Civilizing the Machine: Technology and Republican Values in America, 1776–1900* (New York: Penguin Books, 1976), p. 148.

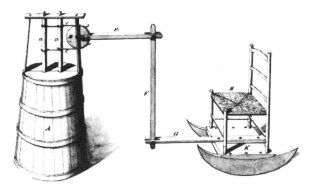

Fig. 12. Rocker-Powered Churn, U.S. Patent 4,878-X to Daniel Sheldon, September 13, 1827. An "X" appended to early patent numbers indicates that the patent was redrawn following the Patent Office fire of 1836. From William Ray and Marlys Ray, *The Art of Invention: Patent Models and Their Makers* (Princeton, N.J.: Pyne Press, 1974), p. 46. (Winterthur Library.)

Still, the work of most machine rockers was to keep their occupants comfortable. Equipped with fans, perfume dispensers, and musical instruments, machine rockers sought to make the rocking experience as pleasurable as possible. Indeed, increasing the comfort of the human race was considered one of the primary achievements of the nineteenth-century American patent system as a whole. In 1860 Edward Everett, a Harvard professor, politician, and renowned orator and booster of technology, lauded American inventors for devising "every implement for the service and comfort of man."[8] Bringing comfort to the world was surely a noble task.

And yet we must ask how comfortable machine rockers really were. It can easily be imagined how tedious lingering perfumes and continuous music might become, or how enduring a gust of air with every rock might quickly become a pneumatic Chinese water torture. If the room

[8] Quoted in Kasson, *Civilizing the Machine*, p. 47.

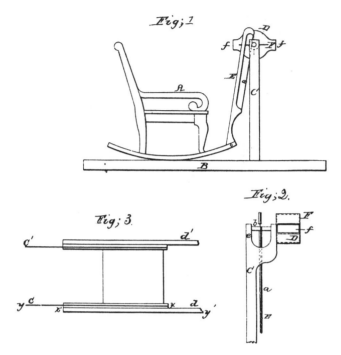

Fig. 13. Rocking-Chair Fan Attachment, U.S. Patent 52,404 to George Fleig, February 6, 1866. (U.S. Patent and Trademark Office.)

were comfortable or too cool, the fans would be useless or worse, and in any case, the accumulation of hardware would have impeded social interaction. Even those rockers that were not fixed in place and surrounded by frames and arms and pulleys usually placed a fan in the occupant's line of vision (figs. 13, 14). At best, such chairs would share the characteristic regimentation of the machine; at worst, they could be a source of constant irritation that added little to the decor of any room. Clearly more thought was put into the mechanical elaboration of machine rockers than into their effectiveness as agents of comfort. The impracticality of many of these rockers seems to verify Giedion's observation: "often [inventors] were completely disinterested in the special use their chair was to serve; they simply wished to contrive a new mechanism."[9]

[9]Giedion, *Mechanization Takes Command*, pp. 390–91.

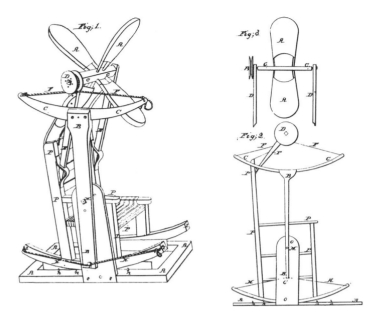

Fig. 14. Improved Fanning and Rocking Chair, U.S. Patent 80,970 to Thomas Kerr, August 11, 1868. (U.S. Patent and Trademark Office.)

That the designers of machine rockers were more interested in the means of harnessing human power than in augmenting human comfort is suggested by their very approach to the task. Despite the impressive diversity of applied mechanisms, the chairs themselves remained essentially untouched. Giedion's history of patent furniture stresses the role of relaxation and physical comfort in motivating new furniture design. According to Giedion, the nineteenth century sought to achieve comfort by adapting furniture mechanically to fit the human body; chairs were made supportive, flexible, adjustable.[10] The idea of comfort embodied in the chairs discussed by Giedion, however, is entirely alien to the machine rocker. Virtually all machine rockers remained rigidly nonadjustable; there was no attempt to adapt them to the human body.

Nor, aside from their purported attention to comfort, do the majority of machine rockers qualify as innovative according to the criteria estab-

---

[10] Giedion, *Mechanization Takes Command*, pp. 389–406.

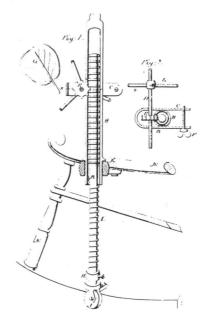

Fig. 15. Rocking-Chair Fan-Attachment, U.S. Patent 78,965 to Augustus R. Hobbs, June 16, 1868. (U.S. Patent and Trademark Office.)

lished by David Hanks in *Innovative Furniture in America*. Many of the patented rocker-powered devices were actually separate mechanisms designed to be attached to any ordinary rocking chair (figs. 15, 16; see also fig. 8). With the exception of Hobbs and Wright's 1868 rocker, the innovations in machine rockers were external rather than internal; applied to rather than incorporated in the chairs.[11] Despite their ambitions as machinery, machine rockers represent a failure to reconceptualize the rocker as a type of furniture.

[11] David A. Hanks, *Innovative Furniture in America from 1800 to the Present* (New York: Horizon Press, 1981). In his preface Hanks establishes comfort, multiple functions, manufacturing technique, portability, and construction materials as criteria for innovativeness. It is not always possible to determine the nature of an invention from its patent title. The title of Otto Brueck's "Rocking-Chair Fan" gives little indication that it is an attachment for a rocker, while Hobbs and Wright's "Rocking-Chair Fan-Attachment" is not an attachment at all, but an entire piece of furniture.

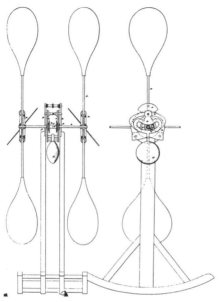

Fig. 16. Automatic Fan, U.S. Patent 14,507 to Benjamin M. Lewy, March 25, 1856. This device was called a "fan rocking-chair" in the patent description and was intended to be "applied to any rocking chair or cradle or other rocking article of furniture." (U.S. Patent and Trademark Office.)

The same additive conception that governed the machine rockers' approach to comfort is evident in their aesthetics as well. Stylistically machine rockers broke no new ground. Daniel Linzie's "odoraeolian seat" of 1849, for example, which pumped air through perfume chambers drilled into its frame, is essentially a robust version of the Boston rocker (figs. 17, 18, 19). Other machine rockers simply adopted the styles of the day. By most customary aesthetic criteria, then, machine rockers must be considered fundamentally conservative artifacts. Approached specifically as machinery, however, these rockers epitomize what John Kasson calls "the aesthetics of machinery." In an effort to define a particularly republican aesthetic, distinct from the decadent

Fig. 17. Watercolor drawing of Daniel Linzie's "odoraeolian" seat, submitted as part of his patent application. (Car-
tographic and Architectural Branch, National Archives and
Records Service.)

arts of Europe, Kasson argues, Americans were drawn to the practical
arts, and utility became the yardstick for measuring both moral and
aesthetic merits. "Nothing is good or beautiful but in the measure that
it is useful," wrote Benjamin Franklin. In the nineteenth century, *Scientific American* was a foremost promoter of both new inventions and
the machine aesthetic, proclaiming, for instance, "inventions are the
poetry of physical science and inventors the poets." In a culture that
equated technology with beauty and morality, machine rockers may
well have been considered exemplars of progressive art.[12]

    Thus far consideration has been given to the physical attributes of
machine rockers: their construction, operation, and purposes. But, as

---

[12] Kasson, *Civilizing the Machine*, pp. 139–80; "The Poetry of Invention," *Scientific
American* 5 (November 24, 1849): 77.

Fig. 18. Official line drawing published by the Patent Office upon granting of U.S. Patent 6,307 to Daniel Linzie, April 10, 1849. Adapted from the original watercolor in figure 17. (U.S. Patent and Trademark Office.)

noted at the outset, objects comprise ideas as well as functions. In *The World of Goods*, anthropologist Mary Douglas argues that objects are a means of communication which is fundamental to the way we structure our reality. "Forget," she urges, "that commodities are good for eating, clothing, and shelter; forget their usefulness and try instead the idea that commodities are good for thinking; treat them as a nonverbal medium for the human creative faculty." Goods, for Douglas, are a nonverbal form of culture communication.[13]

[13] Mary Douglas and Baron Isherwood, *The World of Goods: Towards an Anthropology of Consumption* (New York: Basic Books, 1979), p. 62. Because Douglas and Isherwood's analysis is concerned specifically with the consumption of goods, it is not directly applicable to objects like machine rockers, which were never actually consumed. Nevertheless, their discussion of why people want goods and how they use them is both provocative and illuminating.

Fig. 19. Patent model of Daniel Linzie's Fan-Rocker.
Wood, fabric, steel; H. 8¼", W. 4", D. 6". (Hagley
Museum and Library.)

Although Douglas's work develops an important theoretical under-
pinning for the concept of goods as communication, an intuitive understanding of this idea has long existed in technical circles. Patent drawings
and models are the nineteenth-century heirs to a long tradition of nonverbal thought in technology. As such, they represent an understanding
and a mode of communication that runs parallel to, but is distinct from,
verbal thought. The United States Patent Office demonstrated its faith
in the communicative powers of objects by maintaining a museum of
patent models for most of the nineteenth century, intended to edify the
public and to stimulate inventors. Secretary of State William H. Seward

echoed this position in his introduction to the report on the Paris Universal Exposition of 1867. He proclaimed, "through the universal language of the products of labor . . . the artisans of all countries hold communication."[14]

So palpable has the sense of the communicativeness of objects been that technicians have sometimes turned to linguistic analogies to express it. In the eighteenth century, Swedish mechanician Christopher Polhem constructed a "mechanical alphabet." He considered the "five powers" (screw, pulley, wedge, lever, and winch) to be the vowels of his alphabet and the other machine elements to be consonants; when combined, these would spell out the vocabulary of machines.[15] While Polhem's verbal conceit must be considered metaphorical rather than literal, it was nevertheless an elaborate attempt to articulate the powerful nonverbal meaning latent in objects. If later technicians felt less need than Polhem to systematize and develop this idea, perhaps it is because they, like Seward, simply assumed that objects spoke.

But, as Douglas reminds us, objects do more than simply communicate ideas; they structure them as well. She argues that on a cultural level goods serve as a "live information system" through which people participate in social rituals and maintain both status distinctions and reciprocal obligations: a culture defines itself, in part, by its choice and use of goods. The same is true on a personal level. "The most general objective of the consumer," Douglas points out, "can only be to construct an intelligible universe with the goods he chooses." Douglas's observation owes a great deal to Claude Lévi Strauss's notion of *bricolage*, or the assembling of diverse objects into a personally satisfying model of the universe. Although *bricolage* refers to assemblages of goods rather than to individual artifacts, the notion of objects as a physical means of ordering reality is a powerful one.[16]

Unlike most consumers, the inventors of machine rocking chairs

[14] Eugene S. Ferguson, "The Mind's Eye: Non-Verbal Thought in Technology," *Science* 197, no. 4306 (August 26, 1977): 827–36; William Ray and Marlys Ray, *The Art of Invention: Patent Models and Their Makers* (Princeton, N.J.: Pyne Press, 1974); Eugene S. Ferguson and Christopher Baer, *Little Machines, Patent Models in the Nineteenth Century* (Greenville, Del.: Hagley Museum, 1979); Seward quoted in Oscar Handlin, "Science and Technology in Popular Culture," *Daedalus* 94, no. 1 (Winter 1965): 159.

[15] Ferguson, "Mind's Eye"; Sigvard Strandh, A *History of the Machine* (New York: A and W Publishers, 1979), pp. 54–61.

[16] Douglas and Isherwood, *World of Goods*, p. 65; Claude Lévi-Strauss, *The Savage Mind* (Chicago: University of Chicago Press, 1966), pp. 16–33.

chose to construct a portion of their intelligible universes in an unusually literal way by designing a new machine. It is, of course, difficult to say what each machine rocking chair meant to its inventor. For some, it may have been a cool, insect-free rest on the porch; for others, the means to achieve the wealth or prestige of a Samuel Colt, a Cyrus McCormick, or a Samuel F. B. Morse; for yet others, the satisfaction of having a small portion of human ingenuity recorded in their name. Further research into the lives of these inventors may help to substantiate their personal visions, but until this is done, educated conjecture must suffice.[17]

Here again, Douglas offers a clue into the universe that machine rockers may have represented. In speaking of goods as an information system, she notes that the information content of each term must be readily intelligible to its users; otherwise, its communicative function breaks down, and its users are isolated from their society.[18] Consequently, the consumer must concern himself not only with receiving the information inherent in goods but with controlling it as well. Through their devices, the inventors of machine rockers may have been attempting not only to use the mechanical vocabulary of the mid nineteenth century but also to control it. As witnesses to the century's bewildering proliferation of new technologies that disrupted life as often as they enhanced it, these inventors may well have felt a desire to control that changing technology. All patented objects stand poised between inno-

---

[17]Wealth and prestige were frequently emphasized in promoting patents and the patent system. The following advertisement ran repeatedly in *Scientific American* in the early 1870s: "Probably no investment of a small sum of money brings a greater return than the expense incurred in obtaining a patent even when the invention is but a small one. Larger inventions are found to pay correspondingly well. The names Blanchard, Morse, Bigelow, Colt, Ericsson, Howe, McCormick, Hoe and others who have amassed immense fortunes from their inventions, are well known. And there are thousands of others who have realized large sums from their patents." Although it is usually frustratingly elusive, the inventor's personal vision is precisely what makes a patented object so emotionally compelling and instantly accessible. Roger Kennedy, director of the Smithsonian Institution's National Museum of American History, describes the impact of patent models in these terms: "These are the kinds of things that are haunted by the ambitions of their makers. That's the thriller. Anybody with any imagination who puts their hands on a patent model has in their hand a whole lifetime of creative dreaming. We're looking here at the objects in which was distilled all of the creative juices of a human being" (*Washington Post*, June 21, 1986).

[18]It might be argued that the commercial failure of the dozens of patented machine rockers was caused by their inventors' failure to make the information content of their devices clear to the rest of the culture. Perhaps the tension that they embodied between work and leisure made machine rockers confusing and unintelligible, hence unmarketable.

vation and obsolescence; the act of patenting an invention harbors an underlying urge to freeze progress in midstride, to appropriate and define a specific segment of technical achievement. Perhaps grafting mechanisms onto such a familiar and homey object as the rocking chair was a literal attempt to domesticate nineteenth-century technology.[19]

To whatever personal visions the inventors of machine rockers may have had we must add the larger cultural meanings that their inventions gained by virtue of being patented. It is important to recognize that the patent system was central to nineteenth-century America's understanding and experience of technology. It helped to define and channel some of the fundamental assumptions and obsessions of American culture. By rewarding the clever inventor with occasionally lucrative monopoly rights, the patent system helped to establish money as the primary motivator in civic life; by institutionalizing the patent process and opening it to all, the patent system reinforced a national belief in individualism, equality, and upward social mobility; and by resolutely identifying technical innovation with human improvement, it asserted an abiding faith in progress through technology. The patent system deeply influenced nineteenth-century America's choice and use of goods and, in so doing, the ways in which the culture defined itself. As patented objects, machine rockers participated in and endorsed this definition.[20]

[19] Douglas and Isherwood, *World of Goods*, p. 95. John Kouwenhoven makes a similar point concerning the dime-novel tradition of presenting steam engines in human forms. The popular "steam-man" stories, argues Kouwenhoven, attempted to "humanize" a frightening technology by housing it in a familiar form. See his "Who's Afraid of the Machine in the Garden?" in John Kouwenhoven, *Half a Truth Is Better Than None* (Chicago: University of Chicago Press, 1982), pp. 125–45.

[20] Platt stated in 1891: "without the stimulus afforded by the prospective reward of the inventor this development of invention would never have occurred . . . the inventor is spurred and lured on by the expectation of a fortune. . . . It is right that the man who benefits mankind should be rewarded" (O. H. Platt, "Invention and Advancement," in U.S. Department of the Interior, Patent Office, *Patent Centennial Celebration: Proceedings and Addresses* [Washington, D.C.: Government Printing Office, 1892], p. 71). Money, in the form of tax incentives, continues to be a major shaper of public policy. Rodris Roth notes that the U.S. patent system was the first to be institutionalized rather than based upon royal charter or special legislation and was thus democratically based (Rodris Roth, "Nineteenth-Century American Patent Furniture," in Hanks, *Innovative Furniture*, pp. 23–46). David Potter presents a lucid explication of the interconnected concepts of individualism, equality, and social mobility in his *People of Plenty: Economic Abundance and the American Character* (Chicago: University of Chicago Press, 1954), pp. 75–141. For various discussions of the connection between progress and technology, see Platt, "Invention and Advancement"; Kasson, *Civilizing the Machine*; John Kouwenhoven, "Waste Not, Have Not," *Harper's* 218, no. 1306 (March 1959): 72–78; and Leo Marx, *The Machine in the Garden* (Oxford: Oxford University Press, 1964).

As patent models and, to a somewhat lesser degree, as drawings, machine rockers communicated meaning in another way as well. An ineffable physical authenticity gives objects much of their expressive power and, to students of material culture, their intellectual attraction. Kendall Dood, of the United States Patent and Trademark Office, has captured some of this physical meaning in describing nineteenth-century patent models. The models, he says, were "uniquely suited both to the state of American technology in the mid-nineteenth century and to the popular conception of technology as *something entirely and immediately apprehendable through the senses.*"[21] The open and easily comprehensible designs of machine rockers effectively express America's former, more intuitive understanding of technology, as well as the inventors' own understandings of mechanics and comfort.

The mechanization of the quintessentially American piece of furniture, symbolic of comfort and the pastoral virtues, in the nineteenth century is an important cultural event. It is in the juxtaposition of leisure and efficiency, comfort and productivity, that the machine rocker is most evocative. Designed to enhance the joy of just sitting, rocking chairs are predicated upon the availability of leisure. In literal terms, *leisure* means only "free" time (in both "self-directed" and "unpaid" senses), but culturally it has also acquired the sense of time to be positively enjoyed. Hanks is aware of this when he notes, "the primary function of the rocker has always been to provide ease and comfort." Indeed, as has been noted, increasing human comfort was a major nineteenth-century objective. In an oration delivered at the centennial celebration of the United States patent system, Senator O. H. Platt pronounced the benediction on nineteenth-century technology. Technology, he felt, created a world in which "as the years go on man can have more of comfort with less of personal effort than ever before. If this does not constitute human advancement," he declared, "I do not know what does."[22]

Certainly machine rockers responded in a very direct way to the cultural and technological imperative to increase comfort, but, as we have seen, they were more mechanically imaginative than they were comfortable. These artifacts of leisure display an underlying antipathy

---

[21] Quoted in Robert C. Post, "Patent Models: Symbols for an Era," in *American Enterprise: Nineteenth Century Patent Models* (New York: Cooper-Hewitt Museum, 1984), p. 11.

[22] Hanks, *Innovative Furniture*, p. 14; Platt, "Invention and Advancement," p. 68.

toward leisure. The machine rocker responded to a different American obsession, that of efficiency. Eugene Ferguson has commented on our national "cult of efficiency" from the timesaving and laborsaving devices of Benjamin Franklin through the domestic economy prescriptions of Catharine Beecher and the scientific management of Fredrick Winslow Taylor. Ferguson notes that efficiency has meant not just a thrifty use of resources, but a complete use of them. Machine rockers shared this definition. In 1871, two years before the magazine featured an adult-powered rocker to perform domestic chores, *Scientific American* endorsed both a small-animal engine for household use and a rocking chair/washing machine to be operated by an infant (fig. 20). Idle members of the household could also be put to work making butter or tending babies (figs. 21, 22; see also fig. 12). Not a whit of available domestic energy was to be wasted. [23]

Perhaps the inventors of these devices perceived unexploited domestic energy to be a moral problem demanding a solution. Or, they may have considered it economically so important to maximize household pro-ductivity that they conscientiously pursued such unlikely energy sources as sheep, infants, and porch sitters. In either case, these devices lend weight to one European observer's opinion that Americans felt "con-tempt for the leisure so much valued by Europeans. Leisure they feel to be a kind of standing still, the unpardonable sin." [24]

If machine rockers were thus ambiguous artifacts, embodying con-tradictory ideals of comfort and efficiency, leisure and work, they were no more ambiguous than the age in which they were conceived. As Senator Platt's comments quoted above indicate, the dream that tech-nology would end drudgery and produce universal leisure was very much alive in the late nineteenth century. The myth of abundance without labor in the New World was by then a venerable one, dating to the earliest European descriptions of North America. [25] On American soil,

[23] Eugene S. Ferguson, "The American-ness of American Technology," *Technology and Culture* 20, no. 1 (January 1979): 3–24; "Small Animal Power for Light Purposes," *Scientific American*, n.s., 24, no. 17 (April 22, 1871): 262; "Infantile Power Washing Machine," *Scientific American*, n.s., 24, no. 10 (March 4, 1871): 146.

[24] G. Lowes Dickinson, as quoted in Potter, *People of Plenty*, p. 96.

[25] Potter, *People of Plenty*, pp. 78–90; William Cronon, *Changes in the Land: Indi-ans, Colonists, and the Ecology of New England* (New York: Hill and Wang, 1983), pp. 34–53. On the concept of "myth" in American history, see Marx, *Machine in the Gar-den*; and Henry Nash Smith, *Virgin Land: The American West as Symbol and Myth* (Cambridge, Mass.: Harvard University Press, 1970).

Fig. 20 Infantile Power Washing Machine, U.S. Patent 68,626 to John Highbarger, September 10, 1867. The description reads: "The clothes are washed by the oscillation of a rocking chair, with ribbed rocker bottom, as shown, the rocking being effected by the hands of the operator, which grasp a hand bar." From *Scientific American*, n.s., 24, no. 10 (March 4, 1871): 146.

the myth of abundance gradually fused with the ideals of democracy and individual social advancement. This hybrid faith endured a setback during the period of the American Revolution, when abundance seemed to smack of European luxury and a rigid class structure, but it re-emerged with renewed vigor in the early nineteenth century. As America's self-confidence and productive capacity grew, the idea of abundance became less and less threatening. Kasson identifies the Reverend Henry W. Bellows's 1853 oration, "The Moral Significance of the Crystal Palace," as a watershed in America's understanding of abundance. According to Bellows, technology was to play a critical role in the nation's

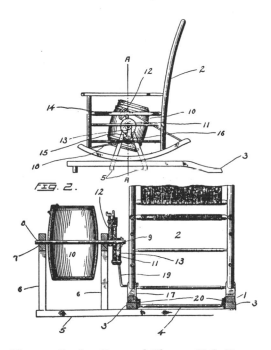

Fig. 21. Rocker-Powered Churn, U.S. Patent
1,051,684, January 28, 1913. (U.S. Patent and
Trademark Office.)

future. "By ostensibly providing the means of wealth for all," Kasson
summarizes, "technology made luxury safe for democracy."[26] Far from
threatening republican virtue, abundance could redeem the political
promises of equal opportunity and social mobility by providing goods
enough for all.

The concepts of technology, wealth, and democracy have been
tightly intertwined throughout America's history, and their connection
has usually been expressed as an overriding, progressive faith that a
benevolent technology would produce both wealth and democracy,
abundance and leisure. But has this faith been borne out in fact? Technology unquestionably increases human productivity, and, in theory, if

[26] Kasson, *Civilizing the Machine*, p. 40.

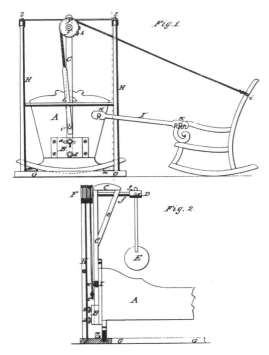

Fig. 22. Automatic Fan, U.S. Patent 138,567
to J. Lehner, May 6, 1873. (U.S. Patent and
Trademark Office.)

a person can produce more goods in the same amount of time, his or
her leisure time may also increase. In practice, however, the dream of
abundance without labor has been an either/or proposition. Increases
in productivity have commonly been devoted to increasing production
and, consequently, consumption, rather than to increasing leisure. This
cardinal urge to expand output produced some of the most disruptive
features of the nineteenth-century economic order: longer working hours,
production speedups and lower rates for piecework, planned obsolescence, and the cycles of overproduction and recession which have characterized industrial capitalism. At the same time, it increased the quantity and variety of goods available to consumers and ultimately created
the state of abundance the West currently enjoys.

Although nineteenth-century America consistently made the choices that would produce abundance rather than leisure, these choices were not made without misgivings. There have always been dissenting voices. As early as 1839, Ralph Waldo Emerson wrote, "This Invasion of Nature by Trade with its Money, its Credit, its Steam, its Railroad threatens to upset the balance of man and establish a new Universal Monarchy more tyrannical than Babylon or Rome."[27] In the last quarter of the nineteenth century, as the scale of industrial production ballooned and as the focus of popular concern shifted from national to personal welfare, dissatisfaction with the industrial and economic order grew. The panic of 1873 signaled the start of an unprecedented series of strikes, riots, and business crises that continued into the twentieth century and brought the fundamental justice of the American economic system into serious question.

For many Americans in the second half of the nineteenth century, particularly working people, the contradictions between the work ethic and dreams of the good life took on crucial importance. In an increasingly industrialized society, the rewards for success must have seemed immeasurably greater and the likelihood of attaining them considerably smaller than ever before. Progress for the few might mean oppression for the many, and instead of leading America into a bright future of universal leisure, technology might be condemning most of her citizens to lives of endless drudgery.

The machine rocker arose in this context of doubt and redefinition of work and leisure, technology and progress. The rocking chair was not unique in being mechanized during the nineteenth century, but it was unique in its symbolic association with comfort. The tension that machine rockers embody between the enjoyment of leisure and the drive to productivity, between the love of comfort and the fear of idleness, is symptomatic of American culture in the second half of the nineteenth century.

What, then, is the fundamental meaning of machine rockers? In Davis's terms, how, by inventing these goods, was the culture helping to define itself? The foregoing thoughts and observations present us with two alternative understandings. The first choice is to consider machine rockers expressions of confidence, artifacts convinced of the benevolent influence of technology. The attempt to mechanize the traditional sym-

---

[27] Quoted in Kasson, *Civilizing the Machine*, p. 118.

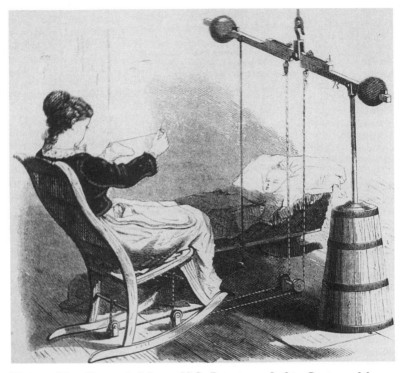

Fig. 23. New Domestic Motor, U.S. Patent 137,856 to Gustavus Meyer, April 15, 1873. From *Scientific American*, n.s., 29, no. 8 (August 23, 1873): 118.

bol of domestic ease may be seen as an assertion of technology's universal applicability. According to this interpretation, machine rockers were a creative resolution, a three-dimensional synthesis of American domestic and industrial ideals.

Alternatively, one may interpret machine rockers as defensive attempts to domesticate and control mechanism in an age of increasingly threatening technology. The rockers' clumsy and inadequate efforts to combine comfort with efficiency may be considered naive denials of the irreconcilable antithesis between the two.

Historical evidence will support both interpretations, and this, of course, is the central problem of the historian. Critic Frederic Jameson has observed, "the past is essentially that about which one must 'make up one's mind': it is sheer fact, inertia, it must be formed from outside by a *decision.*"[28]

Here, then, is my decision on the meaning of machine rockers: machine rockers are both optimistic and opportunistic. They demonstrate a great deal of inventiveness and mechanical playfulness, yet their nod to comfort is unconvincing. Even granting that they were sincerely intended to improve the quality of life, their approach to this task was superficial. At the very least, these objects reveal a devaluation of leisure relative to productivity. Machine rockers emphasized not comfort, but work. A final example, the "New Domestic Motor" of 1873, makes this clear (fig. 23). It was promoted in the following terms:

The inventor of the device . . . not only employs the hitherto wasted female power to oscillate a cradle, but . . . to vibrate the dasher of a churn. By this means . . . the hands of the fair operator are left free for darning stockings, sewing, or other light work, while the entire individual is completely utilized. Fathers of large families of girls, Mormons, and others blessed with a super-abundance of the gentler sex, are thus afforded an effective method of diverting the latent feminine energy, usually manifested in the pursuit of novels, beaux, embroidery, opera-boxes, and bonnets, into channels of useful and profitable labour.

Necessarily this device may be put to a great variety of applications, and may supply motive power for washing-machines, wringers, and other articles of household use, as well as for churns and cradles. At all events it opens a new field for "woman's labour," and one in which she is not likely to be disturbed or encounter competition from the other sex.[29]

The attempt to make a previously and intentionally unproductive artifact productive was, I believe, a misguided attempt to harness leisure

[28] Frederic Jameson, *Marxism and Form* (Princeton, N.J.: Princeton University Press, 1971), p. 210.
[29] "New Domestic Motor," p. 118. The gender implications of machine rockers deserve further research. As a source of power, machine rockers were applied almost exclusively to women's work: washing clothes, tending children, preparing food. Their effort to make women more productive within the home just as women were expanding their economic and social opportunities outside the home places machine rockers at the center of the contemporary debate over women's proper role in society. Machine rockers also complement a small but growing body of literature on women and technology. Two of the best studies are Corlann G. Bush, "The Barn Is His, the House Is Mine: Agricultural Technology and Sex Roles," in *Energy and Transport: Historical Perspectives on Policy Issues*, ed. George H. Daniels and Mark H. Rose (Beverly Hills: Sage Publications, 1982), pp. 235–59; and Ruth Schwartz Cowan, *More Work for Mother: The Ironies of Household Technology from the Open Hearth to the Microwave* (New York: Basic Books, 1983).

to the ends of production. In this, machine rockers are extensions of nineteenth-century America's uncritical trust in the virtue of the machine and the promise of abundance. Certainly not all machine rockers were as blatantly production-oriented as the New Domestic Motor, but all were the products of the same audacious confidence.

Giedion has remarked that in America patent furniture "revealed the century as it liked to relax when wearing none of its masks."[30] Machine rocking chairs represent an alternative tradition: that when wearing none of its masks, nineteenth-century America did not care to relax at all.

[30] Giedion, *Mechanization Takes Command*, p. 390.

Gossip, Rhetoric, and Objects
A Sociolinguistic Approach to Newfoundland Furniture

Gerald L. Pocius

On a snowy May morning in 1981, we drove down the winding road into Keels, a small fishing village of 126 people, located a three-hour drive west of St. John's, Newfoundland's provincial capital (fig. 1). During the trip, a friend from the Newfoundland Museum—Walter Peddle—and I talked about the community. Walter was organizing what would ostensibly be the first exhibition ever on Newfoundland furniture; he had decided to feature Keels objects, and I wanted to come along to see this place that I had heard so much about.[1] Walter had seen literally thousands of pieces of Newfoundland furniture over the

Field research for this essay was funded by the Social Science and Humanities Research Council of Canada. Data analysis took place while the author was at Winterthur Museum as a National Endowment for the Humanities research fellow. Gratitude is expressed to both agencies for their support. The author also thanks Ken Ames, Charlie Bergengren, Peggy Bulger, Hugo Freund, Susan Isaacs, Gene Metcalf, John Moe, Shane O'Dea, Robert Paine, Shelley Posen, Robert St. George, Larry Small, Kevin Sweeney, and Barbara McLean Ward, whose comments have greatly improved this essay. For help in documenting the furniture itself, thanks go to Claude Welcher, John Hofsteter, Alvin Hobbs, Reg Penney, June Fitzgerald, Pam Hall, Mike Byrne, Coleen Lynch, Robert Paine, John Guy, Jack Wheeler, and Jack Kelly. The author especially thanks Walter Peddle for introducing him to both Keels and Newfoundland furniture and for encouraging his research on both of these topics.

[1] For a review of the exhibition, see Christine Cartwright, "Newfoundland Museum: 'Newfoundland Outport Furniture,' " *Material History Bulletin* 14 (Spring 1982): 101–3. The pioneering work on this subject is Walter W. Peddle, *The Traditional Furniture of Outport Newfoundland* (St. John's: Cuff Publications, 1983).

Fig. 1. Keels, Newfoundland, summer 1986. (Photo, Barbara McLean Ward.)

years, yet, according to him, this tiny village had produced the widest variety of objects on the island. A bit puzzled by this diversity, and a bit awed by the furniture, my curiosity was irreversibly aroused.

Not knowing a great deal about furniture, I began to ask questions. Extant goods from Keels spanned a period of roughly a hundred years, from the mid nineteenth to the mid twentieth century. Why did local furniture making not decline then, as it had in other parts of Canada and the United States? Factory-made furniture was available and purchased for use in area houses. What impact did these mass-produced popular objects have on the local furniture tradition? Isolation and lack of communication have often been used to explain the persistence of certain forms of cultural behaviors in Newfoundland (like the archaic technologies used in certain craft traditions).[2] What did Keels furniture indicate about such informational interchange?

[2] Michael Jones points out that there is a general bias in scholarship that assumes that the factory system has had a negative effect on the continuance of craft traditions. See Michael Owen Jones, " 'There's Gotta Be New Designs Once in Awhile': Culture Change and the 'Folk' Arts," *Southern Folklore Quarterly* 36, no. 1 (March 1972): 45. Typical comments on isolation explaining Newfoundland traditions are found in John D. A. Widdowson, Introduction to Aubrey M. Tizzard, *On Sloping Ground:*

Sparked by such questions, I began field research. I decided to focus on a small outport like Keels because it would provide a tight community sample of data with which I could more adequately investigate cultural issues. So many of the furniture studies that I had read were based on unique or exceptional objects, made by families or shops that often had been elevated to an almost reverential status by the furniture-connoisseur community. As well, these artifacts frequently had little connection with their original context, especially since many are now found in museum collections. In my field research, I was not concerned as to where the furniture in each Keels house originated—whether it was made locally or imported—or how it was made—with hand tools or by machine. I was simply interested in the entire range of what ordinary people had in their homes, and only with such a broad basis could I begin to see how furniture functioned as a part of everyday life.[3] For eight months, between May and December 1984, I attempted to record every example of furniture used in Keels between 1850 and 1950, whether folk or factory made. Long dissatisfied with artifact studies that looked for isolated forms distributed over wide areas, I had become convinced that only a tight geographic focus would provide more representative inventories. Much of the furniture recorded was still being used in the Keels area, while other items were tracked down through a St. John's antiques dealer. In all, I recorded 153 Keels artifacts, 83 objects from the eight neighboring communities whose furniture exhibited stylistic similarities, 133 other examples from the region, and 165 from the rest

Reminiscences of Outport Life in Notre Dame Bay, Newfoundland, Memorial University of Newfoundland Folklore and Language Publications, Community Studies 2, ed. John D. A. Widdowson (St. John's: Department of Folklore, Memorial University of Newfoundland, 1979), p. xvii. An example of an archaic material culture technology persisting in Newfoundland is boat-framing techniques (see David A. Taylor, *Boat Building in Winterton, Trinity Bay, Newfoundland*, Canadian Centre for Folk Culture Studies Paper 41 [Ottawa: National Museum of Man, 1982], pp. 91–94). Although certain material culture traditions continued in Newfoundland long after they had disappeared in other areas of North America, the island was certainly anything but an isolated region when it came to artifacts. For comments on this, see Gerald L. Pocius, "Eighteenth- and Nineteenth-Century Newfoundland Gravestones: Self-Sufficiency, Economic Specialization, and the Creation of Artifacts," *Material History Bulletin* 12 (Spring 1981): 1–16.

[3] The concepts of "everyday life" and "ordinary people" are becoming increasingly used in what has been often called the "new social history." For introductions to these topics, see *American Quarterly* 34, no. 3 (Bibliography 1982), a special issue on the study of everyday life; and James B. Gardner and George Rollie Adams, eds., *Ordinary People and Everyday Life: Perspectives on the New Social History* (Nashville: American Association for State and Local History, 1983).

of the island, for comparisons. It immediately struck me that Keels furniture was quite diverse, unlike so many other communities on the Bonavista Peninsula, let alone Newfoundland. I could easily recognize regional styles from other areas on the peninsula—for example, the Renaissance-revival–influenced sideboards from communities around English Harbour and the geometric bracket feet on the chests of drawers from around Trinity. In contrast, Keels had an enormous range of forms and finishes for such a small community, and just when I thought I had seen every conceivable style in my fieldwork, a new artifact would completely surprise me with its design. While some objects exhibited features similar to nearby communities like Kings Cove and Open Hall, there were ultimately more differences than similarities, and Keels furniture did not easily fit into a wider homogeneous regional style. The diversity of this community tradition was something that I had not expected, given the theoretical leanings of much scholarship on furniture design and form.

Folklorists, social historians, museum researchers, and others interested in the study of material culture have often stressed homogeneity over individuality, repetition over variation, and tradition over change in researched objects. This focus comes largely from romantic and nationalist leanings of scholars in search of people and products untouched by the terrible twos: machines and manners. Both the "folk" and their creations have often been described by these repetitive, tradition-bound, homogeneous models. There are historical reasons for this.

In the first few decades of the twentieth century, anthropologists created the concept of "folk society" to argue that a major difference in world view existed between the urbanite and the simple folk living off the land. Robert Redfield is probably the most well known writer on folk society, and many researchers trace an intellectual lineage to his work. Redfield's study of the Mexican community of Tepoztlan laid out what he believed were the main characteristics of folk communities: a relatively homogeneous, isolated, smoothly functioning, and well-integrated society made up of a contented and well-adjusted people. Yet, when Oscar Lewis, one of Redfield's most illustrious students, went back to restudy Tepoztlan, his findings on the nature of such a folk community were different, to say the least. Lewis found, instead, that the same culture was characterized by the "underlying individualism of . . . institutions and character, the lack of co-operation, the tensions between villages . . . , the schisms within the village, the pervading quality of fear, envy, and distrust in interpersonal relations." Scholars often inadvertently cling to Redfield's model when looking at rural, subsistence cultures, although anthropologists no longer even use the terms "folk culture" or "folk society."[4] This homogeneous culture that Redfield wrote about usually exists only in the minds of romantics who have rarely lived in the stereotypical folk society believed riddled with the epithets of community, cooperation, and coziness. Along with the actual people studied, a similar viewpoint stressing homogeneity surrounds the study of folk artifacts. According to various writers, to be considered "folk," objects must exhibit little change over time, the same form must be made by different craftsmen over a wide geographic area, and the design must be dominated by conservative ideals.[5] Quite apart from the problem of determining what is folk from nonfolk without knowing the actual choices the craftsman made at the time the object was created, we often use these ideal characteristics to assemble our data bases. Collections of objects that exhibit preconceived similarities are grouped together as folk, while deviations are considered aberrant and idiosyncratic. Some researchers even imply that a culture cannot be studied through such idiosyncratic and unique works,

[4] Robert Redfield, *Tepoztlan, a Mexican Village: A Study of Folk Life* (Chicago: University of Chicago Press, 1930); Robert Redfield, "The Little Community," in Robert Redfield, *The Little Community and Peasant Society and Culture* (Chicago: University of Chicago Press, 1967); Oscar Lewis, "Tepoztlan Restudied: A Critique of the Folk-Urban Conceptualization of Social Change," in Oscar Lewis, *Anthropological Essays* (New York: Random House, 1970), p. 38. Instead of "folk culture/society," anthropologists generally use the term "peasant culture" to refer to those societies that are still largely resource-based and exist close to larger urbanized centers. A good introduction is Jack M. Potter, May N. Diaz, and George M. Foster, eds., *Peasant Society: A Reader* (Boston: Little, Brown, 1967).
[5] Theoretical statements are Richard C. Poulsen, *The Pure Experience of Order: Essays on the Symbolic in the Folk Material Culture of Western America* (Albuquerque: University of New Mexico Press, 1982), chap. 8; Kenneth L. Ames, *Beyond Necessity: Art in the Folk Tradition* (New York: W. W. Norton, 1977), pp. 22–27; Henry Glassie, *Pattern in the Material Folk Culture of the Eastern United States,* University of Pennsylvania Publications in Folklore and Folklife (Philadelphia: University of Pennsylvania Press, 1968), pp. 4–36; John Michael Vlach, "The Concept of Community and Folklife Study," in *American Material Culture and Folklife: A Prologue and Dialogue,* American Material Culture and Folklife Series, ed. Simon J. Bronner (Ann Arbor: UMI Research Press, 1985), pp. 63–75; and Bruce R. Buckley, "A Folklorist Looks at the Traditional Craftsman," in *Country Cabinetwork and Simple City Furniture,* ed. John D. Morse (Charlottesville: University Press of Virginia, 1970), p. 271. For a discussion of the problems of attempting to set up an ideal typology involving the concepts of "tradition" and "change," see M. Estellie Smith, "The Process of Sociocultural Continuity," *Current Anthropology* 23, no. 2 (April 1982): 127–42.

as if to imply that the makers themselves are not part of the culture.[6] Some research does not seem to be able to reconcile group norms with the pervasive forces of individuality, deviation, and the prospects of culture change.

The uniformity that is perceived to dominate what are labeled folk objects is a product, as well, of a concentration on certain *types* of artifacts that depend on greater stability over time. Much of the scholarship on the objects owned by ordinary people has dealt with vernacular houses (artifacts that are formally stable) and focused specifically on floor plan and house form, aspects that exhibit the greatest uniformity. Researchers of vernacular buildings have not been particularly interested in studying architecture of the late nineteenth century or later, partly, again, because of romantic biases, but as well because of the greater diversity of these house forms (and thus a perceived lack of "folkness"). As more research is done on other kinds of objects more susceptible to change—such as furniture—this overemphasis on objects that exhibit formal stability over time may wane.

Within the discipline of folklore, researchers looking at oral and customary behavior have redirected the theoretical focus toward the study of everyday life, past and present, through a synthesis of ideas borrowed from three currently popular approaches: semiotics, structuralism, and sociolinguistics.[7] Material culture researchers seem to be the last holdouts, not in using these innovative approaches, but in applying them to material—whether people or objects—that is anything but that per-

---

[6] A theoretical discussion of this issue is found in Daniel F. Biebuyck, Introduction to *Tradition and Creativity in Tribal Art*, ed. Daniel F. Biebuyck (Berkeley: University of California Press, 1969), pp. 7, 14. The necessity of having a community basis for objects designated as folk art is argued in John Michael Vlach, "American Folk Art: Questions and Quandaries," *Winterthur Portfolio* 15, no. 4 (Winter 1980): 346–47. Individuality seems to have long been valued in Western culture, and the claim that community norms were more significant than those of personal needs before the onslaught of modernization may be more an analytical construct than an actuality; see Alan Macfarlane, *The Origins of English Individualism: The Family, Property and Social Transition* (New York: Cambridge University Press, 1978); and Raymond Williams, *The Country and the City* (New York: Oxford University Press, 1973).

[7] The early statement by folklorists borrowing from these related approaches is *Toward New Perspectives in Folklore*, Publications of the American Folklore Society, Bibliographical and Special Series 23, ed. Américo Paredes and Richard Bauman (Austin: University of Texas Press for the American Folklore Society, 1972). For a discussion of the biases in contemporary artifact research by folklorists, as well as suggestions for future study, see Gerald L. Pocius, "Material Folk Culture Research in English Canada: Antiques, Aficionados, and Beyond," *Canadian Folklore canadien* 4, nos. 1–2 (1982): 27–41.

ceived to be uniform and uncorrupted. Models must be used to move the study of objects of everyday life into the realm of interaction, regardless of *how* the particular artifacts were made, *who* made them, or *where* the design originated. In my own research in Keels, I wanted not so much to arrive at culturally sweeping statements based on group norms, but rather to examine the realm of individual strategic interaction, being concerned not with community cohesion, but with individual self-interest. I wanted to shift from broad cultural norms to the dynamics of social manipulations through objects.

To understand the Keels furniture that I documented, I decided to treat objects in ways similar to how we treat language—not a new approach by any means, given the various linguistic analogies already applied to artifacts.[8] Metaphors in our theoretical essays abound with such notions: we want to learn how to "read objects," hoping that artifacts will "speak to us." Treating objects like language does not mean only a search for the complicated building blocks of individual artifact design (using Noam Chomsky's model of linguistic competence), but, as well, the actual ways of use (borrowing Dell Hymes's models of linguistic performance). Instead of concentrating on the linguistic writings of transformational grammar, I wanted to use the number of recent sociolinguistic studies to investigate the nature of furniture performance in the community. We must realize that there are different *ways* that people speak with objects, different dialects, different tones of the artifactual voice, different inflections, different meanings. Both the spoken and the artifactual word are used in ways of strategic interaction—drawing on Erving Goffman's many writings—in ways that are often socially competitive.[9] The more I thought about Keels furniture, the more I

[8] Probably the most influential example is Henry Glassie, *Folk Housing in Middle Virginia: A Structural Analysis of Historic Artifacts* (Knoxville: University of Tennessee Press, 1975). See also Marie Jeanne Adams, "Structural Aspects of a Village Art," *American Anthropologist* 75, no. 1 (February 1973): 265–79; Jon Muller, "Structural Studies of Art Styles," in *The Visual Arts: Plastic and Graphic*, ed. Justine M. Cordwell (The Hague: Mouton, 1980), pp. 139–211; Robert F. Trent, *Hearts and Crowns: Folk Chairs of the Connecticut Coast, 1720–1840* (New Haven: New Haven Colony Historical Society, 1977); and James Deetz, *Invitation to Archaeology* (Garden City, N.Y.: Natural History Press, 1967), pp. 81–101.
[9] Noam Chomsky, *Aspects of the Theory of Syntax* (Cambridge, Mass.: MIT Press, 1965); Dell Hymes, *Foundations in Sociolinguistics: An Ethnographic Approach* (Philadelphia: University of Pennsylvania Press, 1974). The best introduction to Goffman's work is Erving Goffman, *The Presentation of Self in Everyday Life* (Garden City, N.Y.: Doubleday/Anchor, 1959).

was convinced that through its artifactual language, people managed information and furthered their own interests. I realized that Keels furniture was acting in many ways like what has seemed to be one of the mainstays of community life: gossip.

Treating Keels furniture as gossip means that the objects themselves operated in many of the same ways as verbal forms of this activity. I was not attempting to investigate what people said—gossiped—*about* furniture in my research, but rather how the furniture *itself* gossiped in ways that people found useful. The table, just as the whispered comment, operated in socially strategic ways. To the uninitiated reader, the notion of gossip carries with it a first impression of scurrilous activities, false data, and social criticism of those who do not conform to group norms; however, recent anthropological research has shifted emphasis in other directions, from community to individual concerns.

Gossip in a small community like Keels involves literally everyone. With a tightly clustered nucleated settlement pattern, the daily—and often nightly—activities of everyone are on full view. People visit one another extensively, doors are never locked, and knocking for permission to enter is unknown. Everyone in the community engages in some form of daily gossip, and news travels quickly and thoroughly. Gossip ensures that there is little privacy, and all avail themselves of the gossip system in varying degrees.

Recent research has pointed out that gossip, whether verbal or artifactual, has to do with two major concerns: information management and the fostering of self-interest.[10] These concern the message and the gossiper respectively, or, with furniture, the object's form and its maker. I will discuss these two major issues in an attempt to understand Keels furniture as a form of gossip. First, the message, the furniture form.

When we look at the message contained in gossip, we realize that it is concerned primarily with information management. The person who gossips is involved in combining information in specific ways so, as anthropologist Robert Paine argues, the gossiper's own status is enhanced by creating information that is of interest to the community at large.[11] To be effective, gossip must be of interest, and three crucial

---

[10] I use the major points outlined by Robert Paine in his research on gossip as the basis for my own comments. See Robert Paine, "What Is Gossip About? An Alternative Hypothesis," *Man*, n.s., 2, no. 2 (June 1967): 278–85.

[11] Paine, "What Is Gossip," p. 280.

factors ensure this interest: the information is new, it competes with other accounts, and it pieces together events that are seemingly unconnected. Keels furniture does all three; let me start with newness. Later I will briefly discuss *why* gossip has such a central role in the community. To ensure that gossip be of interest, the information that it contains must be new.[12] Gossip depends largely for its popularity on being ever changing; as one event becomes examined ad infinitum, then a new topic appears. The gossiper must be on a constant lookout for the new in order to keep his audience interested in what he says.

Keels residents have always been concerned with ensuring that some of the objects found in their houses were new. Whereas old furniture forms continued to be made, new forms—new ideas—were always incorporated into local households. By even the early nineteenth century, certain kinds of furniture types, especially chairs, were almost always bought from distant factories, rather than being made locally. Fancy chairs of all sorts, as well as common kitchen chairs, were purchased frequently for the home (fig. 2). Only one example of a locally made chair was found in Keels, and for various reasons it is likely that it was made in Conception Bay rather than the Keels area (fig. 3).[13] Chairs, then, were always bought new for use in the community.

This penchant for the new also meant that the Keels resident often accepted new furniture *types* into his house, and these would be bought from local merchants. The circular-top dining table found its way from factory to front room in many homes (fig. 4). More ubiquitous was the lounge, often placed in the parlor as well (fig. 5). These were bottom-of-the-line manufactured goods, new to the owner simply by being in

[12] Besides Paine's comments on this need to have information that is new when gossiping, see Max Gluckman, "Gossip and Scandal," *Current Anthropology* 4, no. 3 (June 1963): 311.

[13] Early nineteenth-century St. John's newspapers are filled with advertisements for chairs, often imported from the United States; for example, see Judith Tulloch, *Goods and Services Advertised in St. John's Newspapers, 1830–1840*, Research Bulletin 220 (Ottawa: Parks Canada, 1984), pp. 15–17. Howard Pain, in his study of Upper Canadian furniture, points out that quite early on, as well, there was a scarcity of locally made chairs and that imported goods were obviously preferred (Howard Pain, *The Heritage of Upper Canadian Furniture: A Study in the Survival of Formal and Vernacular Styles from Britain, America and Europe, 1780–1900* [Toronto: Van Nostrand Reinhold Co., 1978], p. 42). An almost identical Newfoundland chair to this one located in Keels is illustrated in Donald B. Webster, *English-Canadian Furniture of the Georgian Period* (Toronto: McGraw-Hill Ryerson, 1979), pl. 26.

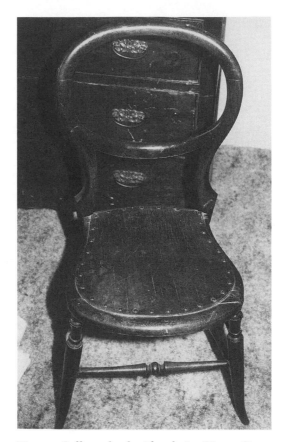

Fig. 2. Balloon-back side chair, Kings Cove, Newfoundland, late nineteenth century. Maple; H. 33″, W. 14¼″, D. 15½″. (Private collection: Photo, Gerald L. Pocius.)

Fig. 3. Side chair, Keels, Newfoundland, nine-teenth century. Birch and pine; H. 33½", W. 16¾", D. 15¼". (Private collection: Photo, Gerald L. Pocius.)

Fig. 4. Factory-made dining table, Keels, Newfoundland, early twentieth century. Oak; H. 30", diam. 45". (Private collection: Photo, Gerald L. Pocius.)

the local home; newness did not come from competing through buying a fancier or larger factory version.[14]

If concern with new ideas sometimes involved buying new furniture types made in a factory, more frequently the local person actually made these factory ideas by hand. Dining tables appeared, sometimes reduced in stature—not surprising given the small size of the typical

[14] For the few essays that treat the cultural importance of such factory furniture, see Michael J. Ettema, "Technological Innovation and Design Economics in Furniture Manufacture," *Winterthur Portfolio* 16, nos. 2/3 (Summer/Autumn 1981): 197–223; Kenneth L. Ames, "Material Culture as Nonverbal Communication: A Historical Case Study," *Journal of American Culture* 3, no. 4 (Winter 1980): 619–41; Kenneth L. Ames, "Meaning in Artifacts: Hall Furnishings in Victorian America," *Journal of Interdisciplinary History* 9, no. 1 (Summer 1978): 19–46; and Lizabeth A. Cohen, "Embellishing a Life of Labor: An Interpretation of the Material Culture of Working-Class Homes, 1885–1915," *Journal of American Culture* 3, no. 4 (Winter 1980): 752–75. Good illustrations of the typical range of factory goods available in North America at the time can be found in *A Victorian Chair for All Seasons: A Facsimile of the Brooklyn Chair Company Cata-*

Keels parlor where they were placed (fig. 6). Lounges of all forms were made, the basic form being a bench with a low back and one scrolled end, but varied in the decorative treatment found on the backboard, apron, and legs (fig. 7). Several locally made rockers borrowed from new factory products: the framing of one, for example, resembled the mass-produced folding chairs of the late nineteenth century. And finally, a pervasive Victorian factory idea was extensively made: the sideboard. The Keels sideboards have a full range of treatments, from the earlier objects inspired by Gothic-revival forms (fig. 8), to taller forms resembling the prolifically produced varieties made of imitation quarter-sawed oak by numerous factories at the end of the century; these indicate that makers had a varied range of actual artifacts that served as models.[15]

If furniture as gossip had to be concerned with new ideas to stay interesting, then this newness did not just mean copying the latest factory piece verbatim. Factory design *elements* could be incorporated on local pieces, and Keels craftsmen often devised ways of reproducing machine designs and technologies by hand. Given many of the English furniture reformers' goals of returning to a preindustrial design aesthetic, some Keels pieces are an ironic statement of man imitating machine, or, in David Pye's terms, the workmanship of risk copying the workmanship of certainty.[16] With pocketknife and saw, many creators attempted to reproduce by hand the machine-made features of factory goods. The towel rails on a Keels washstand, for example, were carved to imitate factory lathe-turned spindles, as were the legs (fig. 9). A later commode embodies several elements of maker imitating machine: plywood panels in the doors imitate decorative inlays, and a small, hand-carved button and finials on the backboard echo factory elements (fig. 10).

logue of 1887 (Watkins Glen, N.Y.: American Life Foundation, 1978); and Eileen Dubrow and Richard Dubrow, *Furniture Made in America: 1875–1905* (Exton, Pa.: Schiffer Publishing, 1982). The standard work on the effects of mechanization in the production of furniture is still Siegfried Giedion, *Mechanization Takes Command: A Contribution to Anonymous History* (1948; reprint, New York: W. W. Norton, 1969), esp. pt. 5. Also see Polly Anne Earl, "Craftsmen and Machines: The Nineteenth-Century Furniture Industry," in *Technological Innovation and the Decorative Arts*, ed. Ian M. G. Quimby and Polly Anne Earl (Charlottesville: University Press of Virginia, 1974), pp. 307–29.

[15] A typical Gothic-revival sideboard much like the one that could have served as the model for this Keels example is depicted in Philip Shackleton, "Ontario Furniture," in *The Book of Canadian Antiques*, ed. Donald B. Webster (Toronto: McGraw-Hill Ryerson, 1974), p. 126.

[16] David Pye, *The Nature and Art of Workmanship* (Cambridge: At the University Press, 1968), pp. 4–8.

Fig. 5. Factory-made lounge, Keels, Newfoundland, late nineteenth century. Original red canvas upholstery; H. 29″, W. 59⅞″, D. 20″. (Private collection: Photo, Gerald L. Pocius.)

Fig. 6. Dining table, Keels, Newfoundland, early twentieth century. Pine, brown paint; H. 29″, diam. 38″. (Private collection: Photo, Gerald L. Pocius.)

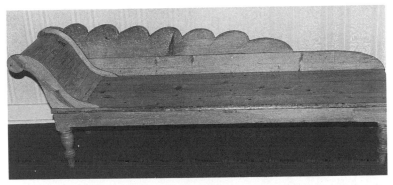

Fig. 7. Lounge, Keels, Newfoundland, late nineteenth century. Spruce, pine, birch; original finish removed; H. 23⅞″, W. 62½″, D. 18¼″. (Private collection: Photo, Gerald L. Pocius.)

When making furniture that had to be new in some respect, a man could, to a certain extent, never create something that was too new. Obviously the ability to create the new is really the innovative combining of existing ideas; no one maker creates something new completely out of nothing. But factory forms gave the maker more options, more choices, and more ideas to expand his creative range. Rather than destroying the local tradition, mass-produced factory forms expanded design possibilities and in some ways contributed to a flourishing of the local craft.[17]

If gossip is concerned with the new to remain interesting, then its second major requirement is that it be competitive. People try to outdo one another in knowing the latest news. As well, each gossiper must attempt to convince his audience that his version of an event (his way

[17] Raymond Williams, *The Long Revolution* (1961; reprint, Westport, Conn.: Greenwood Press, 1975), pp. 3–4, 15, 23; H. G. Barnett, *Innovation: The Basis of Cultural Change* (New York: McGraw-Hill, 1953), pt. 3. Benefits of factory forms seem to hold for some other regions where the forms came in contact with vibrant local furniture-making traditions. See, for example, Connie Morningstar, *Early Utah Furniture* (Logan: Utah State University Press, 1976); *Made in Ohio: Furniture, 1788–1888* (Columbus: Columbus Museum of Art, 1984); and Lonn Taylor and David B. Warren, *Texas Furniture: The Cabinetmakers and Their Work, 1840–1880* (Austin: University of Texas Press, 1975), esp. pp. 52–53, 56, 120, 127, 236.

Fig. 8. Sideboard, possibly by Frank Penney, Keels, Newfoundland, late nineteenth century. Spruce, pine; H. 65¾", W. 60", D. 14¼". (Private collection: Photo, Gerald L. Pocius.)

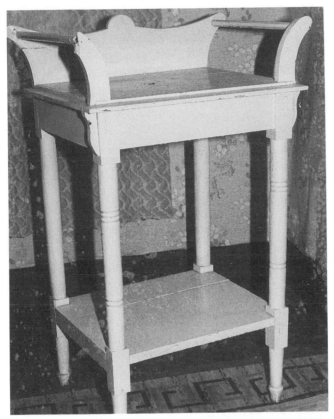

Fig. 9. Washstand, Keels, Newfoundland, late nineteenth century. Spruce, pine, birch; H. 36¼", W. 18¼", D. 16¼". (Private collection: Photo, Gerald L. Pocius.)

of defining a table or a rocker) is the right one. Again drawing on Paine's work, the gossiper wishes to manage information that his audience will receive so that "his, and not their, definition of the situation prevails."[18]

[18] Paine, "What Is Gossip," p. 283. See also Erving Goffman, *Strategic Interaction* (Philadelphia: University of Pennsylvania Press, 1969), p. 12; and Peter J. Wilson, "Filcher of Good Names: An Enquiry into Anthropology and Gossip," *Man*, n.s., 9, no. 1 (March 1974): 99.

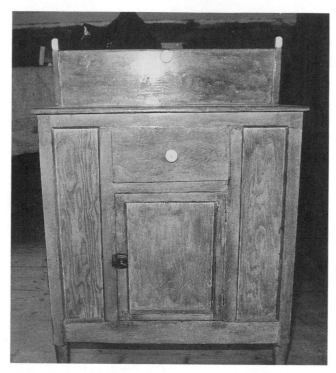

Fig. 10. Commode, Keels, Newfoundland, mid twentieth century. Packing crates, plywood, spruce; original brown stain; H. 43⅞″, W. 31½″, D. 12¾″. (Private collection: Photo, Gerald L. Pocius.)

Furniture, then, makes a competitive statement, where one maker tries to outdo another.

When people verbally compete in order to convince one another of their own proficiency with certain material, they use particular words in special ways: they perform them persuasively. These words are used in what Roger Abrahams (borrowing from Kenneth Burke) has called rhetorical modes to convince an audience of the skill of the performer, that his or her use of language, and therefore performance, is better than others'. Furniture becomes competitive through the use of similar persuasive rhetorical devices, elements that convince the audience of the special nature of the artifact and thus the skills of the maker. I would argue that the competitive aspects of furniture are manifested through their rhetorical devices, what I would call the presentational aspects of each piece: backboards, aprons, drawer fronts, legs (often front legs), and so on—minor components with major rhetorical impact. These elements have often been dismissed by researchers other than art historians as secondary—merely decorative—especially when formal stability is stressed. Mary Douglas argues, however, that where standardization of artifact traditions occurs, small differences matter a lot.[19] If we take any particular furniture type from my research, the rhetorical intent of objects is obvious.

The only real rhetorical elements on tables are the legs, given that the top surface was usually covered. Legs as presentational elements become square and tapered; tapered and chamfered (fig. 11); tapered with decorative feet; sawed legs that formally resemble turnings but have decorative notchings; turnings with a minimal hint of disks; and simple turnings (fig. 12). Each class of tables has basically the same form, but the rhetorical element—the legs—differs greatly.

Chests of drawers, again, to scholars looking for stability of form, appear related: case pieces have similar dimensions and drawer configurations. Obviously a certain stability of form was necessary in order to have a furniture piece a particular height, providing a top as display and work space and drawers for storage space. Even if the maker had to include a dummy drawer to maintain the desired form, the basic configuration and look were still there (fig. 13). But chests became rhetorical, persuasive, and competitive in their aprons, backboards, and drawer fronts. Perhaps borrowing from factory pieces such as cottage-style commodes, chests of drawers began to sport geometric backs, some more abstracted than others. Some had gallery-like railings (fig. 14)—an idea probably borrowed from a sideboard—while others had geometrical backboards with a wide range of shapes.

[19] Roger D. Abrahams, "Introductory Remarks to a Rhetorical Theory of Folklore," *Journal of American Folklore* 81, no. 320 (April–June 1968): 143–58. For background, see Kenneth Burke, *A Rhetoric of Motives* (New York: Prentice-Hall, 1952), pp. 46, 55, 60. One important recent study that briefly mentions this rhetorical impact of furniture is Jack Michel, " 'In a Manner and Fashion Suitable to Their Degree': A Preliminary Investigation of the Material Culture of Early Rural Pennsylvania," *Working Papers from the Regional Economic History Research Center* 5, ed. Glenn Porter and William H. Mulligan, Jr. (Wilmington, Del.: Eleutherian Mills-Hagley Foundation, 1981), p. 20. Mary Douglas and Baron Isherwood, *The World of Goods: Towards an Anthropology of Consumption* (New York: W. W. Norton, 1979), p. 145.

Fig. 11. Kitchen table, Keels, Newfoundland, late nineteenth century. Pine, birch; H. 28¾″, W. 41½″, D. 21¾″. (Private collection: Photo, Gerald L. Pocius.)

So far I have discussed gossip as both new and competitive; I want now to discuss its third major characteristic. Gossip often links two events which are seemingly unconnected in an attempt to create new information. A recent Keels example. Event one: George's truck is usually parked in one spot; George's truck is not seen in that spot all night. Event two: George occasionally visits Mary. Gossip connects events one and two: George spent the night at Mary's house. Gossip has linked two known phenomena to create new information. So it is with furniture. A maker is continually challenged to link elements in new ways: combining mass-produced, local, and idiosyncratic elements like Claude Lévi-Strauss's *bricoleur* creates objects never before conceived. Indeed, this linking of previously unconnected elements, on a basic level, may be considered the mechanism the gossiper actually uses to create continually the new and, therefore, the interesting. Keels's creations do not indicate that makers poorly copied mass or elite styles (the "folk stupid-

Fig. 12. Kitchen table, Keels, Newfoundland, late nineteenth century. Pine, birch; H. 29¾", W. 40", D. 27¼". (Private collection: Photo, Gerald L. Pocius.)

ity" fallacy). Craftsmen were unconcerned with whether their objects followed what we now perceive as a unified, particular, widely made style. In most cases the creator did not intend to copy completely another piece (which some certainly had the ability to do); they simply wanted to link elements in new ways. Furniture research often implies that when high-style craftsmen idiosyncratically interpret a prevailing style,

Fig. 13. Chest of drawers, Keels, Newfoundland, early twentieth century. Packing crates, pine; H. 36¾", W. 32⅞", D. 7¼". (Newfoundland Museum.)

they are being creative, while such an interpretation from a folk crafts-man is basically a misunderstanding.[20]

Every conceivable combination was potentially possible; local makers obviously broke down specific furniture types into cognitive compo-

[20]Gerald L. Pocius, " 'Interior Motives': Rooms, Objects and Meaning in Atlantic Canada Homes," *Material History Bulletin* 15 (Summer 1982): 6. Typical comments along these lines can be found in John G. Shea, *Antique Country Furniture of North America* (New York: Van Nostrand Reinhold Co., 1975), preface.

Fig. 14. Chest of drawers, Keels, Newfoundland, late nineteenth century. Pine, original red ocher finish; H. 53″, W. 42″, D. 12¾″. (Private collection: Photo, Gerald L. Pocius.)

nents, so that elements could be joined together in ways different from the original creative intention. Take washstands, for example. We are dealing with what is essentially a form with a long history of local use; four legs held a roughly square platform where a bowl could be placed. Factory washstands or commodes in the late nineteenth century often had a lyre back to hold a towel. Local makers considered this lyre a distinct element that could be combined with the older washstand forms. The result: open washstands with lyre backs (fig. 15). Conversely, a maker might construct a closed, commodelike object—borrowing from factory forms—but reduce its proportions to make it closely resemble the local open varieties.

In this same vein of linking perceived elements in previously unrecognized ways, chests of drawers also combined local and mass-

Fig. 15. Washstand, Keels, Newfoundland, early twentieth century. Birch, pine,
packing crates; H. 51¼″, W. 20½″, D.
20½″. (Private collection: Photo, Gerald L.
Pocius.)

produced ideas. Lyre backs for holding mirrors were incorporated on
chests of drawers (lyre mirror plus chest of drawers form); in one instance
it was simply a household mirror that was mounted within the lyre
brackets on the chest. Sideboards, as another example, were products
of such syncretism. A sideboard was needed in one Keels household,
but the maker reduced it in form so that proportionally it approximated
the standard chest of drawers in size (fig. 16). But as a sideboard, doors
were used instead of drawers, and the craftsman wanted decorative gal-

Fig. 16. Sideboard, Keels, Newfoundland, early twentieth century. Pine; H. 62⅜″, W. 49″, D. 11½″. (Private collection: Photo, Gerald L. Pocius.)

lerics of some sort. Thus, a few flourishes were cut and a religious motif added for good measure. The result: a linking of sideboard concepts, chest-of-drawers dimensions, and local ideas never before connected.

Even simple factory design ideas could be exclusively combined in new ways to produce objects never seen in a factory. Small Victorian fancy lamp tables with elaborately sawed legs were popular elsewhere but rarely made their way into the Keels home. One craftsman, however, took the idea of this type of decorative leg and combined it with the more ubiquitous, larger dining table to produce a new form for his front room, blending the design of a dining-table top with a smaller lamp-table base.

In short, furniture was perceived as a number of conceptual components—some major (backboards, aprons, facings), others as decorative motifs (buttons, diamonds, incising)—combined using strategies only limited by the maker's ability to bring together seemingly disparate ideas. Like talk, forms were linked in ways not connected, whose ultimate acceptance and validity would be confirmed by how widely they were repeated, or how quickly they were dismissed.

To this point I have been discussing primarily how furniture as gossip manages information. Furniture, like verbal forms, searches for the new, often in a competitive vein, combining ideas—new and old—in different ways. Let me turn now to my other major assertion, that furniture, like verbal gossip, basically acts to serve self-interest. Again, gossip is not primarily a way of maintaining conformity to group values. Rather, as Paine notes, "it is the individual and not the community that gossips. What he gossips about are his own and other's aspirations, and only indirectly the values of the community."[21] Those who create new and interesting gossip—verbal or artifactual—enhance their own social position by focusing attention on themselves as sources of ideas. Those who gossip the best are sought out not as deviants, but as skillful manipulators of particular cultural forms. They ensure social attention, which translates into many and frequent visitors. Thus, furniture becomes purposive behavior that as a component of social relations fosters individual interests. To understand Keels furniture in this regard, let me say a few words first about the network of the local furniture maker.

Furniture making in Keels (and Newfoundland) remained different from this activity in other parts of North America. In other regions craftsmen were often specialists, in most cases at least part-time, if not full-time, woodworkers. Often they were engaged in some minimal

---

[21] Paine, "What Is Gossip," pp. 280–81. This status-enhancing character of gossip is also noted in Roger D. Abrahams, "A Performance-Centered Approach to Gossip," *Man*, n.s., 5, no. 2 (June 1970): 291–93; Ralph L. Rosnow and Gary Alan Fine, *Rumor and Gossip: The Social Psychology of Hearsay* (New York: Elsevier, 1976), pp. 4, 90–91; and John Beard Haviland, *Gossip, Reputation, and Knowledge in Zinacantan* (Chicago: University of Chicago Press, 1977), p. 9.

economic enterprise, with a shop, assistants, and at leaᵗ some concern for the tastes of clients. Whether they made so-called high-style or country goods, they usually had a socially recognized role as craftsman. As time goes on, and perhaps earlier in urban centers, furniture making becomes professionalized, in many ways similar to the phenomenon described by Dell Upton for architecture.[22]

In Keels, however, furniture remained like gossip. Male family members continued to make most objects found in the home long after specialization and professionalization had contributed to a decline in other regions. Although some fishermen at times made a piece or two for a neighbor, people would rarely think of selling such objects to make a living. While some kinds of social activity were limited to those with specialized talents or knowledge (such as the local oral historian or folk healer), furniture making, like verbal gossip, was open to every male in the community, and most men would try their hand at it.[23]

Like all such broadly based social activities, some men were better at furniture making than others. A system of local aesthetics could identify who made furniture out of the ordinary, just as a good singer or storyteller could be clearly identified. Some could build furniture for strictly utilitarian purposes and were proficient in only the basic necessary construction techniques. Others were noted for their design ideas; they were better furniture gossipers.

Looking briefly at the work of several individuals whose lives roughly overlapped indicates the range of ways in which a furniture maker could alter his status through his creations. Frank Penney worked from around 1880 to 1930, obviously borrowing Gothic ideas from either factory goods, other local pieces, or recently built churches in the area.[24] The surviving furniture by Penney indicates that he eventually arrived at a formulaic configuration of the object and then repeated it with similar

[22] Dell Upton, "Pattern Books and Professionalism: Aspects of the Transformation of Domestic Architecture in America, 1800–1860," *Winterthur Portfolio* 19, nos. 2/3 (Summer/Autumn 1984): 107–50.

[23] It was similarly noted that gossip was often a male activity in the community studied by Abrahams, "Performance-Centered Approach," p. 300.

[24] An introduction to the Gothic-revival style as it influenced furniture is Katherine S. Howe and David B. Warren, *The Gothic Revival in America, 1830–1870* (Houston: Museum of Fine Arts, 1976). Typical models for Penney's sideboards are depicted in Charles H. Foss, *Cabinetmakers of the Eastern Seaboard* (Toronto: M. F. Feheley, 1977), p. 77; and Shackleton, "Ontario Furniture," p. 126.

Fig. 17. Kitchen dresser, by Frank Penney, Keels, Newfoundland, late nineteenth century. Pine, original finish removed; H. 88″, W. 56½″, D. 12½″. (Private collection: Photo, Gerald L. Pocius.)

pieces or used components of it on smaller artifacts. Repetition governed his designs. Four of his dressers survive; two are almost identical, except for an original finish that has been removed (figs. 17, 18). Penney's use of arches—pointed and rounded—is an identifiable characteristic, and he used them on all kinds of objects. For some people,

Fig. 18. Kitchen dresser, by Frank Penney, Keels, Newfoundland, late nineteenth century. Pine; H. 75¼", W. 54", D. 12". (Private collection: Photo, Gerald L. Pocius.)

Penney obviously represented the epitome of skill, as his finish work is found on both furniture and interior details throughout the community. His creations demonstrated both his woodworking skills and his ability to introduce a new design idea into Keels.

More diverse were the creations of Billy Wheeler. Working in Keels between about 1910 and 1964, Wheeler made furniture mainly for his own personal use. He drew far and wide for inspiration, ranging from simple forms to elaborate creations. He made pieces that were close approximations of the factory items of his day: the lounge in his front room (factory-like in everything except the carved diamonds on the backboard) (fig. 19) and the rocker in his kitchen (a factory form, but legs carved with a pocketknife to simulate turnings). Some of his creations were the stereotypical folk furniture piece: a solid-board child's rocker, complete with folkloric heart (and a back of nonfolkloric plywood), similar to solid-board rockers still in use (fig. 20). Or a kitchen dresser, plain in most details except for a rather heavy cornice fabricated from several layers of mass-produced molding (fig. 21). Other examples of Wheeler's work, however, were obviously more imaginative in their design strategies. One of his washstands was basically a local form with decorative factory elements including a cross-diagonal stretcher shelf (fig. 22). A bedroom chest of drawers most likely borrowed its design from factory Eastlake-style commodes, with decorative door trim, backboard and apron designs common on furniture influenced by English-reform designers. Finally, his sideboard, with applied circular drawer fronts derived from Renaissance revival factory goods, sports a design that includes upper carved shelf supports borrowed from later factory sideboard designs, keyhold door motifs that may have mass-produced origins as well—perhaps from Moorish-inspired furniture—with several stars and rosettes just to remind you that it is folk (fig. 23).[25]

Wheeler's ability to create the new, to combine all sorts of ideas, obviously gave him a different reputation in Keels than Penney. When discussing the work of both men, a friend who knew them recently remarked that most people could make furniture, but Wheeler insisted on making his creations "tasty"—that is, somehow new and different. Wheeler was obviously considered one of the innovators in the community; he could be counted on for the latest "artifactual news" through

[25] A complete discussion of Billy Wheeler and his work can be found in Walter W. Peddle, *The Forgotten Craftsmen* (St. John's: Cuff Publications, 1984), chap. 4. All of Wheeler's works discussed in my essay are illustrated in Peddle's book. A typical Eastlake piece that likely influenced Wheeler's chest of drawers is shown in Mary Jean Madigan, "Eastlake-Influenced Furniture," in *Nineteenth Century Furniture: Innovation, Revival and Reform*, ed. Mary Jean Madigan (New York: Art and Antiques, 1982), p. 58. An introduction to this style is Mary Jean Madigan, *Eastlake-Influenced American Furniture, 1870–1890* (Yonkers, N.Y.: Hudson River Museum, 1974). An example of a Renaissance-revival sideboard with such drawer treatment can be found in Huia G. Ryder, "New Brunswick Furniture," in *Book of Antiques*, p. 109. An introduction to this furniture style generally is *Renaissance Revival Victorian Furniture* (Grand Rapids: Grand Rapids Art Museum, 1976). The Moorish vogue in furniture styles is discussed in Eileen Dubrow and Richard Dubrow, *American Furniture of the Nineteenth Century, 1840–1880* (Exton, Pa.: Schiffer Publishing, 1983), pp. 231–36.

Fig. 19. Lounge, by Billy Wheeler, Keels, Newfoundland, early twentieth century. Pine, spruce, birch, original cloth upholstery with seagrass stuffing; H. 27″, W. 69½″, D. 23″. (Private collection: Photo, Gerald L. Pocius.)

his furniture. Like anyone else skilled in the art of gossip, he received more attention, enhancing his reputation. By constantly altering the furniture he made, as, for example, a settle and a commode (fig. 24), both using grooved ceiling boards for decorative effects, he fostered his self-interest: he was considered in the community a man of ideas, not just skill.[26]

Penney brought new elements—Gothic elements—into Keels, altering and expanding them to fit a wide range of forms. Unlike Wheeler, however, when he perfected a particular idea to his liking, he simply made the form again and again. Penney brought in a new idea and then repeated it a number of times. Like verbal gossip, he created a new story, but then continued to tell it simply with different permutations.

[26]*Tasty* was an eighteenth- and nineteenth-century dialect term for *attractive* or *agreeable* (see Joseph Wright, *The English Dialect Dictionary*, vol. 6 [London: Henry Fowde, 1905], p. 37). These objects may have been influenced by similar decorative treatments on Eastlake-inspired factory goods; for example, see Madigan, *Eastlake-Influenced Furniture*, no. 55.

Fig. 20. Child's rocker, by Billy Wheeler, Keels, Newfoundland, mid twentieth century. Pine, plywood; H. 20½", W. 16¼", D. 20". (Newfoundland Museum.)

In contrast, Wheeler pushed for the new time and time again; whenever he needed a new piece of furniture, he tried to create a different idea from the various information sources available at the time. Like the verbal gossiper, Wheeler always wanted something new to tell.

Billy Wheeler and Frank Penney are just the better-known furniture makers in Keels. Many men obviously attempted to create idiosyncratic pieces only once or twice in their lives, not trying to excel in other creations. Sideboards were frequently the vehicle for makers competing in this artifactual gossip system; one maker—perhaps Alf Moss—designed several sideboards with esoteric geometric motifs that seem

Fig. 21. Kitchen dresser with bottom dummy drawer, by Billy Wheeler, Keels, Newfoundland, mid twentieth century. Spruce, pine; H. 79″, W. 39¼″, D. 14¼″. (Private collection: Photo, Gerald L. Pocius.)

literal inversions of some of Penney's designs (fig. 25). Nick Kelly decided on a bit of a backboard flare for his otherwise simple sideboard (fig. 26), while his nephew Jack borrowed from the more standard high sideboard designs of the early twentieth century (fig. 27).

Like other aspects of community life, then, furniture making was a broadly based group activity, open to all males. Ultimately, such a

Fig. 22. Washstand, by Billy Wheeler, Keels, New-foundland, early twentieth century. Assorted woods; H. 38½″, W. 24½″, D. 24½″. (Private collection: Photo, Gerald L. Pocius.)

broad social base did not require that everyone necessarily participate at the same level with equal skills. Indeed, many aspects of social life in such a small community are marked by individuality and variation. Unlike furniture making in other regions tied to economic constraints like the tastes of clients or marketability, the person making furniture

Fig. 23. Sideboard, by Billy Wheeler, Keels, Newfoundland, early twentieth century. Pine, spruce,
original brown stain; H. 66¾", W. 47", D. 19½".
(Private collection: Photo, Gerald L. Pocius.)

in Keels generally answered to his own personal concerns. In such a
system, furniture was indeed like verbal gossip, everyone competing to
create objects that demonstrated not just technological competence but
new ideas as well. And with new ideas came new status.

To summarize my arguments so far: certain men who made furniture—like certain verbal gossipers—were extremely good at what they
did, and this reputation enhanced their general community image in

Fig. 24. Commode, by Billy Wheeler, Keels, Newfoundland, mid twentieth century. Assorted woods; H. 50¾″, W. 25″, D. 17″. (Private collection: Photo, Gerald L. Pocius.)

Keels. Men were skillful furniture gossipers because the objects they made managed information through a common social channel: information that was new, competitive, and combined seemingly unrelated facts.

My treatment of Keels furniture as artifactual gossip, however, does

Fig. 25. Sideboard, possibly by Alf Moss, Keels, Newfoundland, early twentieth century. Pine, spruce, original finish removed; H. 48⅞", W. 58½", D. 16". (Private collection: Photo, Gerald L. Pocius.)

not mean that these objects exhibit *all* the characteristics of their verbal counterparts. Verbal forms of gossip have the ability to be new and constantly changing since their life is relatively fleeting; they disappear after perhaps several days of scrutiny in numerous conversations. Once a new object was made, however, it was not discarded simply when it ceased to be new and interesting information. Tempering the concern with things new was a pragmatic strain in local Keels households that basically dictated that objects were used until they wore out. Furniture was kept until it no longer was functional, but even then it might be relegated to the stable for some continued use. Only then did replacement take the form of making an object new and different. Yet it remains that furniture was not rapidly replaced simply when the look of the object was no longer new. However, residents did have a way of creating variety in the appearance of their furniture before it wore out. Often objects were repainted in different colors every year or so, and many have numerous layers of paint. I have even seen the door panels of a cabinet wallpapered each year when the kitchen received its annual redecorating.

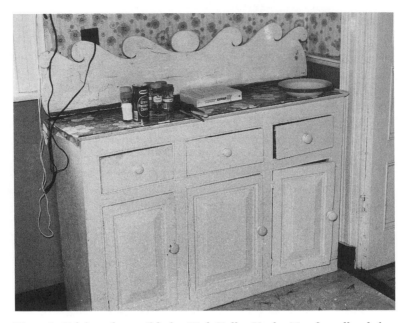

Fig. 26. Sideboard, possibly by Nick Kelly, Keels, Newfoundland, late nineteenth century. Pine, packing crates; H. 40⅞", W. 46½", D. 12". (Private collection: Photo, Gerald L. Pocius.)

Newness was constrained as well by each furniture type having basically to follow the accepted norms as to form. A kitchen table had to have four legs, a bedroom chest of drawers had to be roughly a certain height with a certain number of drawers, and so on. An object could not be so esoteric that it did not approximate an accepted functional norm. It was important that the maker followed this basic configuration, for if the audience recognized and thus accepted the basic form, only then could the craftsman demonstrate his rhetorical skills through the object's presentational elements.[27]

Billy Wheeler's sideboard is a good indication of how complex the informational exchange system was among community craftsmen. Most

[27] Robert Paine, "When Saying Is Doing," in *Politically Speaking: Cross-Cultural Studies of Rhetoric*, Social and Economic Papers no. 10, ed. Robert Paine (St. John's: Institute of Social and Economic Research, Memorial University of Newfoundland, 1981), p. 12.

Fig. 27. Sideboard, by Jack Kelly, Keels, Newfoundland, early twentieth century. Pine, spruce; H. 58⅜″, W. 42¼″, D. 13″. (Private collection: Photo, Gerald L. Pocius.)

likely, Wheeler used ideas (drawer fronts, upper shelf supports, door motifs) from at least three different sideboards, as well as his own personal ideas (rosettes), to create this new artifact. Some of these design elements may have been brought in from outside Keels, and thus these elements and the entire sideboard design per se were new information for local furniture makers. While the content of verbal gossip could span an almost limitless number of topics, obviously furniture gossip was concerned primarily with design issues. Yet this narrow focus of the actual topic of artifactual gossip does not diminish in any way the elaborate network of informational interchange that each new item of furniture set in motion, much like its verbal counterpart. When a new design idea, such as Wheeler's sideboard, was created, it could potentially serve as a model for future objects made by the same craftsman (if he were conservative) or as likely be adapted by others. Some craftsmen, like Wheeler, never made the same design twice. Once made, an artifact soon became old news. Yet old news for one maker served as new news for another. Thus, while someone like Wheeler never exactly copied a previous creation of his, the copying by others was usually widespread; for other craftsmen, it *was* something new. This rapid dissemination of new designs explains why forms never stayed new for very long and why they as frequently were dropped after a brief popularity. Rather than being inherently conservative in the acceptance of new ideas, some makers constantly were interested in seeing what others had done. New information, then, circulated widely through the harbor, whether it came from outside the community or from the genius of one of the local craftsmen. These new ideas disappeared, finally—and often quickly—when they became all too familiar, as with verbal gossip.

If furniture in Keels can be treated as gossip, then it not only explains the diversity and range of artifact forms but also casts doubts on many previous models that emphasize a conservative nature for all folk forms. It is inappropriate to assume that all so-called folk furniture should obey similar rules, as it would be inappropriate to think that all ways of speaking are the same. A wide range of artifact behaviors is subsumed under the categories "folk" or "country"—terms that can easily blur important differences. All folk or country furniture is not the same simply because it is made of local woods and simple technologies, just as all ways of speaking are not the same just because they all use words. The gossip of Keels furniture reveals as well something about the myth of isolation that surrounds rural areas like Newfoundland. Certainly Keels was not in the vanguard of every new idea, but furniture indicates that ideas were known long before the age of mass communication. [28] As far back as existing artifacts go, they indicate that the tiny community of Keels was not populated by unknowledgeable and uncontaminated folk. But finally, why gossip? Why is gossip of such a central concern for communities like Keels? Why is new information eagerly, perhaps desperately, sought out? Furniture, like verbal varieties of gossip, strikes at the heart of one pervasive facet of Keels life: boredom. To our simplicity-seeking psyches, life in tiny Keels might be many things, but to residents at times it seems that life has little new to offer. The same faces, the same neighbors, the same people to work with, the same people to marry—all groups who are there by chance of birth rather than choice. The furniture I have discussed as gossip was important to people who made it, not as signs of knowledge of the outside world, not as symbols of aspirations to an emerging bourgeoisie world view, but as ways to overcome so much of what always seemed the same. Gossip was so pervasive because boredom was as well. Miles Richardson pointed out, "even the rooted people seek relief from the stifling monotony of the everyday world," and in Keels, furniture was a channel that offered such relief. [29] Furniture stands as a surviving counterpart to the thou-

[28] Typical statements that introduce the notion of "country furniture" are William C. Ketchum, Jr., *Chests, Cupboards, Desks and Other Pieces*, Knopf Collector's Guide to American Antiques (New York: Alfred A. Knopf, 1982), p. 16; Marvin D. Schwartz, *Chairs, Tables, Sofas and Beds*, Knopf Collector's Guide to American Antiques (New York: Alfred A. Knopf, 1982), p. 20; Jane Toller, *Country Furniture* (Newton Abbot: David and Charles, 1973), pp. 9–10, 15; Thomas M. Voss, *Antique American Country Furniture* (Philadelphia: J. B. Lippincott Co., 1978), pp. 27, 29–30; Henry Lionel Williams, *Country Furniture of Early America* (New York: Barnes, 1963), pp. 11–12; Ralph Kovel and Terry Kovel, *American Country Furniture, 1780–1875* (New York: Crown Publishers, 1965), p. v; and "Country Furniture: A Symposium," *Antiques* 93, no. 3 (March 1968): 342–71. Unlike my Keels objects, some furniture traditions may have a formal stability, while demonstrating greater variation in finish. See Edwin A. Churchill, *Simple Forms and Vivid Colors: An Exhibition of Maine Painted Furniture, 1800–1850* (Augusta: Maine State Museum, 1983), p. 6. The relatively rapid spread of new furniture styles among rural North American craftsmen is discussed in Warren Roberts, "Ananias Hensel and His Furniture: Cabinetmaking in Southern Indiana," *Midwestern Journal of Language and Folklore* 9, no. 2 (Fall 1983): 113–14.
[29] The connection between gossip and boredom is discussed in Patricia Meyer Spacks, *Gossip* (New York: Alfred A. Knopf, 1985), p. 165. Although I say that boredom *was* pervasive, I suspect that the situation remains largely unchanged. While at Winterthur in February 1985, I called a friend in Keels and asked him what was new. His reply: "Nothing, boy, we're frozen and we're bored." Miles Richardson, Introduction to *Place: Experience and Symbol*, Geoscience and Man 24, ed. Miles Richardson (Baton Rouge: Department of Geography and Anthropology, Louisiana State University, 1984), p. 1.

Fig. 28. Washstand, Keels, Newfoundland, early twentieth century. Pine, spruce; original finish of yellow and blue restored; H. 33⅝″, W. 17⅛″, D. 15½″. (Private collection: Photo, Gerald L. Pocius.)

sands of verbal utterances that were aimed at the same goal: to provide any information, new and different, to create variety.

Keels furniture, then, became a powerful vehicle through which residents could competitively assert their individuality. In some types of behavior, Keels residents strove to be the same, but in other forms, such as gossip, they could dare to be different. As in our own lives, the person in Keels was pulled by the polar forces of needing to conform and needing to be different. Scrutinizing romantics often laud the conformist models of community while ironically championing such homogeneity as a solution to the Orwellian uniformity that surrounds so much of modern life. Keels folk knew better and struggled to escape a boring sameness that to outsiders often seems appealing. Their furniture indicates, perhaps, that they were more successful than most in creating identities that answered to individual goals. Their humble washstands (fig. 28), finally, speak loudly (gossip loudly?) to people striving to be different in a context that was in many ways oppressively uniform. I suspect that they succeeded; maybe a bit better than many of us naive observers would ever imagine.

Index

Page numbers in **boldface** refer to illustrations.

347